504 ABSOLUTELY ESSENTIAL WORDS

Sixth Edition

Murray Bromberg
Former Professor, Touro College

Julius Liebb
Former Assistant Principal, Andrew Jackson H.S.

Arthur Traiger
Former Assistant Principal, Martin Van Buren H.S.
Instructor, Japan University

All inquiries should be addressed to:
Barron's Educational Series, Inc.
250 Wireless Boulevard
Hauppauge, New York 11788
www.barronseduc.com

Library of Congress Catalog Card No. 2011033127

ISBN: 978-0-7641-4781-4

Library of Congress Cataloging-in-Publication Data

Bromberg, Murray.
 504 absolutely essential words / Murray Bromberg, Julius Liebb, Arthur Traiger. — 6th ed.
  p. cm.
 Includes bibliographical references and index.
 ISBN 978-0-7641-4781-4 (alk. paper)
 1. Vocabulary—Problems, exercises, etc. I. Liebb, Julius. II. Traiger, Arthur. III. Title.
IV. Title: Five hundred four absolutely essential words.

PE1449.B68 2012
428.1–dc23   2011033127

CONTENTS

PRONUNCIATION GUIDE

The pronunciation of the *504 absolutely essential words* included in this book are those used by educated, cultured speakers in everyday, relaxed informal conversation.

Below are a list of symbols; the sound that each symbol represents can be easily understood from the key word in which it is shown.

a	back	ô	horn	f	fall	s	sit
ā	hay	oo	look	g	get	t	tin
ä	car	ōō	too	h	hotel	v	voice
ã	care	oi	toy	j	joy	w	win
e	then	u	up	k	kill	ch	church
ē	easy	ú	toot	l	let	hw	white
ė	bird	ū	you	m	man	zh	leisure
i	it	ou	out	n	not	y	yes
ī	kite	b	bed	p	put	z	zebra
ō	home	d	done	r	rose	ŋ	drink

The unstressed vowel sound is symbolized as follows:

ə   for **a** as in a**r**ound   for **i** as in san**i**ty   for **u** as in foc**u**s
     for **e** as in glitt**e**r   for **o** as in compl**e**te

INTRODUCTION

This is a self-help book. If you use it intelligently, you will help yourself to strengthen and expand your word knowledge. The words you will learn, moreover, are essential in that they are known and used regularly by educated people. You will find that such words as *squander, rehabilitate, blunder, obesity,* and five hundred more will turn up in your newspapers, in the magazines you read, in books, on television, in the movies, and in the conversation of the people you meet daily.

504 Absolutely Essential Words is divided into 42 lessons, each containing 12 new words. Those words are first presented to you in three sample sentences; next, the new words appear in a brief passage; the last part of each lesson is a set of exercises that give you practice using the new words. One of the most important features of **504 . . . Words** is that each of the new words is repeated over and over again throughout this book so that you will have a greater chance to become familiar with it.

Included are seven Word Review sections, each containing challenging exercises that will help you to test your mastery of the new words.

Newly added are interesting exercises in letter writing and parts of speech that will familiarize you with our basic 504 essential words. Finally, this 6th edition features frequently misspelled words, a Bonus Review, a Bonus Lesson with 125 More Difficult (But Essential) Words, and a new section called Panorama of Words.

HOW TO USE THIS BOOK

504 Absolutely Essential Words can be used in a number of ways, depending upon the needs and the status of the reader. A student in a high school English class, for example, could work with the book over a period of one school year, learning a dozen words each week for 42 weeks. Pupils who are studying vocabulary in an individualized program can move through the text at their own speed, mastering the new words as rapidly as they are able. Adults, out of school, can dip into the book on a selective basis, paying attention to the new words and skipping over those with which they are already familiar.

The High School English Class Some teachers prefer to set aside one day a week for intensive vocabulary study. At such time the sentences containing the new words are often read aloud so that the students hear them used in context. The definitions may be copied into a vocabulary notebook to reinforce the learning. Next, the accompanying paragraph(s) containing the 12 new words should be read aloud, followed by the exercise in which the blanks are to be filled in. Some discussion of the "Spotlight On" word is appropriate, preceding a homework assignment in which the students compose original sentences for each of the new words.

Independent Study An interesting way to approach **504 Absolutely Essential Words** on one's own is to take an informal pretest on each week's words, comparing the definitions with the ones provided in the text. After studying the three sample sentences, the reader should compose several original ones, using the model paragraph(s) for resource material.

The "Spotlight On" word introduces students to the fascinating history of the English language. They are advised to look up other words in each lesson in order to find out about their origin and to expand their vocabulary in the process.

Finally, students who are working on their own should complete the exercises at the end of each section, filling in the blanks and striving for a perfect score.

Repetition The words with asterisks (*) are those that have been taught in previous lessons. They are planted everywhere in the book since the repetition of newly learned material is a recognized road to mastery. If you come across such a word but cannot remember its meaning, turn back to the lesson in which that word first appeared. (See the index on pages 200-202 for such information.)

LESSON

1

1. **abandon** (ə ban' dən) desert; leave without planning to come back; quit
   a. When Roy **abandoned** his family, the police went looking for him.
   b. The soldier could not **abandon** his friends who were hurt in battle.
   c. Because Rose was poor, she had to **abandon** her idea of going to college.

Words to Learn This Week

abandon
keen
jealous
tact
oath
vacant
hardship
gallant
data
unaccustomed
bachelor
qualify

2. **keen** (kēn) sharp; eager; intense; sensitive
   a. The butcher's **keen** knife cut through the meat.
   b. My dog has a **keen** sense of smell.
   c. Bill's **keen** mind pleased all his teachers.

3. **jealous** (jel' əs) afraid that the one you love might prefer someone else; wanting what someone else has
   a. A detective was hired by the **jealous** widow to find the boyfriend who had abandoned* her.
   b. Although my neighbor just bought a new car, I am not **jealous** of him.
   c. Being **jealous**, Mona would not let her boyfriend dance with any of the cheerleaders.

4. **tact** (takt) ability to say the right thing
   a. My aunt never hurts anyone's feelings because she always uses **tact.**
   b. By the use of **tact**, Janet was able to calm her jealous* husband.
   c. Your friends will admire you if you use **tact** and thoughtfulness.

5. **oath** (ōth) a promise that something is true; a curse
   a. The president will take the **oath** of office tomorrow.
   b. In court, the witness took an **oath** that he would tell the whole truth.
   c. When Terry discovered that he had been abandoned,* he let out an angry **oath**.

6. **vacant** (vā' kənt) empty; not filled
   a. Someone is planning to build a house on that **vacant** lot.
   b. I put my coat on that **vacant** seat.
   c. When the landlord broke in, he found that apartment **vacant**.

7. **hardship** (härd' ship) something that is hard to bear; difficulty
   a. The fighter had to face many **hardships** before he became champion.
   b. Abe Lincoln was able to overcome one **hardship** after another.
   c. On account of **hardship**, Bert was let out of the army to take care of his sick mother.

8. **gallant** (gal' ənt) brave; showing respect for women
   a. The pilot swore a **gallant** oath* to save his buddy.
   b. Many **gallant** knights entered the contest to win the princess.
   c. Ed is so **gallant** that he always gives up his subway seat to a woman.

9. **data** (dāt' ə or dat' ə) facts; information
   a. The **data** about the bank robbery were given to the F.B.I.
   b. After studying the **data**, we were able to finish our report.
   c. Unless you are given all the **data**, you cannot do the math problem.

10. unaccustomed (ən ə kəs' təmd) not used to something
    a.   Coming from Alaska, Claude was **unaccustomed** to Florida's heat.
    b.   The king was **unaccustomed** to having people disobey him.
    c.   **Unaccustomed** as he was to exercise, Vic quickly became tired.

11. bachelor (batch' ə lər) a man who has not married
    a.   My brother took an oath* to remain a **bachelor**.
    b.   In the movie, the married man was mistaken for a **bachelor**.
    c.   Before the wedding, all his **bachelor** friends had a party.

12. qualify (kwal' ə-fī) become fit; show that you are able
    a.   I am trying to **qualify** for the job that is now vacant.*
    b.   Since Pauline can't carry a tune, she is sure that she will never **qualify** for the Girls' Chorus.
    c.   You have to be taller than 5'5'' to **qualify** as a policeman in our town.

Words in Use

Read the following passage to see how the new words are used in it.

My Brother, the Gentleman

The story of Sir Walter Raleigh, who spread his cloak on the ground to keep Queen Elizabeth from the **hardship** of crossing a muddy puddle, can **qualify** that nobleman for an award as a man of **tact** and good breeding. My brother Kenny, a **bachelor** with a **keen** interest in history, was impressed by that anecdote and thought he might demonstrate his excellent upbringing in a parallel situation. Accordingly he decided to **abandon** his subway seat in favor of a woman standing nearby.

Although **unaccustomed** to such generous treatment, the young woman was pleased to accept Kenny's kind offer. However, her **jealous** boyfriend swore an **oath** under his breath because he thought my brother was flirting with his girlfriend. I don't have any **data** on the number of young men who get into similar trouble as a result of a **gallant** gesture, but it's probably one in a thousand. Poor Kenny! He pointed to the now **vacant** seat.

Picture It

Which of the words studied in this lesson is suggested by the picture?

Fill in the Blanks

Place one of the new words in each of the blanks below.

1. As I looked at all the _____ the salesman showed me, I knew that I was getting more and more mixed up.
2. I used _____ when I told my fat uncle that his extra weight made him look better.
3. When the guard saw that the cot was _____ , he realized that the prisoner had left the jail.
4. Although he took an _____ on the Bible, Sal lied to the jury.
5. My aunt was so _____ of our new couch that she bought one just like it.
6. I enjoyed reading the story of the _____ man who put his cloak over a mud puddle so that the queen would not dirty her feet.
7. The loss of Claudia's eyesight was a _____ which she learned to live with.
8. The driver was forced to _____ his car when two of the tires became flat.
9. Betty could not _____ for the Miss Teenage America Contest because she was twenty years old.
10. The blade was so _____ that I cut myself in four places while shaving.
11. _____ to being kept waiting, the angry woman marched out of the store.
12. Because he was a _____ , the movie actor was invited to many parties.

Answer key, p. 196

Word Detective

From the list of 12 new words that follows, choose the one that corresponds to each definition below.

abandon	keen	jealous	tact
oath	vacant	hardship	gallant
data	unaccustomed	bachelor	qualify

1. a promise that something is true _____
2. sharp; eager; intense _____
3. to desert; to leave without planning to come back _____
4. something that is hard to bear _____
5. to become fit _____
6. wanting what someone else has _____
7. brave; showing respect for women _____
8. a man who has not married _____
9. facts; information _____
10. the ability to say the right thing _____
11. empty; not filled _____
12. not used to something _____

Answer key, p. 196

Spotlight On

abandon—This is an interesting word with a French background; in that language it meant "to put under another's control," hence, "to give up." In Lesson 19 you will find the new word *ban*, and may discover how it is related to *abandon*. A good dictionary will also show you the connection with other words such as *bandit* and *contraband*.

LESSON 2

Words to Learn This Week

corpse
conceal
dismal
frigid
inhabit
numb
peril
recline
shriek
sinister
tempt
wager

1. **corpse** (kôrps) a dead body, usually of a person
   a. When given all the data* on the **corpse**, the professor was able to solve the murder.
   b. The **corpse** was laid to rest in the vacant* coffin.
   c. An oath* of revenge was sworn over the **corpse** by his relatives.

2. **conceal** (kən sēl') hide
   a. Tris could not **conceal** his love for Gloria.
   b. Count Dracula **concealed** the corpse* in his castle.
   c. The money was so cleverly **concealed** that we were forced to abandon* our search for it.

3. **dismal** (diz' məl) dark and depressing
   a. When the weather is so **dismal**, I sometimes stay in bed all day.
   b. I am unaccustomed* to this **dismal** climate.
   c. As the **dismal** reports of the election came in, the senator's friends tactfully* made no mention of them.

4. **frigid** (frij' id) very cold
   a. It was a great hardship* for the men to live through the **frigid** winter at Valley Forge.
   b. The jealous* bachelor* was treated in a **frigid** manner by his girlfriend.
   c. Inside the butcher's freezer the temperature was **frigid.**

5. **inhabit** (in hab' it) live in
   a. Eskimos **inhabit** the frigid* part of Alaska.
   b. Because Sidney qualified,* he was allowed to **inhabit** the vacant* apartment.
   c. Many crimes are committed each year against those who **inhabit** the slum area of our city.

6. **numb** (num) without the power of feeling; deadened
   a. My fingers quickly became **numb** in the frigid* room.
   b. **A numb** feeling came over Mr. Massey as he read the telegram.
   c. When the nurse stuck a pin in my **numb** leg, I felt nothing.

7. **peril** (per' əl) danger
   a. The hunter was abandoned* by the natives when he described the **peril** that lay ahead of them.
   b. There is great **peril** in trying to climb the mountain.
   c. Our library is filled with stories of **perilous** adventures.

8. **recline** (ri klīn') lie down; stretch out; lean back
   a. Richard likes to **recline** in front of the television set.
   b. After **reclining** on her right arm for an hour, Maxine found that it had become numb.*
   c. My dog's greatest pleasure is to **recline** by the warm fireplace.

9. **shriek** (shrēk) scream
   a. The maid **shrieked** when she discovered the corpse.*
   b. With a loud **shriek**, Ronald fled from the room.
   c. Facing the peril* of the waterfall, the boatman let out a terrible **shriek.**

10. sinister (sin' is tər) evil; wicked; dishonest; frightening
   a.   The **sinister** plot to cheat the widow was uncovered by the police.
   b.   When the bank guard spied the **sinister**-looking customer, he drew his gun.
   c.   I was frightened by the **sinister** shadow at the bottom of the stairs.

11. tempt (tempt) try to get someone to do something; test; invite
   a.   A banana split can **tempt** me to break my diet.
   b.   The sight of beautiful Louise **tempted** the bachelor* to change his mind about marriage.
   c.   Your offer of a job **tempts** me greatly.

12. wager (wā ' jər) bet
   a.   I lost a small **wager** on the Super Bowl.
   b.   After winning the **wager**, Tex treated everyone to free drinks.
   c.   It is legal to make a **wager** in the state of Nevada.

Words in Use

Read the following passage to see how the new words are used in it.

Terror in the Cemetery

I like to bet on anything that is exciting, so when my friends tried to **tempt** me with an offer, I took it. The idea was for me to spend a **frigid** December night in a cemetery, all alone, in order to win twenty dollars. Little did I realize that they would use dirty tricks to try to frighten me into abandoning the cemetery, therefore losing my **wager**.

My plan was to **recline** in front of a large grave, covered by a warm blanket, with a flashlight to help me cut through the **dismal** darkness. After midnight, I heard a wild **shriek**. I thought I saw the grave open and a **corpse** rise out of it! Although I was somewhat **numb** with fear, I tried to keep my senses. Using good judgment, I knew that no **peril** could come to me from that **sinister** figure. When I did not run in terror, my friends, who had decided to **conceal** themselves behind the nearby tombstones, came out and we all had a good laugh. Those spirits that may **inhabit** a cemetery must have had a good laugh, too.

Fill in the Blanks

Place one of the new words in each of the blanks below.

1. The chances of my winning the election were so _____ that I decided to quit before the votes were counted.
2. I won the _____ that my bachelor* friend would be married by June.
3. Kit Carson's keen* eyesight protected him from the _____ in the forest.
4. While escaping from the bank, the robbers forced the teller to _____ on the floor of their car.
5. Since the shack was vacant,* we did not expect to hear the terrible _____ which came from it.
6. With a _____ smile, the gangster invited Martha into his Cadillac.
7. You cannot _____ the truth when you are questioned by the keen* lawyer.
8. It is said that many ghosts _____ the old Butler house.
9. In _____ weather I always wear three or four sweaters.
10. After standing guard duty for four hours, I became completely _____ .
11. As the closet was opened, the _____ fell out, frightening the janitor out of one year's growth.
12. With the promise of a raise in pay, my boss tried to _____ me to stay on in the job.

Answer key, p. 196

Creativity Exercise

Now make up your own sentences, one for each of the new words you have just been taught.

1. _____
2. _____
3. _____
4. _____
5. _____
6. _____
7. _____
8. _____
9. _____
10. _____
11. _____
12. _____

Spotlight On

sinister—In Latin this word means "on the left." According to ancient belief, that which appeared on the left-hand side brought bad luck. Another explanation for connecting bad luck with the left side is that the west (left) is toward the setting sun.

Picture It

Which of the words studied in this lesson is suggested by the picture?

"Good words anoint a man, ill words kill a man."

—John Florio, *First Fruites*

---

1. typical (tip' ə kəl) usual; of a kind
   a. The sinister* character in the movie wore a **typical** costume, a dark shirt, loud tie, and tight jacket.
   b. The horse ran its **typical** race, a slow start and a slower finish, and my uncle lost his wager.*
   c. It was **typical** of the latecomer to conceal* the real cause of his lateness.

2. minimum (min' ə məm) the least possible amount; the lowest amount
   a. Studies show that adults need a **minimum** of six hours sleep.
   b. The **minimum** charge for a telephone, even if no calls are made, is about $60 a month.
   c. Congress has set a **minimum** wage for all workers.

3. scarce (skãrs) hard to get; rare
   a. Chairs that are older than one hundred years are **scarce**.
   b. Because there is little moisture in the desert, trees are **scarce**.
   c. How **scarce** are good cooks?

4. annual (an' ū əl) once a year; something that appears yearly or lasts for a year
   a. The **annual** convention of musicians takes place in Hollywood.
   b. The publishers of the encyclopedia put out a book each year called an **annual**.
   c. Plants that live only one year are called **annuals**.

5. persuade (pər swād') win over to do or believe; make willing
   a. Can you **persuade** him to give up his bachelor* days and get married?
   b. No one could **persuade** the captain to leave the sinking ship.
   c. Beth's shriek* **persuaded** Jesse that she was in real danger.

6. essential (ə sen' shəl) necessary; very important
   a. The **essential** items in the cake are flour, sugar, and shortening.
   b. It is **essential** that we follow the road map.
   c. Several layers of thin clothing are **essential** to keeping warm in frigid* climates.

7. blend (blend) mix together thoroughly; a mixture
   a. The colors of the rainbow **blend** into one another.
   b. A careful **blend** of fine products will result in delicious food.
   c. When Jose **blends** the potatoes together, they come out very smooth.

8. visible (viz' ə bəl) able to be seen
   a. The ship was barely **visible** through the dense fog.
   b. Before the stars are **visible**, the sky has to become quite dark.
   c. You need a powerful lens to make some germs **visible**.

9. expensive (eks pen' səv) costly; high-priced
   a. Because diamonds are scarce* they are **expensive**.
   b. Margarine is much less **expensive** than butter.
   c. Shirley's **expensive** dress created a great deal of excitement at the party.

10. talent (tal'ənt) natural ability
    a. Medori's **talent** was noted when she was in first grade.

   b.   Feeling that he had the essential* **talent**, Carlos tried out for the school play.
   c.   Hard work can often make up for a lack of **talent**.

11.   devise (də vīz') think out; plan; invent
   a.   The burglars **devised** a scheme for entering the bank at night.
   b.   I would like to **devise** a method for keeping my toes from becoming numb* while I am ice skating.
   c.   If we could **devise** a plan for using the abandoned* building, we could save thousands of dollars.

12.   wholesale (hō l' sāl) in large quantity; less than retail in price
   a.   The **wholesale** price of milk is six cents a quart lower than retail.
   b.   Many people were angered by the **wholesale** slaughter of birds.
   c.   By buying my eggs **wholesale** I save fifteen dollars a year.

Words in Use
Read the following passage to see how the new words are used in it.

An Unusual Strike

The baseball strike of 1994–95, which kept the public from seeing the **annual** World Series, was not a **typical** labor dispute in which low-paid workers try to **persuade** their employers to grant a raise above their **minimum** wage. On the contrary, players who earned millions of dollars yearly, who were **visible** on TV commercials, drove **expensive** autos, and dined with presidents, withheld their **essential** skills until the executive, legislative, and judicial branches of our government were forced to **devise** solutions to the quarrel.

The team owners, a **blend** of lawyers, manufacturers, corporate executives, etc., felt that something had to be done about the huge salaries that the players were demanding. Since the **talent** beyond the major leagues was **scarce**, they had to start spring training in 1995 with a **wholesale** invitation to replacement players. The regular athletes returned in late April but there was a feeling that the strike could happen again.

Fill in the Blanks
Place one of the new words in each of the blanks below.

   1. The March of Dimes makes its _____ appeal in the early spring.
   2. Oil paints _____ easily to form thousands of different shades.
   3. The _____ passing mark in most schools is 65%.
   4. The producer always had her eye out for young _____ .
   5. Your gifts do not tempt* me and will not _____ me to change my mind.
   6. In the cemetery the corpse* was _____ in the bright moonlight.
   7. A _____ day in Florida is full of sunshine and warm breezes.
   8. Let's _____ a plan for doing away with homework.
   9. Everyone agrees that friendship is _____ for all of us.
   10. A sharp rise in _____ prices is bound to affect the prices in our neighborhood stores.
   11. The buffalo, which once roamed the plains, is quite _____ today.
   12. Government experts told us to buy chicken without realizing how _____ it had become.

Answer key, p. 196

Creativity Exercise
Now make up your own sentences, one for each of the new words you have just been taught.

   1. _____

   2. _____

3. _____

4. _____

5. _____

6. _____

7. _____

8. _____

9. _____

10. _____

11. _____

12. _____

Spotlight On

expensive—The definition given to you was "costly, high-priced." Other synonyms could have been provided because English is quite rich in that area. Webster's *Dictionary of Synonyms,* for example, contains ten entries that explain *expensive* or show us slight variations of the word: *costly, dear, valuable, precious, invaluable, priceless, exorbitant, excessive, immoderate.* When would you use *costly* as a synonym for *expensive* and when would you use *excessive*?

Picture It

Which of the words studied in this lesson is suggested by the picture?

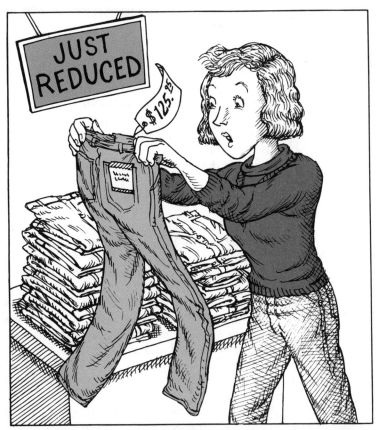

LESSON 4

"Good words are worth much and cost little."
—George Herbert, *Jacula Prudentum*

Words to Learn This Week

vapor
eliminate
villain
dense
utilize
humid
theory
descend
circulate
enormous
predict
vanish

1. **vapor** (vā' pər) moisture in the air that can be seen; fog; mist
   a. Scientists have devised* methods for trapping **vapor** in bottles so they can study its makeup.
   b. He has gathered data* on the amount of **vapor** rising from the swamp.
   c. A **vapor** trail is the visible* stream of moisture left by the engines of a jet flying at high altitudes.

2. **eliminate** (i lim' ə nāt) get rid of; remove; omit
   a. When the railroad tracks are raised, the danger of crossing will be **eliminated**.
   b. When figuring the cost of a car, don't **eliminate** such extras as air conditioning.
   c. If we were to **eliminate** all reclining* chairs, no one would fall asleep while watching television.

3. **villain** (vil' ən) a very wicked person
   a. A typical* moving picture **villain** gets killed at the end.
   b. The **villain** concealed* the corpse* in the cellar.
   c. When the **villain** fell down the well, everyone lived happily ever after.

4. **dense** (dens) closely packed together; thick
   a. The **dense** leaves on the trees let in a minimum* of sunlight.
   b. We couldn't row because of the **dense** weeds in the lake.
   c. His keen* knife cut through the **dense** jungle.

5. **utilize** (ū' tə līz) make use of
   a. No one seems willing to **utilize** this vacant* house.
   b. The gardener was eager to **utilize** different flowers and blend* them in order to beautify the borders.
   c. Does your mother **utilize** leftovers in her cooking?

6. **humid** (hū' mid) moist; damp
   a. It was so **humid** in our classroom that we wished the school would buy an air conditioner.
   b. New Yorkers usually complain in the summer of the **humid** air.
   c. Most people believe that ocean air is quite **humid**.

7. **theory** (thē' ə rē) explanation based on thought, observation, or reasoning
   a. Einstein's **theory** is really too difficult for the average person to understand.
   b. My uncle has a **theory** about the effect of weather on baseball batters.
   c. No one has advanced a convincing **theory** explaining the beginnings of writing.

8. **descend** (di send') go or come down from a higher place to a lower level
   a. If we let the air out of a balloon, it will have to **descend**.
   b. The pilot, thinking his plane was in peril,* **descended** quickly.
   c. Knowing her beau was waiting at the bottom of the staircase, Eleanor **descended** at once.

9. **circulate** (sər' kū lāt) go around; go from place to place or person to person
   a. A fan may **circulate** the air in summer, but it doesn't cool it.

b.   My father **circulated** among the guests at the party and made them feel comfortable.
c.   Hot water **circulates** through the pipes in the building, keeping the room warm.

10. enormous (i nôr' məs) extremely large; huge
a.   The **enormous** crab moved across the ocean floor in search of food.
b.   Public hangings once drew **enormous** crowds.
c.   The gallant* knight drew his sword and killed the **enormous** dragon.

11. predict (pri dikt') tell beforehand
a.   Weathermen can **predict** the weather correctly most of the time.
b.   Who can **predict** the winner of the Super Bowl this year?
c.   Laura thought she could **predict** what I would do, but she was wrong.

12. vanish (van' ish) disappear; disappear suddenly
a.   Even in California the sun will sometimes **vanish** behind a cloud.
b.   Not even a powerful witch can make a jealous* lover **vanish**.
c.   Give him a week without a job and all his money will **vanish**.

Words in Use

Read the following passage to see how the new words are used in it.

A Fan in the Air

Fog, tiny droplets of water **vapor**, is the **villain** of the airports. In an effort to **eliminate dense** fog from airports, weathermen **utilize** giant fans, nylon strings, and chemicals dropped from planes or shot upwards from strange machines on the ground. Nothing works as well, though, as a new weapon in the fight against fog: the helicopter. Researchers believe that if warm dry air above the fog could somehow be driven down into the **humid** blanket of fog, the droplets would evaporate, thus clearing the air. In a recent experiment to test their **theory** the researchers had a helicopter **descend** into the fog above barely visible* Smith Mountain Airport near Roanoke, Virginia. The blades of the helicopter caused the air to **circulate** downwards and an **enormous** hole in the clouds opened above the airport. Weathermen **predict** that with larger, more expensive* helicopters they will be able to make the thickest fog **vanish**.

Picture It

Which of the words studied in this lesson is suggested by the picture?

Fill in the Blanks

Place one of the new words in each of the blanks below.

1. If we have one more hot, _____ day, you will be able to persuade* me to move to Alaska.
2. In the show the magician waved his wand to make a lady _____ .
3. The hair on his head was so _____, a special pair of scissors was used to thin it.
4. Since he has passed all his subjects, I'll _____ that he will graduate.
5. The _____ in the movie was played by an actor who was able to look mean.
6. _____ rose out of the valve on top of the steam engine.
7. The basketball player was _____ ; he could practically drop the ball through the hoop.
8. What _____ can you suggest to explain the frequent changes in women's clothing?
9. Why don't you _____ all the space on that page?
10. Sooner or later the elevator will _____ and we'll be able to go up.
11. I heard a doctor on a television show say that if we _____ one slice of bread each day, we'll lose weight.
12. Copies of some magazines are so scarce,* the librarian won't allow them to _____ .

Answer key, p. 196

Synonym Search

Circle the word that most nearly expresses the meaning of the word printed in blue type.

1. **circulate** the news
   (a) report   (b) spread   (c)interpret   (d) watch
2. **eliminate** a problem
   (a) perceive   (b) wipe out   (c) aggravate   (d) create
3. an **enormous** ocean liner
   (a) incredible   (b) extravagant   (c) unforgettable   (d) huge
4. **dense** fog
   (a) misty   (b) thick   (c) invisible   (d) dismal*
5. **descend** the stairs
   (a) slip on   (b) fortify   (c) come down   (d) use
6. the suspected **villain**
   (a) wicked person   (b) schemer   (c) gossip   (d) dictator
7. **humid** climate
   (a) frigid*   (b) moist   (c) perilous*   (d) sunny
8. **predict** the future
   (a) plan for   (b) look forward to   (c) foretell   (d) accept
9. deadly **vapors** from the chemical explosion
   (a) forces   (b) explosives   (c) gases   (d) sleet
10. **vanish** into thin air
    (a) change   (b) crumble   (c) disappear   (d) vacate
11. science **theory**
    (a) knowledge of facts   (b) laboratory equipment   (c) explanation based on thought
    (d) experiment
12. **utilize** their services
    (a) pay for   (b) make use of   (c) extend   (d) regain

Answer key, p. 196

Spotlight On

villain—We see from this how social attitudes can affect the meanings of words. In Latin a *villa* was a small farm and its buildings; a connection of such buildings became a *village*, and a person who lived on such a farm was a *villain*. Some who lived in the cities looked down on the country folk, regarding them as stupid, low-minded, and evil. In that way, country people earned a reputation (*villains*) they did not deserve.

LESSON 5

Words to Learn This Week

tradition
rural
burden
campus
majority
assemble
explore
topic
debate
evade
probe
reform

1. **tradition** (tra dish' ən) beliefs, opinions, and customs handed down from one generation to another
   a. The father tried to persuade* his son that the **tradition** of marriage was important.
   b. All religions have different beliefs and **traditions**.
   c. As time goes on, we will eliminate* **traditions** that are meaningless.

2. **rural** (rŭr' əl) in the country
   a. Tomatoes are less expensive* at the **rural** farm stand.
   b. **Rural** areas are not densely* populated.
   c. The **rural** life is much more peaceful than the city one.

3. **burden** (bėr' dən) what is carried; a load
   a. The **burden** of the country's safety is in the hands of the president.
   b. Irma found the enormous* box too much of a **burden**.
   c. Ricky carried the **burden** throughout his college career.

4. **campus** (kam' pəs) grounds of a college, university, or school
   a. The **campus** was designed to utilize* all of the college's buildings.
   b. Jeff moved off **campus** when he decided it was cheaper to live at home.
   c. I chose to go to Penn State because it has a beautiful **campus**.

5. **majority** (me jôr' ə tē) the larger number; greater part; more than half
   a. A **majority** of votes was needed for the bill to pass.
   b. The **majority** of people prefer to pay wholesale* prices for meat.
   c. In some countries, the government does not speak for the **majority** of the people.

6. **assemble** (əs sem' bl) gather together; bring together
   a. The rioters **assembled** outside the White House.
   b. I am going to **assemble** a model of a spacecraft.
   c. All the people who had **assembled** for the picnic vanished* when the rain began to fall.

7. **explore** (eks plôr') go over carefully; look into closely; examine
   a. Lawyer Spence **explored** the essential* reasons for the crime.
   b. The weather bureau **explored** the effects of the rainy weather.
   c. Sara wanted to know if all of the methods for solving the problem had been **explored**.

8. **topic** (täp' ik) subject that people think, write, or talk about
   a. Predicting* the weather is our favorite **topic** of conversation.
   b. Valerie only discussed **topics** that she knew well.
   c. The speaker's main **topic** was how to eliminate* hunger in this world.

9. **debate** (di bāt') a discussion in which reasons for and against something are brought out
   a. The **debate** between the two candidates was heated.
   b. **Debate** in the U.S. Senate lasted for five days.
   c. Instead of shrieking* at each other, the students decided to have a **debate** on the topic.*

10. **evade** (i vād') get away from by trickery or cleverness
    a. Juan tried to **evade** the topic* by changing the subject.

13

b. In order to **evade** the police dragnet, Ernie grew a beard.
c. The prisoner of war **evaded** questioning by pretending to be sick.

11. probe (prōb) search into; examine thoroughly; investigate
a. The lawyer **probed** the man's mind to see if he was innocent.
b. After **probing** the scientist's theory,* we proved it was correct.
c. King Henry's actions were carefully **probed** by the noblemen.

12. reform (ri fôrm') make better; improve by removing faults
a. After the prison riot, the council decided to **reform** the correctional system.
b. Brad **reformed** when he saw that breaking the law was hurting people other than himself.
c. Only laws that force companies to **reform** will clear the dangerous vapors* from our air.

Words in Use

Read the following passage to see how the new words are used in it.

Shape Up at Shaker

Each summer at the Shaker Work Group, a special school in **rural** Pittsfield, Massachusetts, where teenagers learn by working, it has been a **tradition** to have the teenagers take on the **burden** of setting their own rules and living by them. Although there are some adults on the **campus**, teenagers are a **majority**.

One summer the group **assembled** to **explore** the **topic** of lights-out time. There was little **debate** until 10:30 P.M. was suggested. Why? Everyone at the Shaker Work Group works a min-imum* of several hours each morning on one project and several hours each afternoon on another. Since everyone has to get up early, no one wanted to stay up later at night anyway.

Few teenagers at the Shaker Work Group try to **evade** the rules. When one does, the entire group meets to **probe** the reasons for the "villain's"* actions. Their aim is to **reform** the rule breaker. However, at Shaker Village, the theory* is that teenagers who are busy working will have no time to break rules.

Fill in the Blanks

Place one of the new words in each of the blanks below.

1. I left the city for a peaceful _____ farm.
2. Professor Dixon liked the atmosphere of the university _____ .
3. He tried to _____ questions he didn't know how to answer.
4. The _____ of people wanted him to be president.
5. The guests began to _____ for Thanksgiving dinner.
6. Christmas trees are a popular _____ for many people.
7. Making a living for his family was too much of a _____ .
8. I want to _____ all the cities I haven't visited.
9. If Gene doesn't _____ , he will get into serious trouble.
10. He had to do research on the _____ of biology for a school report.
11. Historians will _____ the causes of the war in Iraq.
12. Whether or not eighteen-year-olds should be allowed to vote was in _____ for a long time.

Answer key, p. 196

Creativity Exercise

Now make up your own sentences, one for each of the new words you have just been taught.

1. _____

2. _____

3. _____

4. _____

5. _____

6. _____

7. _____

8. _____

9. _____

10. _____

11. _____

12. _____

_____

Spotlight On

majority—In the past, we heard politicians talk about the "silent majority," meaning the average Americans who are decent persons, earn livings, follow the laws of the land, all in a quiet way. Those politicians might have been surprised to learn that when the philosophers and writers of old used the term "silent majority" they were referring to dead people.

Picture It

Which of the words studied in this lesson is suggested by the picture?

LESSON 6

Words to Learn This Week

approach
detect
defect
employee
neglect
deceive
undoubtedly
popular
thorough
client
comprehensive
defraud

1. **approach** (ə prōch') come near or nearer to
   a. The lawyers in the trial were often asked to **approach** the bench.
   b. Her beau kissed Sylvia when he **approached** her.
   c. Ben **approached** the burden* of getting a job with a new spirit.

2. **detect** (di tekt') find out; discover
   a. Sam Spade **detected** that the important papers had vanished.*
   b. From her voice it was easy to **detect** that Ellen was frightened.
   c. We **detected** from the messy room that a large group of people had assembled* there.

3. **defect** (di' fekt) fault; that which is wrong
   a. My Chevrolet was sent back to the factory because of a steering **defect**.
   b. His theory* of the formation of our world was filled with **defects**.
   c. The villain* was caught because his plan had many **defects**.

4. **employee** (em ploi ē') a person who works for pay
   a. The **employees** went on strike for higher wages.
   b. My boss had to fire many **employees** when meat became scarce.*
   c. Joey wanted to go into business for himself and stop being an **employee**.

5. **neglect** (ni glekt') give too little care or attention to
   a. The senator **neglected** to make his annual* report to Congress.
   b. Bob's car got dirty when he **neglected** to keep it polished.
   c. It is essential* that you do not **neglect** your homework.

6. **deceive** (di sēv') make someone believe as true something that is false; mislead
   a. Atlas was **deceived** about the burden* he had to carry.
   b. Virginia cried when she learned that her best friend had **deceived** her.
   c. The villain* **deceived** Chief White Cloud by pretending to be his friend.

7. **undoubtedly** (un dout' id lē) certainly; beyond doubt
   a. Ray's team **undoubtedly** had the best debators* in our county.
   b. The pilgrims **undoubtedly** assembled* to travel to Rome together.
   c. If she didn't want to get into an argument, Valerie would have followed the majority* **undoubtedly**.

8. **popular** (pop' ū lar) liked by most people
   a. The Beatles wrote many **popular** songs.
   b. At one time miniskirts were very **popular**.
   c. **Popular** people often find it hard to evade* their many friends.

9. **thorough** (ther' o) being all that is needed; complete
   a. The police made a **thorough** search of the house after the crime had been reported.
   b. My science teacher praised Sandy for doing a **thorough** job of cleaning up the lab.
   c. Mom decided to spend the day in giving the basement a **thorough** cleaning.

10. client (klī' ənt) person for whom a lawyer acts; customer
   a.   The lawyer told her **client** that she could predict* the outcome of his trial.
   b.   My uncle tried to get General Motors to be a **client** of his company.
   c.   If this restaurant doesn't improve its service, all its **clients** will vanish.*

11. comprehensive (käm' pri hen' siv) including much; covering completely
   a.   After a **comprehensive** exam, my doctor said I was in good condition.
   b.   The engineer gave our house a thorough*, **comprehensive** checkup before my father bought it.
   c.   Mrs. Silver wanted us to do a **comprehensive** study of Edgar Allan Poe.

12. defraud (di frôd') take money, rights, etc., away by cheating
   a.   My aunt saved thousands of dollars by **defrauding** the government.
   b.   If we could eliminate* losses from people who **defraud** the government, tax rates could be lowered.
   c.   By **defrauding** his friend, Dexter ruined a family tradition* of honesty.

Words in Use

Read the following passage to see how the new words are used in it.

The Health of Your Car

The newest **approach** to automobile repair is the clinic, a place where car doctors go over an automobile in an attempt to **detect defects.** Since the clinic does no repairs, its **employees** do not **neglect** the truth. So many automobile owners feel that mechanics **deceive** them that the clinics, even though they **undoubtedly** charge high fees, are quite **popular**.

The experts do a **thorough** job for each **client**. They explore* every part of the engine, body, and brakes; they do all kinds of tests with expensive* machines. Best of all, the **comprehensive** examination takes only about half an hour. With the clinic's report in your hand no mechanic will be able to **defraud** you by telling you that you need major repairs when only a small repair is necessary.

Picture It

Which of the words studied in this lesson is suggested by the picture?

Fill in the Blanks

Place one of the new words in each of the blanks below.

1. Each of our workers is trained to give your car a _____ examination. (Which *two* words might fit this sentence?)
2. Tom Jones was _____ the best singer in the choir when he was young.
3. He could _____ the problem from all angles.
4. Mrs. Spector always wanted to be _____ with her friends.
5. Why did you _____ cleaning your room today?
6. The _____ bought his boss a birthday present.
7. Rocco's only _____ was that he walked with a slight limp.
8. None of the other poker players suspected that their friend would _____ them in order to win.
9. When Cynthia realized that nobody liked her, she knew she had been _____ .
10. I could _____ from the tone of his voice that he was in a bad mood.
11. His _____ was happy with the work Terence had been doing for him.
12. I do not want to do anything less than a _____ job on my term paper. (Which *two* words might fit this sentence?)

Answer key, p. 196

Choose the Correct Word

Circle the word in parentheses that best fits the sense of the sentence.

1. Many of today's (popular, comprehensive) songs will become tomorrow's Golden Oldies.
2. My boss insists that all of the (employees, clients) punch a time clock each morning.
3. I (approached, detected) a hint of sarcasm in your seemingly innocent reply to the sales clerk who apologized for the long lines.
4. As the car (approached, detected) the bridge, we could see the dense* fog coming in off the water.
5. Our weekly vocabulary quizzes are (comprehensive, popular), including not only that week's new words, but words we learned in past weeks as well.
6. Even a small (client, defect) in an electric appliance can be the possible* cause of a fire.
7. Ms. Rodriguez (undoubtedly, comprehensively) felt she had been unjustly accused of showing favoritism, but most of her students felt otherwise.
8. Her (thorough, popular) description of the missing bracelet helped police find it.
9. We've all learned that if you (defraud, neglect) your teeth, you will surely develop dental problems of one kind or another.
10. It is probably still true that the majority* of Americans do not think our political leaders would knowingly (defect, defraud) the government.
11. To (defraud, deceive) someone into thinking you are a friend when you are only along for the ride is selfish and unfeeling.
12. Since your livelihood depends on pleasing them, (clients, employees), like customers, are always right.

Answer key, p. 196

Spotlight On

defect—Some of the new words have more than one part of speech—for example, they have meanings as verbs as well as nouns. *Defect* was defined for you as a noun: "fault; that which is wrong." It also serves as a verb, meaning "to quit a country, a political party, or a cause." One is said "to defect from one country to another" or "to defect from the Democratic Party." Which of the other words in Lesson 6 have more than one part of speech?

Word Review #1

In the first six lessons you were taught 72 important words. The following exercises will test how well you learned some of those words.

A. In each of the parentheses below you will find two of the new vocabulary words. Pick the one that fits better. Remember, the sentences should make good sense.

1. It was a (dense, typical) day in July, hot and sticky.
2. 1 could tell that Matt was coming because I knew his (blend, vapor) of tobacco.
3. Please realize that if you try to climb the icy mountain (peril, tradition) awaits you.
4. The mechanic (defected, detected) an oil leak in the engine.
5. How could you (recline, neglect) paying the rent?
6. Felix made a (sinister, frigid) remark that sent chills up and down my spine.
7. Many questions had to be answered before Mrs. Soto could (qualify, evade) for the job.
8. I am (unaccustomed, dismal) to receiving gifts from people I don't know very well.
9. Factory-made goods are plentiful, but farm products are (rural, scarce).
10. When he got to the jail, the people in charge tried to (reform, abandon) him.

Answer key, p. 196

B. Opposites. In Column I are ten words taught in Lessons 1–6. Match them correctly with their opposite meanings, which you will find in Column II.

Column I	Column II
1. approach	a. unseen
2. expensive	b. filled
3. visible	c. hated
4. popular	d. dull
5. vacant	e. dry
6. keen	f. be seen
7. descend	g. leave
8. humid	h. not needed
9. vanish	i. climb
10. essential	j. cheap

Answer key, p. 196

C. Which of the vocabulary choices in parentheses fits best in these newspaper headlines?

1. **Sailors _____ Sinking Ship**   (Defraud, Circulate, Abandon, Devise)
2. **Congress Votes to Raise _____ Wage**   (Hardship, Minimum, Typical, Rural)
3. **_____ Fog Covers Bay Area**   (Dense, Thorough, Scarce, Keen)
4. **Unfit Parents Arrested for Child _____**   (Defect, Tradition, Neglect, Theory)
5. **Escaped Convict Continues to _____ Police**   (Abandon, Evade, Inhabit, Conceal)
6. **College _____ Quiet After Demonstration**   (Client, Campus, Debate, Probe)
7. **Mayor Takes _____ of Office on Steps of City Hall**   (Oath, Data, Majority, Reform)
8. **Rescuers _____ into Mine to Find Lost Workers**   (Descend, Assemble, Circulate, Recline)
9. **New Apartment House to Rise on _____ Land**   (Frigid, Comprehensive, Dense, Vacant)
10. **Poll to _____ Outcome of Election**   (Qualify, Predict, Tempt, Eliminate)

Answer key, p. 196

D. From the list of words below choose the word that means:

deceive	tradition	abandon	persuade	inhabit	gallant
thorough	evade	descend	comprehensive	eliminate	hardship
villain	assemble	circulate	talent	majority	wholesale
client	dense	predict	devise	defraud	recline
probe	theory	tact	conceal	data	tempt

1. in large amounts *as well as* less costly
2. an evil doer, *but originally meant* someone who lived on a farm
3. more than half *as well as* the legal age at which persons can manage their affairs
4. search or investigate *either* by means of an instrument or simply by questioning
5. cheat *and also* deprive someone of rights or property
6. give up on a plan *as well as* neglect one's post
7. gather (data) or just get together
8. reject *and also* expel
9. leaving out little or nothing *and* is related to the word for "understanding"
10. skill in dealing with people *as well as* a fine touch or cleverness

Answer key, p. 196

E. Letter of Complaint. The following business letter uses 10 words that appeared in Lessons 1–6. Fill in the blanks with those words, selected from the group below:

abandon	conceal	employee	expensive	neglect
annual	defect	enormous	gallant	recline
circulate	defraud	essential	hardship	tempt
comprehensive	detect	evade	majority	wholesale

13 Oak Street
Merrick, NY 11566
April 2, 2011

Speedy Catalog Service
200 Beverly Road
Champaign, IL 61821

Dear Sirs:

Three weeks ago, I bought a 20" Royal TV set (Item #996R) from your catalog, which had featured an ___1___ clearance sale at ___2___ savings. I am enclosing a copy of the $200 money order that I sent to you.

When my father and I unpacked the set, we ___3___ (ed) several ___4___ (s), including a scratched screen and a broken volume dial. Since that was not my fault, I believe that I am entitled to receive a new set.

It was a ___5___ for me to save part of my weekly allowance for six months in order to pay for the TV, and I would appreciate your help in this matter. Even though it is not an ___6___ set, and I was getting it at a ___7___ price, I still feel that the merchandise should be perfect.

Obviously, one of your ___8___ (s) had ___9___ (d) to do an ___10___ inspection before the TV was shipped to my home.

Sincerely,
Arthur Karnes

Answer key, p. 196

F. Words That Do Double Duty. Some of the words in this book can be used as different parts of speech. The sample sentences for the word *gallant* show it to be an adjective, a word that describes a noun or pronoun:

> *gallant* oath
> *gallant* knight
> Ed is so *gallant*.

However, gallant can be used as a noun when we say: "The *gallant*, dressed in his finery, approached the queen."

The following words from Lessons 1–6 are capable of serving as more than one part of speech:

abandon (v., n.)	burden (n., v.)
hardship (n., adj.)	debate (n., v.)
wager (n., v.)	probe (n., v.)
annual (n., adj.)	reform (v., adj.)
blend (n., v.)	neglect (n., v.)

Make up two sentences for each of the above words, showing how it could be used as two different parts of speech.

Examples: After I wasted two months, I had to *abandon* (v.) the project.
At the party, Edith danced with reckless *abandon* (n.).

LESSON
7

"A fool and his words are soon parted."

—William Shenstone, *On Reserve*

**Words to Learn
This Week**

postpone
consent
massive
capsule
preserve
denounce
unique
torrent
resent
molest
gloomy
unforeseen

1. **postpone** (pōst pōn') put off to a later time; delay
    a. The young couple wanted to **postpone** their wedding until they were sure they could handle the burdens* of marriage.
    b. I neglected* to **postpone** the party because I thought everyone would be able to come.
    c. The supermarket's owner planned to **postpone** the grand opening until Saturday.

2. **consent** (kən sent') agree; give permission or approval
    a. My teacher **consented** to let our class leave early.
    b. David would not **consent** to our plan.
    c. The majority* of our club members **consented** to raise the dues.

3. **massive** (mas' iv) big and heavy; large and solid; bulky
    a. The boss asked some employees* to lift the **massive** box.
    b. From lifting weights, Willie had developed **massive** arm muscles.
    c. The main building on the campus* was so **massive** that the new students had trouble finding their way around at first.

4. **capsule** (kap' səl) a small case or covering
    a. The small **capsule** contained notes the spy had written after the meeting.
    b. A new, untested medicine was detected* in the **capsule** by the police scientists.
    c. He explored* the space **capsule** for special equipment.

5. **preserve** (pri zėrv') keep from harm or change; keep safe; protect
    a. The lawyers wanted to **preserve** the newest reforms* in the law.
    b. Farmers feel that their rural* homes should be **preserved**.
    c. The outfielder's records are **preserved** in the Baseball Hall of Fame.

6. **denounce** (di nouns') condemn in public; express strong disapproval of
    a. The father **denounced** his son for lying to the district attorney.
    b. Some people **denounce** the government for probing* into their private lives.
    c. The consumer advocate **denounced** the defective* products being sold.

7. **unique** (ū nēk') having no like or equal; being the only one of its kind
    a. Going to Africa was a **unique** experience for us.
    b. The inventor developed a **unique** method of making ice cream.
    c. Albie has a **unique** collection of Israeli stamps.

8. **torrent** (tôr' ənt) any violent, rushing stream; flood
    a. A massive* rain was coming down in **torrents**.
    b. In the debate,* a **torrent** of questions was asked.
    c. After trying to defraud* the public, Lefty was faced with a **torrent** of charges.

9. **resent** (ri zent') feel injured and angered at (something)
    a. Bertha **resented** the way her boyfriend treated her.
    b. The earthquake victim **resented** the poor emergency care.
    c. Columbus **resented** the fact that his crew wanted to turn back.

10. molest (mə lest') interfere with and trouble; disturb
  a. My neighbor was **molested** when walking home from the subway.
  b. The gang did a thorough* job of **molesting** the people in the park.
  c. Lifeguards warned the man not to **molest** any of the swimmers.

11. gloomy (glūm' ē) dark; dim; in low spirits
  a. My cousin was **gloomy** because his best friend had moved away.
  b. The reason Doris wasn't popular* was that she always had a **gloomy** appearance.
  c. Jones Beach is not so beautiful on a **gloomy** day.

12. unforeseen (un fôr sēn') not known beforehand; unexpected
  a. We had some **unforeseen** problems with the new engine.
  b. The probe* into the congressman's finances turned up some **unforeseen** difficulties.
  c. The divers faced **unforeseen** trouble in their search for the wreck.

Words in Use

Read the following passage to see how the new words are used in it.

The Frozen Future

Doctors are always devising* new cures for diseases that kill people. But suppose you are dying from an incurable illness now. If only you could **postpone** death until a cure was found! Now some people are trying to do just that. One young man **consented** to having his body frozen and placed in a **massive capsule** in order to **preserve** it until doctors find a cure for his disease. Some people have **denounced** this **unique** experiment with a **torrent** of angry words. They **resent** human attempts to **molest** the natural order of life and death. There is also a **gloomy** fear that the world is already overcrowded and that people have to die to make room for those who are about to be born. If the experiment works, **unforeseen** problems undoubtedly* will arise.

Picture It

Which of the words studied in this lesson is suggested by the picture?

Fill in the Blanks

Place one of the new words in each of the blanks below.

1. We have tried for over 200 years to _____ the United States Constitution.
2. The _____ weather predictions* upset him.
3. Will Karen _____ to having her baby picture published in the school newspaper?
4. I found a _____ collection of old books in the attic.
5. Dave knew that if he mistreated her, she would _____ it.
6. The president _____ the criminal activities that were going on.
7. Lori feared that if she walked the streets, she would be _____ .
8. Owning a house created _____ difficulties.
9. The new movie invited a _____ of disapproval.
10. A telephone call told us that the employees'* picnic was _____ until next week.
11. The _____ was filled with records of the past.
12. It was a _____ job for just one person to unload the big truck.

Answer key, p. 196

Creativity Exercise

Now make up your own sentences, one for each of the new words you have just been taught.

1. _____
2. _____
3. _____
4. _____
5. _____
6. _____
7. _____
8. _____
9. _____
10. _____
11. _____
12. _____

Spotlight On

preserve—Would you expect any connection between this word and *family*? Well, there is. In ancient times man was master of his household (*familia*) and the person who *served* him was the woman who had been captured and *preserved* from slaughter in order to work for the conqueror. In the 1500s a servant was called a *familiar*.

LESSON 8

1. **exaggerate** (eg zaj' ər āt) make something greater than it is; overstate
   a. He wasn't trying to deceive* you when he said that his was the best car in the world; he was just **exaggerating**.
   b. The bookkeeper **exaggerated** her importance to the company.
   c. When he said that O'Neal was eight feet tall, he was undoubtedly* **exaggerating**.

Words to Learn This Week

exaggerate
amateur
mediocre
variety
valid
survive
weird
prominent
security
bulky
reluctant
obvious

2. **amateur** (am' e tər) person who does something for pleasure, not for money or as a profession
   a. The **amateur** cross-country runner wanted to be in the Olympics.
   b. After his song, Don was told that he wasn't good enough to be anything but an **amateur**.
   c. Professional golfers resent* **amateurs** who think they are as good as the people who play for money.

3. **mediocre** (mē di ō' kər) neither good nor bad; average; ordinary
   a. After reading my composition, Mrs. Evans remarked that it was **mediocre** and that I could do better.
   b. Howard was a **mediocre** scientist who never made any unique* discoveries.
   c. The movie wasn't a great one; it was only **mediocre**.

4. **variety** (və rī' ə tē) lack of sameness; a number of different things
   a. Eldorado Restaurant serves a wide **variety** of foods.
   b. The show featured a **variety** of entertainment.
   c. He faced unforeseen* problems for a **variety** of reasons.

5. **valid** (val' id) supported by facts or authority; sound; true
   a. The witness neglected* to give **valid** answers to the judge's questions.
   b. Rita had **valid** reasons for denouncing* her father's way of life.
   c. When Dave presented **valid** working papers, the foreman consented* to hiring him immediately.

6. **survive** (sər vīv') live longer than; remain alive after
   a. It was uncertain whether we would **survive** the torrent* of rain.
   b. Some people believe that only the strongest should **survive**.
   c. The space capsule* was built to **survive** a long journey in space.

7. **weird** (wêrd) mysterious; unearthly
   a. She looked **weird** with that horrible makeup on her face.
   b. Allen felt that **weird** things were starting to happen when he entered the haunted house.
   c. Becky had a **weird** feeling after swallowing the pills.

8. **prominent** (präm' ə nənt) well-known; important
   a. My client* is a **prominent** businessperson.
   b. Napoleon is a **prominent** figure in the history of France.
   c. Her violet eyes were the **prominent** feature of the model's face.

9. **security** (si kyúr'ə tē) freedom from danger, care, or fear; feeling or condition of being safe
   a. Our janitor likes the **security** of having all doors locked at night.
   b. When the president travels, strict **security** measures are taken.
   c. Pablo wanted to preserve* the **security** of his lifestyle.

10. bulky (bul' kē) taking up much space; large
    a. Charley and Morty removed the **bulky** package from the car.
    b. The massive* desk was quite **bulky** and impossible to carry.
    c. His client* wanted an item that wasn't so **bulky**, Olsen told us.

11. reluctant (ri luk' tənt) unwilling
    a. It was easy to see that Herman was **reluctant** to go out and find a job.
    b. The patient was **reluctant** to tell the nurse the whole gloomy* truth.
    c. I was **reluctant** to give up the security* of family life.

12. obvious (ob' vē əs) easily seen or understood; clear to the eye or mind; not to be doubted; plain
    a. It was **obvious** that the lumberjack was tired after his day's work.
    b. The fact that Darcy was a popular* boy was **obvious** to all.
    c. The detective missed the clue because it was too **obvious**.

Words in Use

Read the following passage to see how the new words are used in it.

The Guitar

It is impossible to **exaggerate** the popularity* of the guitar. One out of every four **amateur** musicians in the United States plays the guitar. Even a **mediocre** player can produce a **variety** of music with this unique* instrument. Trying to find **valid** reasons for the guitar's ability to **survive** through the years isn't hard. One **weird** theory* by a **prominent** musician states that guitarists find **security** hiding behind the **bulky** instrument. But most people are **reluctant** to accept this idea because there are more **obvious** reasons for playing a guitar. It can be carried anywhere, it is inexpensive* to buy, and only a few lessons are required to learn to play it well.

Picture It

Which of the words studied in this lesson is suggested by the picture?

Fill in the Blanks

Place one of the new words in each of the blanks below.

1. Most people agreed that he was a _____ looking man because of the long red beard.
2. Chuck's reason for quitting his job was _____ ; he was not being paid.
3. The answer to the question was so _____ that everyone knew it.
4. The _____ tennis player would never make the Olympic squad.
5. She was _____ to take on any more responsibilities at work.
6. People often tend to _____ stories they hear.
7. The bank is kept under very tight _____ .
8. Because the box was so _____ it took two men to lift it.
9. Even though he was not a professional, the _____ photographer entered the contest.
10. A wide _____ of shows is playing at the concert hall.
11. Mrs. Meyers is a _____ member of the staff.
12. We all hoped that the small boat would _____ the storm.

Answer key, p. 196

Matching

Match the 12 new words in Column I with the definitions in Column II.

Column I	Column II
1. reluctant	a. large; taking up much space
2. mediocre	b. true; supported by facts
3. prominent	c. person who does something for pleasure, not as a profession
4. obvious	d. average; ordinary
5. exaggerate	e. mysterious; unearthly
6. bulky	f. unwilling
7. variety	g. easily seen or understood
8. valid	h. well-known; important
9. security	i. remain alive; live on
10. survive	j. overstate; make something greater than it is
11. weird	k. feeling or condition of being safe
12. amateur	l. a number of different things

Answer key, p. 196

Spotlight On

obvious—Like so many of our words, this one comes from Latin roots—*ob* meaning *against* and *via* meaning *way*. Something that met you on the way, therefore, was *obvious*. Look up the meanings of the Latin roots of some of the other words in Lesson 8 such as *exaggerate, survive,* and *prominent*.

LESSON 9

—Benjamin Disraeli, *Contarini Fleming*

---

1. **vicinity** (və sin' ə tē) region near a place; neighborhood
   a. Living in the **vicinity** of New York, Jeremy was near many museums.
   b. The torrent* of rain fell only in our **vicinity**.
   c. We approached* the Baltimore **vicinity** by car.

2. **century** (sen' chə rē) 100 years
   a. George Washington lived in the eighteenth **century**.
   b. The United States is more than two **centuries** old.
   c. Many prominent* men have been born in this **century**.

3. **rage** (rāj) violent anger; something that arouses intense but brief enthusiasm
   a. Joan's bad manners sent her mother into a **rage**.
   b. In a fit of **rage,** Francine broke the valuable glass.
   c. The mayor felt a sense of **rage** about the exaggerations* in the press.

4. **document** (dok' ū mənt) something handwritten or printed that gives information or proof of some fact
   a. Newly discovered **documents** showed that the prisoner was obviously* innocent.
   b. The **documents** of ancient Rome have survived* many centuries.*
   c. We were reluctant* to destroy important **documents**.

5. **conclude** (kən klōōd') end; finish; decide
   a. Most people are happy when they **conclude** their work for the day.
   b. The gloomy* day **concluded** with a thunderstorm.
   c. Work on the building could not be **concluded** until the contract was signed.

6. **undeniable** (un di nī' ə bəl) not to be denied; cannot be questioned
   a. The jury concluded* that the teenagers were **undeniably** guilty.
   b. It is **undeniable** that most professionals can beat any amateur.*
   c. That Leon resented* Rita's good marks in school was **undeniable.**

7. **resist** (rē zist') act against; strive against; oppose
   a. Totie could not **resist** eating the chocolate sundae.
   b. Tight security* measures **resisted** Jimmy's entrance into the bank.
   c. Harold **resisted** the opportunity to poke fun at the weird* man.

8. **lack** (lak) be entirely without something; have not enough
   a. Your daily diet should not **lack** fruits and vegetables.
   b. His problem was that he **lacked** a variety* of talents.*
   c. As an amateur* dancer, Vincent knew that he **lacked** the professional touch.

9. **ignore** (ig nôr') pay no attention to; disregard
   a. Little Alice realized that if she didn't behave, her parents would **ignore** her.
   b. The student could not answer the question because he **ignored** the obvious* facts.
   c. Older brothers and sisters often feel **ignored** when their parents only spend time with a new baby.

Words to Learn This Week

vicinity
century
rage
document
conclude
undeniable
resist
lack
ignore
challenge
miniature
source

10. challenge (chal' ənj) call to a fight
   a.   Aaron Burr **challenged** Alexander Hamilton to a duel.
   b.   No one bothered to **challenge** the prominent* lawyer.
   c.   Trying to become a doctor was quite a **challenge**, Dick discovered.

11. miniature (min' ē ə tūr) represented on a small scale
   a.   The young boy wanted a **miniature** sports car for his birthday.
   b.   Instead of buying a massive* dog, Teddy got a **miniature** poodle.
   c.   We were seeking a **miniature** model of the bulky* chess set.

12. source (sôrs) place from which something comes or is obtained
   a.   The college student knew that he needed more than a basic textbook as a **source** for his report.
   b.   The **source** of Buddy's trouble was boredom.
   c.   Professor Smith's speech was a valid* **source** of information on chemistry.

Words in Use

Read the following passage to see how the new words are used in it.

More About the Guitar

The guitar is one of the oldest instruments known to man. It probably originated in the **vicinity** of China. There were guitars in ancient Egypt and Greece as well, but the written history of the guitar starts in Spain in the 13th **century**. By 1500 the guitar was popular in Italy, France, and Spain. A French **document** of that time **concludes** that many people were playing the guitar. Stradivarius, the **undeniable** king of violin makers, could not resist creating a variety* of guitars. Also, there was no **lack** of music written for the instrument. Haydn, Schubert, and others wrote guitar music. When the great Beethoven was asked to compose music for the guitar, he went into a **rage** and refused, but eventually even Beethoven could not **ignore** the **challenge**; legend tells us he finally called the guitar a **miniature** orchestra. Indeed the guitar does sound like a little orchestra! Perhaps that is why in rural* areas around the world the guitar has been a **source** of music for millions to enjoy.

Picture It

Which of the words studied in this lesson is suggested by the picture?

Fill in the Blanks

Place one of the new words in each of the blanks below.

1. Ernesto would constantly _____ his father's questions.
2. Historical _____ are kept in a special section of the library.
3. Great scientific progress has been made in this _____ .
4. The massive* wrestler accepted the _____ of the newcomer.
5. Not wearing warm clothing was the _____ of his illness.
6. "When do you expect to _____ your investigation of the case?"
7. It is _____ that this restaurant's food is delicious.
8. Lena showed a _____ of good judgment.
9. Everyone who lived in the _____ of the bomb test was in peril.*
10. Anita's habit of interrupting him sent her husband into a _____ .
11. My nephew was given a set of _____ soldiers for Christmas.
12. When you are tired it is hard to _____ staying in bed all day.

Answer key, p. 196

Synonym Search

Circle the word that most nearly expresses the meaning of the word printed in blue type.

1. **century**
   (a) countless years   (b) three score years   (c) one hundred years   (d) generation
2. **document**
   (a) official paper   (b) critical review   (c) decree   (d) composition
3. **undeniable**
   (a) essential*   (b) unforeseen*   (c) comprehensive   (d) unquestionable
4. **vicinity**
   (a) region near a place   (b) division of a city or town   (c) residential district
   (d) metropolitan area
5. **challenge**
   (a) banish permanently   (b) verify easily   (c) call to a fight   (d) join together
6. **lack**
   (a) take responsibility   (b) correct   (c) be without   (d) give freely
7. **miniature**
   (a) balanced   (b) tiny   (c) eager   (d) forbidden
8. **rage**
   (a) extreme anger   (b) foolish explanation   (c) rapid movement   (d) bad habit
9. **conclude**
   (a) show   (b) reorganize   (c) examine   (d) decide
10. **source**
    (a) origin   (b) task   (c) onlooker   (d) chart
11. **resist**
    (a) discuss honestly   (b) change completely   (c) strive against   (d) pay attention
12. **ignore**
    (a) disregard   (b) complete   (c) exaggerate*   (d) offer

Answer key, p. 196

Spotlight On

century—In our slang, a *C-note* (*century*) stands for $100. Other slang references to money are *fin* ($5), *sawbuck* ($10), and *grand* ($1,000). Look up the origins of these colorful terms for our dollars.

LESSON 10

**Words to Learn
This Week**

excel
feminine
mount
compete
dread
masculine
menace
tendency
underestimate
victorious
numerous
flexible

1. **excel** (ek sel') be better than; do better than
   a. Because he was so small, Larry could not **excel** in sports.
   b. At least Hannah had the security* of knowing that she **excelled** in swimming.
   c. Clarence Darrow wanted to become a prominent* lawyer, but he felt that he must first **excel** in the study of history.

2. **feminine** (fem' ə nin) of women or girls
   a. When my sister wants to look **feminine** she changes from dungarees into a dress.
   b. Aunt Sarah can always be counted on to give the **feminine** viewpoint.
   c. My brother is ashamed to cry at a sad movie because people might think he is behaving in a **feminine** manner.

3. **mount** (mount) get up on
   a. Congressman Jones **mounted** the platform to make his speech.
   b. The watchman **mounted** the tower to see if there were any people in the vicinity.*
   c. My sister couldn't **mount** the horse so they gave her a pony instead.

4. **compete** (kəm pēt') try hard to get something wanted by others; be a rival
   a. The former champion was challenged* to **compete** for the tennis title.
   b. The runner was reluctant* to **compete** in front of his parents for the first time.
   c. When the amateur* became a pro he had to **compete** against better men.

5. **dread** (dred) look forward to with fear; fear greatly; causing great fear
   a. The poor student **dreaded** going to school each morning.
   b. He had a **dread** feeling about the challenge* he was about to face.
   c. I **dread** going into that deserted house.

6. **masculine** (mas' kū lin) of man; male
   a. The boy became more **masculine** as he got older.
   b. It is undeniable* that his beard makes him look **masculine.**
   c. The girls liked Jerry because of his **masculine** ways.

7. **menace** (men' is) threat
   a. Irv's lack* of respect made him a **menace** to his parents.
   b. The torrents* of rain were a **menace** to the farmer's crops.
   c. Sergeant Foy's raw language was an obvious* **menace** to the reputation of the entire police department.

8. **tendency** (ten' den sē) leaning; movement in a certain direction
   a. My algebra teacher has a **tendency** to forget the students' names.
   b. His **tendency** was to work hard in the morning and then to take it easy in the afternoon.
   c. The **tendency** in all human beings is to try to survive.*

9. **underestimate** (un dər es' tə māt) set too low a value, amount, or rate
   a. I admit that I **underestimated** the power in the bulky* fighter's frame.

b.   Undoubtedly* the boss **underestimated** his employee's* ability to work hard.
c.   The value of our house was **underestimated** by at least two thousand dollars.

10. **victorious** (vik tô' rē əs) having won a victory; conquering
     a.   Playing in New Jersey, the Jets were **victorious** two years in a row.
     b.   Terry faced the challenge* with the bad attitude that he could not be **victorious**.
     c.   Our girls' volleyball squad was **victorious** over a taller team.

11. **numerous** (noo' mər əs) very many; several
     a.   Critics review **numerous** movies every week.
     b.   Dr. Fischer had resisted* accepting money from the poor woman on **numerous** house calls.
     c.   The debater* used **numerous** documents* to back up his statements.

12. **flexible** (fiek' sə bəl) easily bent; willing to yield
     a.   The toy was **flexible**, and the baby could bend it easily.
     b.   Remaining **flexible**, Nick listened to arguments from both sides.
     c.   A mouse's **flexible** body allows it to squeeze through narrow openings.

Words in Use

Read the following passage to see how the new words are used in it.

Bet on the Blond

Can women **excel** as jockeys in big-time horse racing? Years ago the **feminine** touch was kept out of racing, but now at tracks all over the country women **mount** horses and **compete** with men, many of whom **dread** the whole idea. Their **masculine** image, they feel, may be threatened.* Also, some offer the **weak** argument that females are a **menace** on the track. But, as we all know, we should resist* the **tendency** to **underestimate** the power of women. A few female jockeys have been **victorious** in **numerous** races, and this is probably what has put the male jockeys in a rage.* It would be wise if the men were more **flexible** in their attitudes toward women athletes.

Fill in the Blanks

Place one of the new words in each of the blanks below.

1. The massive* tree on the corner was a _____ to traffic.
2. At parties, the shy girl would _____ being asked to dance.
3. My uncle has a _____ to repeat the same story over and over again.
4. The modest man used to _____ his own strength.
5. No person can ever _____ in all things he does.
6. Being _____ is far better than being stubborn.
7. We went to the beach on _____ occasions last summer.
8. Playing with dolls is traditionally* a _____ pastime.
9. Only the brightest students were invited to _____ for the prize.
10. Carole was ten years old before her parents finally let her _____ a horse.
11. The amateur* tennis player completed many matches without being _____ .
12. When Stuart started growing a mustache, it was obvious* he was becoming more _____ .

Answer key, p. 196

Creativity Exercise

Now make up your own sentences, one for each of the new words you have just been taught.

1. _____

2. _____

3. _____

4. _____

5. _____

6. _____

7. _____

8. _____

9. _____

10. _____

11. _____

12. _____

Spotlight On

mount—A salesman of worthless goods and phony remedies would often gather a crowd at a fair by juggling or doing some other lively antics. Sometimes he *mounted* a bench (bank) on which goods were displayed, and in that manner our English word *mountebank* came to mean *quack* or *fake*.

Picture It

Which of the words studied in this lesson is suggested by the picture?

LESSON 11

"We tie knots and bind up words in double meanings, and then try to untie them."

—Seneca, *Epistalae ad Lucilium*

Words to Learn This Week

evidence
solitary
vision
frequent
glimpse
recent
decade
hesitate
absurd
conflict
minority
fiction

1. **evidence** (ev' ə dəns) that which makes clear the truth or falsehood of something
   a. Each juror felt he needed more **evidence** before voting to convict the former football star.
   b. Her many awards were **evidence** enough that Leona excelled* in dancing.
   c. Our teacher ignored* the **evidence** that Simon had cheated on the test.

2. **solitary** (sal' ə ter ē) alone; single; only
   a. Sid's **solitary** manner kept him from making new friendships.
   b. There was not a **solitary** piece of evidence* that Manuel had eaten the cheesecake.
   c. The convict went into a rage* when he was placed in a **solitary** cell.

3. **vision** (vizh' ən) power of seeing; sense of sight
   a. With the aid of the binoculars, my **vision** improved enough to see the entire vicinity.
   b. Ted had perfect **vision**, and that helped to make him a good baseball player.
   c. The glasses that Irma bought corrected her nearsighted **vision**.

4. **frequent** (frē' kwint) happening often; occurring repeatedly
   a. We made **frequent** visits to the hospital to see our grandfather.
   b. On **frequent** occasions Sam fell asleep in class.
   c. Dr. Bonner gave me some pills for my **frequent** headaches.

5. **glimpse** (glimps) a short, quick view
   a. This morning we caught our first **glimpse** of the beautiful shoreline.
   b. One **glimpse** of the very feminine* vision* was enough to tell Romeo that he loved Juliet.
   c. The tall shrubs kept us from getting a **glimpse** of the new people who inhabited* the beach house.

6. **recent** (rē' sənt) done, made, or occurring not long ago
   a. At a **recent** meeting, the Board of Education provided the evidence* we had been asking for.
   b. Bessie liked the old silent movies better than the more **recent** ones.
   c. **Recent** studies have concluded* that more people are unemployed than ever before.

7. **decade** (dek' ād) ten years
   a. After a **decade** of granting salary increases, my boss ended the practice.
   b. Many people moved out of this city in the last **decade**.
   c. I have a vision* that this **decade** will be better than the last one.

8. **hesitate** (hez' ə tāt) fail to act quickly; be undecided
   a. Nora **hesitated** to accept the challenge.*
   b. When he got to the robbers' vicinity,* he **hesitated** before going on.
   c. The proverb tells us that he who **hesitates** is lost.

9. absurd (ab sėrd') plainly not true or sensible; foolish
  a. It was **absurd** to believe the fisherman's tall tale.
  b. The flabby boy realized that the suggestion to diet was not **absurd**.
  c. Underestimating* the importance of reading is **absurd**.

10. conflict (kän' flikt) direct opposition; disagreement
  a. Our opinions about the company's success in the last decade* are in **conflict** with what the records show.
  b. There was a noisy **conflict** over who was the better tennis player.
  c. The class mediation team was invited to settle the **conflict**.

11. minority (mə nôr' ə tē) smaller number or part; less than half
  a. Only a small **minority** of the neighborhood didn't want a new park.
  b. A **minority** of our athletes who competed* in the Olympics were victorious.*
  c. Native Americans are a **minority** group in the United States.

12. fiction (fik' shen) that which is imagined or made up
  a. The story that the president had died was **fiction**.
  b. We hardly ever believed Vinny because what he said was usually **fiction**.
  c. Marge enjoys reading works of **fiction** rather than true stories.

Words in Use

Read the following passage to see how the new words are used in it.

The Famous Monster of the Lake

There seems to be more and more **evidence** that the enormous* monster in Loch Ness, a **solitary** lake in Scotland, is more than a **vision**. Each year there are numerous* **glimpses** of the monster by visitors and neighborhood people; also **recent** films, not easy to ignore,* are making even scientists **hesitate**. The story of **frequent** visits by a monster once seemed **absurd** to them, but now they are not so sure.

Yet the **conflict** is far from over. Those who believe the monster exists are still in the **minority**, and they are constantly competing* for more information to prove that the Loch Ness monster is not a **fiction**. Even now they are trying to get more and clearer moving pictures of what has become the famous inhabitant* of the lake. Perhaps the question of whether the monster exists or not will be answered in this coming **decade**.

Picture It

Which of the words studied in this lesson is suggested by the picture?

Fill in the Blanks

Place one of the new words in each of the blanks below.

1. The old man had lived for seven _____ .
2. He had the _____ that some day there would be peace on earth.
3. Only a _____ of the senators were against welfare.
4. No one has ever had even a _____ of the future.
5. People used to think it was an _____ idea that human beings could ever fly.
6. We make _____ visits to Florida in the winter.
7. If you have any questions, don't _____ to ask.
8. There was only a _____ man on the beach.
9. The _____ was over the high cost of bread.
10. _____ studies have shown that the cost of living has gone up rapidly.
11. The gun alone was _____ enough to convict the killer.
12. The stories Henry told people about his adventures turned out to be merely _____ .

Answer key, p. 196

Matching

Match the 12 new words in Column I with the definitions in Column II.

Column I	Column II
1. vision	a. ten years
2. fiction	b. happening often
3. frequent	c. alone
4. absurd	d. that which makes clear the truth or falsehood of something
5. minority	e. occurring not long ago
6. evidence	f. a short, quick view
7. conflict	g. that which is imagined or made up
8. decade	h. sense of sight
9. glimpse	i. smaller number or part
10. recent	j. direct opposition
11. solitary	k. plainly not true or sensible
12. hesitate	l. fail to act quickly

Answer key, p. 196

Spotlight On

absurd—Here is another example of the ways in which original meanings changed through the centuries. At first, *absurd* meant *quite deaf*. Its Latin roots also had the meanings of *out of tune, harsh, rough*—finally developing into *silly* or *senseless*.

LESSON
12

Words to Learn This Week

ignite
abolish
urban
population
frank
pollute
reveal
prohibit
urgent
adequate
decrease
audible

1. **ignite** (ig nīt') set on fire
   a. Spark plugs **ignite** in an automobile engine.
   b. One match can **ignite** an entire forest.
   c. A careless remark helped to **ignite** the conflict* between the brothers and the sisters.

2. **abolish** (ə bäl' ish) do away with completely; put an end to
   a. The death penalty has recently* been **abolished** in our state.
   b. We **abolished** numerous* laws that didn't serve any purpose in this decade.*
   c. My school has **abolished** final exams altogether.

3. **urban** (ėr' bən) of or having to do with cities or towns
   a. Many businesses open offices in **urban** areas.
   b. I plan to exchange my **urban** location for a rural* one.
   c. Only a small minority* of the people of the United States live far from any **urban** area.

4. **population** (pop ū lā' shən) people of a city or country
   a. China has the largest **population** of any country.
   b. The **population** of the world has increased in every decade.*
   c. After the recent* floods, the **population** of Honduras was reduced by 10,000.

5. **frank** (frangk) free in expressing one's real thoughts, opinions, or feelings; not hiding what is in one's mind
   a. Never underestimate* the value of being **frank** with one another.
   b. Eretha was completely **frank** when she told her friend about the sale.
   c. People liked Duffy because they knew he would be **frank** with them.

6. **pollute** (pə lo͞ot') make dirty
   a. The Atlantic Ocean is in danger of becoming **polluted**.
   b. There is much evidence* to show that the air we breathe is **polluted**.
   c. It is claimed that soap powders **pollute** the water we drink.

7. **reveal** (ri vēl') make known
   a. Napoleon agreed to **reveal** the information to the French population.*
   b. The evidence* was **revealed** only after hours of questioning.
   c. The auto company **revealed** reluctantly* that there were defects* in their new models.

8. **prohibit** (prȯ' hib' it) forbid by law or authority
   a. Elvin's manager **prohibited** him from appearing on television.
   b. Many homeowners **prohibit** others from walking on their property.
   c. The law **prohibits** the use of guns to settle a conflict.*

9. **urgent** (ėr' jənt) demanding immediate action or attention; important
   a. An **urgent** telephone call was made to the company's treasurer.
   b. The principal called an **urgent** meeting to solve the school's numerous* problems.
   c. When he heard the **urgent** cry for help, the lifeguard did not hesitate.*

10. **adequate** (ad' ə kwit) as much as is needed; fully sufficient
    a. Rover was given an **adequate** amount of food to last him the whole day.
    b. A bedroom, kitchen, and bath were **adequate** shelter for his living needs.
    c. Carlos was **adequate** at his job but he wasn't great.

11. **decrease** (di krēs') make or become less
    a. As he kept spending money, the amount he had saved **decreased.**
    b. In order to improve business, the store owner **decreased** his prices.
    c. The landlord promised to **decrease** our rent.

12. **audible** (ô də bəl) able to be heard
    a. From across the room, the teacher's voice was barely **audible**.
    b. After Len got his new hearing aid, my telephone calls became **audible**.
    c. Commands from Ann's drill sergeant were always easily **audible**.

Words in Use

Read the following passage to see how the new words are used in it.

The Electric Auto Is on Its Way

Ignite gasoline and you have noise and smoke; turn on an electric motor and you **abolish** two headaches that are dreaded* by **urban populations**. Automobile manufacturers are **frank** about the way their motors **pollute** the air, and that is why there are frequent* hints that the big companies will soon **reveal** a practical electric car.

So far, lack* of knowledge of storing electricity in the car **prohibits** wide production of electric autos, but recently* Congress called **urgently** for **adequate** research into the battery or fuel cell problem. Electric autos would be inexpensive* to run and would **decrease** air pollution.* It might be weird,* however, to live in the quiet surroundings of a city where autos that used to be noisily **audible** would be whisper-quiet.

Picture It

Which of the words studied in this lesson is suggested by the picture?

Fill in the Blanks

Place one of the new words in each of the blanks below.

1. The doctor was completely _____ with the dying man.
2. In an _____ whisper, Maria called for my attention.
3. We didn't need any evidence* to see that the poor man was in _____ need of money and food.
4. All his life the child was used to living in _____ areas.
5. Dry matches to _____ the campfire were sought by the boy scout.
6. Smoking is _____ in the medical building.
7. Gasoline fumes help to _____ the air.
8. The _____ in the number of people voting in national elections is due to lack* of interest.
9. Some citizens believe that we will never be able to _____ war.
10. The _____ of New York City is about eight million people.
11. In the comics, Superman never _____ his true identity.
12. They needed an _____ supply of water to last for the entire trip through the desert.

Answer key, p. 196

Word Detective

From the list of 12 new words that follows, choose the one that corresponds to each definition below.

ignite	abolish	urban	population
frank	pollute	reveal	prohibit
urgent	adequate	decrease	audible

1. having to do with cities or towns   _____
2. make known   _____
3. as much as is needed; sufficient   _____
4. make dirty   _____
5. do away with completely   _____
6. make or become less   _____
7. free in expressing one's thoughts   _____
8. demanding immediate action   _____
9. set on fire   _____
10. people of a city or country   _____
11. able to be heard   _____
12. forbid by law or authority   _____

Answer key, p. 196

Spotlight On

ignite—Some years ago, much attention was given to the fiery comet Kohoutek, which was supposed to blaze spectacularly across the sky. The people of medieval times spoke of four such types of natural history: *aerial meteors* (winds), *aqueous meteors* (rain, snow), *luminous meteors* (rainbow, halo) and *igneous meteors* (lightning, shooting stars). Now that you know the definition of ignite, you can see why such heavenly occurrences were called *igneous*.

Word Review #2

Here are some of the words that were covered in Lessons 7–12. The following exercises will test how well you learned them.

A. In each of the parentheses below you will find two of the new vocabulary words. Choose the one that fits better.

1. We will have to (postpone, decrease) our meeting unless more members show up.
2. Rex (underestimated, resisted) the skill of the other tennis player, and he was beaten badly.
3. With only a (frank, mediocre) typing ability, Veronica never expected to be hired.
4. Germs are a (menace, dread) to our health.
5. Although Rip was (challenged, reluctant) to tell all he knew, he remained silent.
6. We invited only the most (prominent, undeniable) people in town to our fund-raising party.
7. When her job in the city was (molested, abolished), Daisy went home to the farm.
8. (Unforeseen, Amateur) problems kept coming up each day, making it harder and harder for me to finish my work.
9. I believe in our doctor and like the (absurd, adequate) reasons he gave us for keeping Grandma in the hospital.
10. Don't you get angry when someone (ignores, concludes) your questions?

Answer key, p. 196

B. Opposites. In Column I are ten words that were taught in Lessons 7–12. Match them correctly with their *opposite* meanings, which you will find in Column II.

Column I	Column II
1. consent	a. put out
2. valid	b. not important
3. ignite	c. die
4. reveal	d. refuse
5. urgent	e. allow
6. victorious	f. large
7. survive	g. get off
8. mount	h. hide
9. prohibit	i. beaten
10. miniature	j. untrue

Answer key, p. 196

C. Which of the vocabulary choices in parentheses fits best in these newspaper headlines?

1. **"Charges Against Me Are _____," Complains Governor**   (Undeniable, Frank, Absurd, Mediocre)
2. **High School Principal to _____ Student Autos**   (Preserve, Prohibit, Abolish, Underestimate)
3. **_____ Flight of Space Shuttle for 48 Hours**   (Unforeseen, Ignite, Preserve, Postpone)
4. **Witness Promises to _____ Truth Today**   (Reveal, Denounce, Exaggerate, Challenge)
5. **"Best Novel in a _____," Says Critic**   (Conflict, Decade, Variety, Fiction)
6. **Sick Child Visited by _____ Specialist**   (Obvious, Prominent, Amateur, Dread)
7. **Flu Germs _____ Elderly Citizens**   (Menace, Resist, Pollute, Prohibit)
8. **Stolen Jewels Are Objects of _____ Search**   (Adequate, Valid, Unforeseen, Massive)
9. **Huge Unemployment in _____ Areas**   (Reluctant, Recent, Urban, Urgent)
10. **Weatherman Apologizes for _____ Weekend Forecast**   (Valid, Gloomy, Obvious, Solitary)

Answer key, p. 196

D. From the list of words below choose the word that means:

conclude	solitary	excel	massive	fiction	preserve
urban	obvious	menace	denounce	vision	century
torrent	unique	compete	tendency	security	source
frank	glimpse	dread	numerous	mediocre	undeniable
decrease	conflict	hesitate	document	reluctant	absurd

1. be undecided *as well as* show reluctance
2. an untruth *but* one that is practiced by even the best writers
3. ponderous or large *and* is the opposite of *capsule*
4. ten decades *and* has the same root as *cent*
5. finish *as well as* make an inference
6. ridiculous *yet in a certain phrase* is close to *sublime*

7. *easily understood as well as* evident and apparent
8. save *and in its origin* bears a relation to *family*
9. a dream or hope *as well as* sight
10. one of a kind *and also* rare or without equal

Answer key, p. 196

E.   The Friendly Letter. With our reliance on the telephone, and now on the new technologies, letter writing among friends has become less important. Still and all, there is no substitute for a personal letter, which friends will appreciate. In the following letter, fill in the blanks, using words selected from the group below:

abolish	decrease	glance	prohibit	urban
adequate	dread	glimpse	security	urgent
conclude	excel	hesitate	source	valid
consent	frank	obvious	tendency	vision

May 17, 2011

Dear Rona,

My first day at the Herricks Junior High here in Sandy, Utah was a weird* one. Everyone knew each other, and I was like an alien from outer space. After having spent seven years in classes with you in Miami, I have to adjust to a new state, a new city, a new neighborhood, and a new school!

To be perfectly __1__ , I __2__ to guess how I'll manage to survive* because I really miss you and the whole gang back in sunny Florida. You and I always talked about swimming and scuba diving but here all the kids are into skiing. I'm sure that I'll __3__ my first time on the big slopes because I have a __4__ to fear new experiences. To start with, I'll have to swap my swim gear for down jackets, mittens, and ear muffs. Brrr!

Back to Herricks Jr. High. We have only 140 kids in this less than __5__ school where there is absolutely no need for a __6__ guard. A quick __7__ of my program reveals* that I have five major subjects, including French. In addition, *ma cherie*, I have Phys. Ed. three times a week, plus Computer Lab., Home Eco. (we made jello the first day!) and Music. It's __8__ I won't have time to loaf.

There is a Senior Prom and a class trip to Los Angeles, if I can get my Mom to __9__ . I have to __10__ this letter now because they gave me a ton of homework.

Fondly,
Blanche

Answer key, p. 196

F.   Words That Do Double Duty. As we noted in Word Review #1, there are many words that can serve as different parts of speech. For example, *burden* may be a noun (a heavy load) or a verb (to burden someone). The following words from Lessons 7–12 are capable of being used as two different parts of speech.

consent (v., n.)	challenge (v., n.)
preserve (v., n.)	menace (v., n.)
security (n., adj.)	frequent (v., adj.)
rage (v., n.)	conflict (v., n.)
document (v., n.)	dread (v., adj.)

Make up two sentences for each of the above words, showing how it could be used as different parts of speech.

Examples: My mother gave her *consent* (n.) to our trip.
Mr. De Poto would not *consent* (v.) to giving me a raise.

LESSON
13

"He can compress the most words into the smallest ideas of any man I ever met."

—Abraham Lincoln, of a fellow lawyer

1. **journalist** (jėr' nəl ist) one who writes for, edits, manages, or produces a newspaper or magazine
   a. There were four **journalists** covering the murder story.
   b. Barbara's experience working at a book store wasn't adequate* preparation for becoming a **journalist**.
   c. **Journalists** must have a comprehensive* knowledge* of the city where they work.

Words to Learn This Week

journalist
famine
revive
commence
observant
identify
migrate
vessel
persist
hazy
gleam
editor

---

2. **famine** (fam' ən) starvation; great shortage
   a. **Famine** in Africa caused the death of one tenth of the population.*
   b. There has been a **famine** of good writing in the last decade.*
   c. The rumor of a **famine** in Europe was purely fiction.*

3. **revive** (ri vīv') bring back or come back to life or consciousness
   a. There is a movement to **revive** old plays for modern audiences.
   b. The nurses tried to **revive** the heart attack victim.
   c. Committees are trying to **revive** interest in population* control.

4. **commence** (kə mens') begin; start
   a. Graduation will **commence** at ten o'clock.
   b. Bella hesitated* before **commencing** her speech.
   c. The discussion **commenced** with a report on urban* affairs.

5. **observant** (ab zer' vənt) quick to notice; watchful
   a. We were **observant** of the conflict* between the husband and his wife.
   b. Because Cato was **observant**, he was able to reveal* the thief's name.
   c. Milt used his excellent vision* to be **observant** of everything in his vicinity.*

6. **identify** (ī den' tə fī) recognize as being, or show to be, a certain person or thing; prove to be the same
   a. Numerous* witnesses **identified** the butcher as the thief.
   b. Mrs. Shaw was able to **identify** the painting as being hers.
   c. With only a quick glimpse,* Reggie was able to **identify** his girlfriend in the crowd.

7. **migrate** (mī' grāt) move from one place to another
   a. The fruit pickers **migrated** to wherever they could find work.
   b. Much of our population* is constantly **migrating** to other areas of the country.
   c. My grandfather **migrated** to New York from Italy in 1919.

8. **vessel** (ves' əl) a ship; a hollow container; tube containing body fluid
   a. The Girl Scouts were permitted a glimpse* of the **vessel** being built when they toured the Navy Yard.
   b. My father burst a blood **vessel** when he got the bill from the garage.
   c. Congress voted to decrease* the amount of money being spent on space **vessels**.

9. **persist** (pər sist') continue firmly; refuse to stop or be changed
   a. The humid* weather **persisted** all summer.
   b. Would Lorraine's weird* behavior **persist**, we all wondered?
   c. Lloyd **persisted** in exaggerating* everything he said.

10. hazy (hā' zē) misty; smoky; unclear
    a. The vicinity* of London is known to be **hazy**.
    b. Factories that pollute* the air create **hazy** weather conditions.
    c. Although Cora had a great memory, she was unusually **hazy** about the details of our meeting on January 16th.

11. gleam (glēm) a flash or beam of light
    a. A **gleam** of light shone through the prison window.
    b. The only source* of light in the cellar came in the form of a **gleam** through a hole in the wall.
    c. My grandmother gets a **gleam** in her eyes when she sees the twins.

12. editor (ed' ə tər) person who prepares a publication; one who corrects a manuscript and helps to improve it
    a. The student was proud to be the **editor** of the school newspaper.
    b. Meredith's journalistic knowledge* came in handy when she was unexpectedly given the job of **editor** of The Bulletin.
    c. It is undeniable* that the magazine has gotten better since Ellis became **editor**.

Words in Use

Read the following passage to see how the new words are used in it.

Flying Saucers Again

Whenever **journalists** face a news **famine** they **revive** the undeniably* interesting question: How can we explain UFOs—unidentified flying objects? The story usually **commences** with a description of the object by some **observant** night watchman who doesn't hesitate* to **identify** the object as having **migrated** from outer space. The **vessel**, he persists, appeared over the **hazy** lake at about 30 feet. A greenish **gleam** prohibited* him from seeing its exact shape, he admits. Newspaper **editors** love these stories because they keep the population* interested in knowledge about UFOs and keep them buying newspapers.

Fill in the Blanks

Place one of the new words in each of the blanks below.

1. The wedding will _____ at eight o'clock.
2. When Abe lost his job, he had to _____ to a place where he could find work.
3. We could tell Ira was happy by the bright _____ in his eyes.
4. Because of the _____, people were dying in the streets.
5. Many people claim to have seen a ghostly _____ sailing through the fog.
6. Can you _____ the flags of all the states in the United States?
7. He was _____ of all the rules of his religion.
8. The _____ sent five reporters to cover the big story.
9. They were trying to _____ interest in old movies.
10. The travelers were stupid to _____ in eating the food after they were told it was spoiled.
11. _____ weather kept the pilot from seeing the airfield clearly.
12. The young _____ applied for his first job at a small newspaper.

Answer key, p. 197

Creativity Exercise

Now make up your own sentences, one for each of the new words you have just been taught.

1. _____

2. _____

3. _____

4. _____

5. _____

6. _____

7. _____

8. _____

9. _____

10. _____

11. _____

12. _____

Picture It

Which of the words studied in this lesson is suggested by the picture?

Spotlight On

commence—Many people have wondered why the end of someone's school days should be celebrated by *Commencement* Exercises, which, ordinarily, refer to a beginning. The reason for that term is that we often think of the completion of an education as the time to *commence* or begin to earn a livelihood.

LESSON 14

> "Words, like fine flowers, have their colors, too."
>
> —Ernest Rhys, *Words*

1. **unruly** (un roo' lē) hard to rule or control; lawless
   a. **Unruly** behavior is prohibited* at the pool.
   b. When he persisted* in acting **unruly**, Ralph was fired from his job.
   c. His **unruly** actions were a menace* to those who were trying to work.

2. **rival** (ri' vəl) person who wants and tries to get the same thing as another; one who tries to equal or do better than another
   a. The boxer devised* an attack that would help him to be victorious* over his young **rival**.
   b. Sherry didn't like to compete* because she always thought her **rival** would win.
   c. Seidman and Son decided to migrate* to an area where they would have fewer **rivals**.

3. **violent** (vī' ə lənt) acting or done with strong, rough force
   a. Carefully, very carefully, we approached* the **violent** man.
   b. **Violent** behavior is prohibited* on school grounds.
   c. Vernon had a tendency* to be **violent** when someone angered him.

4. **brutal** (broo' təl) coarse and savage; like a brute; cruel
   a. Dozens of employees* quit the job because the boss was **brutal** to them.
   b. The **brutal** track coach persisted* in making the team work out all morning under the hot sun.
   c. Swearing to catch the murderer, the detectives revealed* that it had been an unusually **brutal**, violent* crime.

5. **opponent** (ə pō' nənt) person who is on the other side of a fight, game, or discussion; person fighting, struggling or speaking against another
   a. The Russian chess player underestimated* his **opponent** and lost.
   b. He was a bitter **opponent** of costly urban* reform.
   c. Seeing his flabby* **opponent**, Slugger was sure he would be victorious.*

6. **brawl** (brôl) a noisy quarrel or fight
   a. The journalist* covered all the details of the **brawl** in the park.
   b. Larry dreaded* a **brawl** with his father over finding a job.
   c. What started out as a polite discussion soon became a violent* **brawl**.

7. **duplicate** (doo' plə kāt) an exact copy; make an exact copy of; repeat exactly
   a. Elliott tried to deceive* Mrs. Held by making a **duplicate** of my paper.
   b. We **duplicated** the document* so that everyone had a copy to study.
   c. The so-called expert did a mediocre* job of **duplicating** the Van Gogh painting.

8. **vicious** (vish' əs) evil; wicked; savage
   a. Liza was unpopular* because she was **vicious** to people she had just met.
   b. The **vicious** editor* published false stories about people he disliked.
   c. Mr. Voss was reluctant* to talk about his **vicious** pit bull.

9. **whirling** (hwər' ling) turning or swinging round and round; spinning
   a. The space vessel* was **whirling** around before it landed on earth.
   b. As they tried to lift the bulky* piano, the movers went **whirling** across the living room.
   c. Because Angelo drank too much, he commenced* to feel that everything was **whirling** around the bar.

10. **underdog** (un' dər dôg) person having the worst of any struggle; one who is expected to lose
    a. Minority* groups complain about being the **underdogs** in this century.*
    b. I always feel sorry for the **underdog** in a street fight.
    c. The Jets were identified* as **underdogs** even though they had beaten the Steelers earlier in the season.

11. **thrust** (thrust) push with force
    a. Once the jet engine was ignited,* it **thrust** the rocket from the ground.
    b. He had adequate* strength to **thrust** himself through the locked door.
    c. Eva was in a terrible rage* when she **thrust** herself into the room.

12. **bewildered** (bi wil' dérd) confused completely; puzzled
    a. The lawyer was **bewildered** by his client's* lack* of interest in the case.
    b. His partner's weird* actions left Jack **bewildered**.
    c. **Bewildered** by the sudden hazy* weather, he decided not to go to the beach.

Words in Use

Read the following passage to see how the new words are used in it.

Roller Derby

The most **unruly** game known to man or woman is the Roller Derby. Revived* every so often on television, it has no **rival** for **violent**, **brutal** action. The game commences* with two teams on roller skates circling a banked, oval track. Then one or two skaters try to break out of the pack and "lap" the **opponents**. When the skater leaves the pack, the **brawl** begins. No sport can **duplicate** the **vicious** shrieking,* pushing, elbowing, and fighting, all at high speed while the skaters are **whirling** around the track. And women are just as much of a **menace*** as the men. Often considered the **underdog**, the female skater can thrust a pointed fingernail into the face of a **bewildered** enemy.

Picture It

Which of the words studied in this lesson is suggested by the picture?

Fill in the Blanks

Place one of the new words in each of the blanks below.

1. Rory was thrown out of school because of his _____ behavior.
2. The _____ lion attacked the lost child in the forest.
3. They had a _____ over who was a better swimmer.
4. The magician _____ his hand into his hat, and out came a rabbit.
5. A man was caught trying to _____ documents* that were top secret.
6. His _____ was a man who was trying to win the heart of his girl.
7. The experienced chess player tried to keep his _____ guessing.
8. The boy was _____ by the fact that his parents had abandoned* him.
9. Whenever the skinny boy got into a fight he was the _____ .
10. When some animals aren't fed on time they become very _____ .
11. The ball was hit so hard that it went _____ down the field.
12. Five hundred men were killed in that _____ battle.

(NOTE: The same words could be used in Sentences 2, 10, and 12; similarly, you may have a
    problem in deciding about the proper words to use in Sentences 6 and 7.)

Answer key, p. 197

True or False

Based on the way the new word is used, write T (true) or F (false) next to the sentence.

1. A **violent** person is someone who uses strong, rough force.
2. An **underdog** is someone who is likely to win.
3. A **brawl** is a noisy quarrel or fight.
4. To **thrust** means to push forcibly.
5. A **rival** is someone who wants and tries to get the same thing as another.
6. **Unruly** means easy to control.
7. **Brutal** means sweet-tempered and easygoing.
8. An **opponent** is a person or group who is on the other side of a fight, game, or discussion.
9. A **duplicate** is something that is imagined or made up.
10. To be **bewildered** is to be ready for action.
11. A **vicious** act is one that is evil, wicked, and savage.
12. **Whirling** means turning or swinging round and round.

Answer key, p. 197

Spotlight On

rival—Probably comes from the Latin *rivus* (stream). Those who lived on the opposite banks of a river
were likely to be *rivals*. Today, in big cities, it is likely to be a matter of *turf* (neighborhood streets) over
which *rival* gangs sometimes fight.

LESSON 15

"Speak clearly, if you speak at all; Carve every word before you let it fall."
—Oliver Wendell Holmes, A *Rhymed Lesson*

Words to Learn This Week

expand
alter
mature
sacred
revise
pledge
casual
pursue
unanimous
fortunate
pioneer
innovative

1. **expand** (ik spand') increase in size; enlarge; swell
   a. We will **expand** our business as soon as we locate a new building.
   b. Present laws against people who pollute* the air must be **expanded**.
   c. **Expanding** the comic strips, the editor* hoped that more people would buy his paper.

2. **alter** (ôl' ter) make different; change; vary
   a. I **altered** my typical* lunch and had a steak instead.
   b. Dorothy agreed to **alter** my dress if I would reveal* its cost to her.
   c. It's absurd* to spend money to **alter** that old candy store.

3. **mature** (mə choor' or mətur') ripe; fully grown or developed
   a. I could tell that Mitch was **mature** from the way he persisted* in his work.
   b. Only through **mature** study habits can a person hope to gain knowledge.*
   c. It is essential* that you behave in a **mature** way in the business world.

4. **sacred** (sā' krid) worthy of respect; holy
   a. Her **sacred** medal had to be sold because the family was in urgent* need of money.
   b. It was revealed* by the journalist* that the **sacred** temple had been torn down.
   c. Kate made a **sacred** promise to her parents never to miss a Sunday church service.

5. **revise** (ri vīz') change; alter*; bring up to date
   a. My family **revised** its weekend plans when the weather turned hazy.*
   b. The dictionary was **revised** and then published in a more expensive* edition.
   c. Under the **revised** rules, Shane was eliminated* from competing.*

6. **pledge** (plej) promise
   a. Before the grand jury, the sinister* gangster **pledged** to tell the whole truth.
   b. Monte was reluctant* to **pledge** his loyalty* to his new girlfriend.
   c. **Pledged** to discovering the facts, the journalist* began to dig up new evidence* for his readers.

7. **casual** (kazh' ū əl) happening by chance; not planned or expected; not calling attention to itself
   a. As the villain* stole the money from the blind man, he walked away in a **casual** manner.
   b. The bartender made a **casual** remark about the brawl* in the backroom.
   c. Following a **casual** meeting on the street, the bachelor* renewed his friendship with the widow.

8. **pursue** (pər soo') follow; proceed along
   a. We **pursued** the bicycle thief until he vanished* from our vision.*
   b. Ernie rowed up the river, **pursuing** it to its source.*
   c. The senior wanted to **pursue** urban* affairs as his life's work.

9. unanimous (yü nan' ə məs) in complete agreement
  a.   The class was **unanimous** in wanting to eliminate* study halls.
  b.   There has never been an election in our union that was won by a **unanimous** vote.
  c.   The Senate, by a **unanimous** vote, decided to decrease* taxes.

10. fortunate (fôr' chə nit) having good luck; lucky
  a. Wesley was **fortunate** to have an adequate* sum of money in the bank.
  b. It is **fortunate** that the famine* did not affect our village.
  c. The underdog* was **fortunate** enough to come out a winner.

11. pioneer (pī ə nēr') one who goes first or prepares a way for others
  a.   My grandfather was a **pioneer** in selling wholesale* products.
  b.   England was a **pioneer** in building large vessels* for tourists.
  c.   In the fourth grade I assembled* a picture collection of great American **pioneers**.

12. innovative (in ə vā' tiv) fresh; clever; having new ideas
  a.   The **innovative** ads for the computers won many new customers.
  b.   Everyone in our office praised the boss for his **innovative** suggestions.
  c.   Nicole decided to alter* her approach and become more **innovative**.

Words in Use

Read the following passage to see how the new words are used in it.

John Dewey High School; Brooklyn, New York

The high school of the future may be New York City's John Dewey High School. Located in Brooklyn, this unique* school offers an **expanded**, **altered** course of study for **mature** students. The **sacred** 40 minute period has been abolished* and replaced with 20 minute units, so that some classes are 20, 40, 60 or even 80 minutes long. Courses have been **revised** into seven-week units. In honor study halls, students **pledge** themselves to quiet study. Generally, the teachers' attitude toward students is **casual**. Pupils may utilize* the cafeteria any time they have no class. Pupils **pursue** courses they choose themselves. So far the positive reaction is **unanimous;** everyone senses that the **fortunate** students at John Dewey High School are **pioneers** in the thrust* to find new ways of teaching and learning. We salute this **innovative** school.

Fill in the Blanks

Place one of the new words in each of the blanks below.

  1. Dominick was _____ to have such good friends.
  2. Rhonda didn't believe in divorce because she felt that marriage is _____ .
  3. The pilot had to _____ his course when he ran into bad weather.
  4. Everyone approved of Dave's _____ proposal.*
  5. David wanted to _____ medicine as a career.
  6. He moved out of the house when he became a _____ young man.
  7. The vote to make Jim president of the camera club was _____ .
  8. When his mother died of cancer, the young doctor decided to _____ his life to finding a cure for it.
  9. They had to _____ their plans when a third person decided to join them for lunch.
 10. My grandfather was a _____ in the field of sports medicine.
 11. The relaxed friends spoke in a _____ manner as they talked on the street.
 12. I can feel my stomach _____ when I breathe deeply.

Answer key, p. 197

Creativity Exercise

Now make up your own sentences, one for each of the new words you have just been taught.

  1.

2. _____

3. _____

4. _____

5. _____

6. _____

7. _____

8. _____

9. _____

10. _____

11. _____

12. _____

Spotlight On

pioneer—Originally derived from an old French word for a foot soldier, _peonier_, the word has come to mean much more than the first to settle a region. It now also refers to those who open new fields of inquiry, even new worlds. Thus, we have space _pioneers_ and _pioneers_ in cancer research. Ecologists, who deal with the adaptation of life to the environment, even call a plant or animal that successfully invades and becomes established in a bare area a _pioneer_.

Picture It

Which of the words studied in this lesson is suggested by the picture?

LESSON
16

Words to Learn This Week

slender
surpass
vast
doubt
capacity
penetrate
pierce
accurate
microscope
grateful
cautious
confident

1. **slender** (slen' dər) long and thin; limited; slight
   a. Carlotta's **slender** figure made her look somewhat taller than she was.
   b. There was only a **slender** chance that you could conceal* the truth.
   c. The **slender** thief was able to enter the apartment through the narrow window.

2. **surpass** (sər pas') do better than; be greater than; excel*
   a. The machines of the twenty-first century* surely **surpass** those of earlier times.
   b. Most farmers believe that rural* life far **surpasses** urban* living.
   c. It is undeniable* that a cold lemonade in July cannot be **surpassed**.

3. **vast** (vast) very great; enormous*
   a. Daniel Boone explored* **vast** areas that had never been settled.
   b. Our campus* always seems **vast** to new students.
   c. **Vast** differences between the two sides were made clear in the debate.*

4. **doubt** (dout) not believe; not be sure of; feel uncertain about; lack of certainty
   a. Scientists **doubt** that a total cure for cancer will be found soon.
   b. The question of whether he could survive* the winter was left in **doubt**.
   c. We don't **doubt** that the tradition* of marriage will continue.

5. **capacity** (ke pas' ə tē) amount of room or space inside; largest amount that can be held by a container
   a. A sign in the elevator stated that its **capacity** was 1100 pounds.
   b. The gasoline capsule* had a **capacity** of 500 gallons.
   c. So well-liked was the prominent* speaker that the auditorium was filled to **capacity** when he began his lecture.

6. **penetrate** (pen' ə trāt) get into or through
   a. We had to **penetrate** the massive* wall in order to hang the mirror.
   b. Although Kenny tried to pound the nail into the rock with a hammer, he couldn't **penetrate** the hard surface.
   c. The thieves **penetrated** the bank's security* and stole the money.

7. **pierce** (pērs) go into; go through; penetrate*
   a. My sister is debating* whether or not to get her ears **pierced**.
   b. I tried to ignore* his bad violin playing, but the sound was **piercing**.
   c. Halloran violently* **pierced** the skin of his rival,* causing massive* bleeding.

8. **accurate** (ak' ū rit) exactly right as the result of care or pains
   a. Ushers took an **accurate** count of the people assembled* in the theater.
   b. Emma's vision* was so **accurate** that she didn't need glasses.
   c. In writing on the topic,* Vergil used **accurate** information.

9. **microscope** (mī′ krə skōp) instrument with a lens for making objects larger so that one can see things more clearly
   a. The students used a **microscope** to see the miniature* insect.
   b. When young Oprah's birthday came around, her uncle gave her a **microscope**.
   c. Using a **microscope**, the scientist was able to probe* into the habits of germs.

10. **grateful** (grāt′ fəl) feeling gratitude; thankful
   a. The majority* of pupils felt **grateful** for Mr. Ash's help.
   b. We were **grateful** that the gloomy* weather cleared up on Saturday.
   c. In his letter, Waldo told how **grateful** he was for the loan.

11. **cautious** (kô′ shəs) very careful; never taking chances
   a. Be **cautious** when you choose your opponent.*
   b. Good authors are **cautious** not to exaggerate* when they write.
   c. If the rain is failing in torrents,* it is best to drive **cautiously**.

12. **confident** (kän′ fə dənt) firmly believing; certain; sure
   a. Judge Emery was **confident** he could solve the conflict.*
   b. When he lifted the burden,* Scotty was **confident** he could carry it.
   c. Annette was **confident** she would do well as a nurse.

Words in Use

Read the following passage to see how the new words are used in it.

A Valuable Discovery

The laser is a marvelous device that sends out a **slender**, concentrated beam of light, a light that **surpasses** the light at the sun's surface. So **vast** is the laser beam's power that it has without a **doubt** the **capacity** to vaporize* any substance located anywhere on earth. The laser can **penetrate** steel, **pierce** a diamond, or make an **accurate** die for wire so thin that it can be seen only with a **microscope**.

Grateful eye surgeons report that they have used laser beams to repair the retinas in some fortunate* patients by creating tiny scars that joined the retina to the eyeball. Pioneering* medical men are making **cautious** exploration* into cancer cures with the laser, **confident** that they will alter* the course of this brutal* disease.

Picture It

Which of the words studied in this lesson is suggested by the picture?

Fill in the Blanks

Place one of the new words in each of the blanks below.

1. Little Paul was _____ that he got the Christmas present he asked for.
2. I _____ that you can break Michael's scoring record.
3. My mother used to say that I was as _____ as a toothpick.
4. Be _____ about swimming right after eating a meal.
5. The map he drew of our neighborhood was not very _____ .
6. In Superman comics, the only thing Superman couldn't _____ was lead.
7. When my family went to look for a new house, we had a _____ choice.
8. Modern highways far _____ the old dirt roads of yesterday.
9. The jar was filled to _____ .
10. We were all very _____ that Duane would pass his exams.
11. The _____ used by my biology teacher is very expensive.
12. The music was so loud that I thought that it would _____ my eardrums.

Answer key, p. 197

Synonym Search

Circle the word that most nearly expresses the meaning of the word printed in blue type.

1. **penetrate** the skin
   (a) pass through   (b) moisten   (c) burn   (d) protect
2. electron **microscope**
   (a) rangefinder   (b) reflection mirror   (c) optical enlarging instrument
   (d) three-dimensional focuser
3. **confident** speaker
   (a) certain   (b) aboveboard   (c) reasonable   (d) well informed
4. **slender** forms
   (a) round and curvy   (b) bright and shiny   (c) colorful and attractive   (d) long and thin
5. **accurate** information
   (a) error-free   (b) endless   (c) available   (d) remarkable
6. taste that cannot be **surpassed**
   (a) pursued*   (b) excelled*   (c) seen   (d) approved
7. an unlimited **capacity**
   (a) ability to store   (b) attention to detail   (c) resistance* to change   (d) talent
8. move **cautiously**
   (a) very carefully   (b) with exaggeration   (c) hurriedly   (d) in a satisfying manner
9. **grateful** for the help given
   (a) tearful   (b) proud   (c) thankful   (d) persuaded*
10. **vast** wilderness
    (a) unknown   (b) enormous   (c) untamed   (d) quiet
11. a road that **pierces** the dense* jungle
    (a) cuts through   (b) winds in and out of   (c) runs parallel to   (d) avoids
12. innocent beyond a shadow of a **doubt**
    (a) lack of certainty   (b) lack of freedom   (c) lack of vision*   (d) lack of courage

Answer key, p. 197

Spotlight On

confident—Have you ever wondered why the name Fido is often given to a dog? The root of the word *confident* tells you. *Fidere* meant "trust" in Latin, and the dog, man's best friend, has been traditionally considered trusty and faithful to his master. However, too much trust can bring trouble: look up the meaning of *confidence man*.

LESSON
17

"Word by word the book is made."
                                    —French proverb

Words to Learn This Week

appeal

addict

wary

aware

misfortune

avoid

wretched

keg

nourish

harsh

quantity

opt

---

1. **appeal** (ə pēl') attraction; interest; to urge
   a. Anything Jorge could get at wholesale* price had a great **appeal** for him.
   b. My boss always **appeals** to his employees* to work swiftly and neatly.
   c. I found her clothing designs to be enormously* **appealing**.

2. **addict** (ad' ikt) one who cannot break away from a habit or practice
   a. Because he was a heroin **addict**, it was essential* for Carlos to get the drug each day.
   b. Marcia became flabby* because she was **addicted** to ice cream sodas.
   c. Those who take aspirins and other pain-killers regularly should realize that they may become drug **addicts**, too.

3. **wary** (wār' ē) on one's guard against danger or trickery; cautious*
   a. Marilyn's mother told her to be **wary** of strangers.
   b. After Orlando had been the victim of a cheat, he was **wary** of those who said they wanted to help him.
   c. Living in a polluted* city makes you **wary** of the air you breathe.

4. **aware** (ə wār') knowing; realizing
   a. Donna was **aware** of her tendency* to exaggerate.*
   b. It was some time before the police became **aware** of the brawl* that was taking place on the street.
   c. One way to gain knowledge* is to be **aware** of everything around you.

5. **misfortune** (mis fôr' chən) bad luck
   a. It was my **misfortune** that our car wasn't thoroughly* checked before the trip through the desert.
   b. Being bitten by the vicious* dog was quite a **misfortune** for Tommy.
   c. I had the **misfortune** of working for a greedy* man.

6. **avoid** (ə void') keep away from; keep out of the way of
   a. If you are fortunate* you can **avoid** people who are trying to deceive* you.
   b. There was no way to **avoid** noticing her beautiful green eyes.
   c. **Avoid** getting into a brawl* if you can.

7. **wretched** (retch' id) very unsatisfactory; miserable
   a. I feel **wretched** after a night when I've scarcely* slept.
   b. There was unanimous* agreement that we had seen a **wretched** movie.
   c. Toby had **wretched** luck at the gambling tables.

8. **keg** (keg) small barrel, usually holding less than ten gallons
   a. The corner saloon uses numerous* **kegs** of beer on a Saturday night.
   b. "Get a **keg** of nails," the carpenter shouted at me.
   c. It is obvious* to me that the situation is filled with peril,* a real powder **keg** if I ever saw one.

9. **nourish** (nər' ish) make or keep alive and well, with food; feed; develop an attitude
   a. A diet of **nourishing** food is served to every hospital patient.

53

    b.   It was easy to detect* that the skinny boy was not well **nourished**.
    c.   After the operation, our doctor plans to **nourish** my mother with vitamins and good food.

10. harsh (härsh) rough to the touch, taste, eye, or ear; sharp
    a.   The law is **harsh** on people who go around menacing* others.
    b.   Looking at his cigarette, Phil realized it was absurd* to inhale such **harsh** smoke.
    c.   Hazel altered* her tone of voice from a **harsh** one to a soft tone.

11. quantity (kwän' tə tē) amount
    a.   I never neglect* to carry a small **quantity** of money with me.
    b.   Who believes that **quantity** is better than quality?
    c.   A large **quantity** of meat is always stored in our freezer.

12. opt (opt) choose or favor; select
    a.   If you give me an ice cream choice, I'll **opt** for chocolate.
    b.   Our cheerleaders plan to **opt** for new sweaters.
    c.   On Friday, three of my buddies will **opt** to go into the navy.

Words in Use

Read the following passage to see how the new words are used in it.

A Cup of Coffee?

The drink with the most **appeal** for Americans is still coffee, but coffee **addicts** had better be **wary** of the instant forms. Greedy for customers and confident* they won't lose them, companies will put their product in any instant form—liquid, powder, chips—and the coffee drinker, **aware** of his **misfortune**, finds it hard to **avoid** some of the more **wretched** instant products. The **harsh** fact is that an enormous* **quantity** of instant coffee is being sold, no doubt,* to **nourish** the popular demand for convenience. A **keg** of real coffee may become a museum piece as more and more people opt for instant coffee.

Picture It

Which of the words studied in this lesson is suggested by the picture?

Fill in the Blanks

Place one of the new words in each of the blanks below.

1. Sometimes it is best to _____ being too nice to strangers.
2. I wasn't _____ that there were concerts in the park on Tuesdays.
3. We bought a large _____ of potato chips for the party.
4. Rock 'n roll music just doesn't _____ to me.
5. My aunt was in _____ health and had to have nurses on twenty-four hour duty.
6. The _____ smoke from the fireplace burned my eyes.
7. It was quite a _____ that Beverly's husband died in an automobile accident.
8. If I had to _____ for a new career, it would be medicine.
9. It is smart to be _____ of foods whose contents are not listed on the package.
10. The judge denounced* the thief for stealing a _____ of molasses.
11. A candy bar will not _____ you the way a piece of meat will.
12. Baxter took pep pills regularly and became a drug _____ without realizing it.

Answer key, p. 197

Matching

Match the 12 new words in Column I with the definitions in Column II.

Column I	Column II
1. opt	a. attraction
2. quantity	b. miserable
3. misfortune	c. one who cannot break a habit
4. nourish	d. realizing
5. appeal	e. small barrel
6. harsh	f. cautious
7. addict	g. keep away from
8. keg	h. rough to the touch, taste, eye, or ear
9. wretched	i. amount
10. wary	j. choose or favor
11. avoid	k. bad luck
12. aware	l. make or keep alive and well with food

Answer key, p. 197

Spotlight On

keg—The history of a word tells us something of the habits and traditions of a people. What, for example, can you deduce about the trade and customs of early Englishmen from the fact that the word *keg* came into our language from the Icelandic word *kaggi*? Perhaps the hardy people of that northern land found good use for what they could store in those containers.

"Without knowing the force of words, it is impossible to know men."
—Confucius, *Analects*

1. **tragedy** (traj' ə dē) a very sad or terrible happening; a sad play
   a. It was a **tragedy** that some pioneers* were killed on their way west.
   b. If you had your choice between seeing a comedy or a **tragedy**, which play would you choose?
   c. Harry's enormous* jealousy* led to the **tragedy** in their family.

2. **pedestrian** (pə des' tri ən) person who goes on foot; walker
   a. After driving a bus all day, Norris liked to be a **pedestrian** and take long, casual* walks in the evening.
   b. The police say it is urgent* that **pedestrians** stay on the sidewalk.
   c. I don't doubt* that a **pedestrian** can get places faster than a car in downtown traffic.

3. **glance** (glans) to look at quickly; a quick look
   a. The observant* driver **glanced** at the accident at the side of the road.
   b. I took one **glance** at the wretched* animal and turned away.
   c. Thompson identified* the burglar after a **glance** at the photograph in the police station.

4. **budget** (buj' it) estimate of the amount of money that can be spent for different purposes in a given time
   a. We had to decrease* the **budget** this year because our club is broke.
   b. The prominent* executive presented her **budget** to the Board of Directors.
   c. When my mother draws up her **budget** for the week, she sets aside a goodly sum for nourishing* food.

5. **nimble** (nim' bəl) active and sure-footed; quick moving; light and quick
   a. Although Dusty was a miniature* poodle, he was **nimble** enough to fight bigger dogs.
   b. The **nimble** policeman leaped over the fence to pursue* the car thief.
   c. With my **nimble** fingers, I'm good at text messaging.

6. **manipulate** (mə nip' yə lāt) handle or treat skillfully
   a. Scientists must know how to **manipulate** their microscopes.*
   b. While Mr. Baird **manipulated** the puppets, Fran spoke to the audience.
   c. The wounded pilot **manipulated** the radio dial until he made contact.

7. **reckless** (rek' lis) careless; heedless; wild
   a. We must not ignore* **reckless** drivers; we must take them off the road.
   b. After breaking his hand fighting **recklessly**, Arthur decided to be more cautious* in the future.
   c. The **reckless** smoker ignited* the entire forest.

8. **horrid** (hôr' id) terrible; frightful
   a. Janey avoided* staring at the **horrid** man's face.
   b. It is simply **horrid** the way cars pollute* the air we breathe.
   c. When Mary was good, she was very good, but when she was bad, she was **horrid**.

Words to Learn This Week
tragedy
pedestrian
glance
budget
nimble
manipulate
reckless
horrid
rave
economical
lubricate
ingenious

9. **rave** (rāv) talk wildly
   a.   Shortly after taking the drug, the addict* began to **rave** and foam at the mouth.
   b.   Speedy **raved** that his car had the capacity* to reach 120 miles per hour.
   c.   Sadie was confident* that Mr. Stebbe would **rave** about her essay.

10. **economical** (ē kə näm' i kl) not wasting money or time
    a.   I find it **economical** to shop in the large supermarkets.
    b.   Marissa was praised for her **economical** management of the budget.*
    c.   The President made Congress aware* of the need to be more **economical**.

11. **lubricate** (lōō brə' kāt) make (machinery) smooth and easy to work by putting on oil, grease, or a similar substance
    a.   The bulky* wheels of a railroad train must be **lubricated** each week.
    b.   A large quantity* of grease is needed to **lubricate** an airplane engine.
    c.   When an engine is **lubricated**, it works much better.

12. **ingenious** (in jēn' yəs) having great mental ability; clever
    a.   Bernie devised* an **ingenious** plan to cheat on his income tax.
    b.   Rube Goldberg was a journalist* who won fame for his **ingenious** inventions.
    c.   The master spy had an **ingenious** way of passing secrets to the agent.

Words in Use

Read the following passage to see how the new words are used in it.

The Challenge* of the Small Car

The auto makers in Detroit barely survived* the **tragedy** of 1956. That was the year the consumer became aware* of the Volkswagen, and the auto market was forever altered.* Once Americans got a **glance** at this low-priced, **nimble**, small car that one could **manipulate** so easily, they frequently* refused those **horrid** Detroit monsters with eight cylinders and ten miles to each gallon of gasoline. Many **pedestrians**, previously uninterested in owning a car, began to purchase small foreign cars.

Conservative as well as **reckless** drivers found the price within their **budget** and became customers.

Volkswagen owners would **rave** about their **economical** cars, telling everyone how little gas they used and how infrequently* they needed to be **lubricated**. Volkswagen, once one of the most popular* small cars sold in America, has now fallen behind the autos of the **ingenious** Japanese manufacturers.

Fill in the Blanks

Place one of the new words in each of the blanks below.

1. Try not to be _____ when you drive a car, especially at night.
2. The brilliant investigator found an _____ answer to the problem.
3. I find it more _____ to buy a monthly train ticket than to pay for each ride each day.
4. If you continue to _____ about the play, everyone will think you are a relative of the author.
5. I took one _____ and I knew it was Miley Cyrus.
6. Every week Mrs. Evans made a _____ covering the essential* sums she would have to spend.
7. The coach knew how to _____ the players to do what he wanted.
8. Bobby's job at the gas station was to _____ all the cars after they had been worked on.
9. When someone you love dies, it is a _____ .
10. Journalists* reported that the dropping of the bombs was a _____ act.
11. The car leaped up on the sidewalk, struck a _____, and then crashed into the bakery's window.
12. Whirling* across the stage, the _____ ballet dancer captured our hearts.

Answer key, p. 197

Creativity Exercise

Now make up your own sentences, one for each of the new words you have just been taught.

1. _____

2. _____

3. _____

4. _____

5. _____

6. _____

7. _____

8. _____

9. _____

10. _____

11. _____

12. _____

Spotlight On

pedestrian—You have learned the use of this word as a noun, but the word undergoes an interesting change when it is used as an adjective. A *pedestrian speech,* for example, is very dull and commonplace. It moves along very slowly. Can you see how this meaning is related to "going on foot"? Another uncomplimentary use of the same root is *pedant.* Find the meaning.

Picture It

Which of the words studied in this lesson is suggested by the picture?

Word Review #3
These exercises are based on some of the words included in Lessons 13–18.

A. In each of the parentheses below you will find two choices. Pick the one that fits better.

1. It broke our hearts to see the suffering caused by the (famine, wretched) in Africa.
2. Watching the piano player's (nimble, wary) fingers was great entertainment.
3. The once-rich manufacturer was trying hard to (revive, surpass) interest in his product.
4. Lois received a pat on the back for her (unruly, mature) behavior.
5. Only if you (alter, avoid) the plans for the vacation will I be able to go along with you.
6. Bruce's (reckless, cautious) way of driving caused many accidents.
7. Since you are unwilling to (pursue, duplicate) the matter, I think we ought to forget about it.
8. Parker's (casual, economical) way of handling his money saved a fortune for his family.
9. Every member of our club agreed to the new rule and it was passed (unanimously, confidently).
10. Our cellar is filled to (capacity, quantity) with old furniture and other junk.

Answer key, p. 197

B. Opposites. In Column I are ten words from Lessons 13–18. Match them correctly with their *opposite* meanings in Column II.

Column I	Column II
1. ingenious	a. starve
2. nourish	b. make smaller
3. commence	c. stupid
4. hazy	d. thick
5. slender	e. good luck
6. expand	f. clear
7. misfortune	g. driver
8. harsh	h. stay at home
9. migrate	i. smooth
10. pedestrian	j. finish

Answer key, p. 197

C. Which of the vocabulary choices in parentheses fits best in these newspaper headlines?

1. **"Send Food to Relieve _____ in Africa"**   (Famine, Underdog, Reckless, Economical)
2. **City Council in _____ Vote to Lower Taxes**   (Casual, Fortunate, Unanimous, Ingenious)
3. **Henry Ford Honored as _____ in Auto Industry**   (Sacred, Pioneer, Rival, Brutal)
4. **Millions _____ to Warmth of the Southwest**   (Appeal, Surpass, Expand, Migrate)
5. **Producer to _____ Musical Comedy Hit of the 1920s**   (Appeal, Commence, Revive, Pledge)
6. **"Be _____ of Get-Rich-Quick Schemes," Warns Banker**   (Wary, Reckless, Grateful, Confident)
7. **Referees Fail to Control _____ Hockey Game**   (Nimble, Duplicate, Unruly, Vast)
8. **Dieter Praised for _____ Figure**   (Observant, Slender, Bewildered, Casual)
9. **Training Film Shows How to Avoid Being _____ Driver**   (Nimble, Wary, Reckless, Accurate)
10. **_____ Dog Bites Three Children**   (Vicious, Wary, Harsh, Sacred)

Answer key, p. 197

D. From the list of words below choose the word that means:

manipulate	quantity	thrust	penetrate	rival	bewildered
rave	pioneer	duplicate	capacity	pledge	observant
appeal	casual	whirling	tragedy	gleam	identify
wary	unruly	confidence	expand	nourish	persist
wretched	brawl	surpass	sacred	vessel	revise

1. self-assurance and boldness *but in the phrase* "_____ man" is not complimentary
2. the first in a new field *and* began as the French word for *foot soldier*
3. a competitor *but originally* meant one who lives across the river
4. a ship *as well as* a hollow utensil such as a pot, kettle, or dish
5. push *as well as* pierce or lunge
6. correct *as well as* update
7. volume or ability to learn *and* occurs in the phrases "full to _____" and "operate at _____"
8. give food *as well as* develop an attitude or habit

9. a type of drama *as well as* a sad event
10. talk wildly *but also* a form of praise

Answer key, p. 197

E.   Letter of Application. In the coming years, you may apply for jobs by mail. Your letter of application, if done well, will help you to secure a position. In the following letter, fill in the blanks, using words selected from the group below.

appeal	duplicate	harsh	innovative	pursue
aware	expand	hazy	mature	quantity
capacity	glance	identify	observant	rave
confident	grateful	journalist	pioneer	rival

84 Pine Drive
Stony Point, NY 10980
April 3, 2011

Mr. George Ziotis
Camp Skylark
Mohawk Junction, NJ 07043

Dear Mr. Ziotis:

I am hereby applying for the position of camp counselor, which was advertised in the Sunday edition of this week's *Bergen Record*.

For the past two summers, I served as a counselor-in-training at Camp Tekapusha in Kiamesha, NY. My skills in arts and crafts, as well as at the waterfront, won __1__ reviews from the camp owners. They liked the fact that I was an __2__ junior counselor, always coming up with new ideas.

I am __3__ that I'm now __4__ enough to lead my own group. The parents of the boys I worked with during the last two years said that I related very well to their children.

In addition, I hope to __5__ a career as a __6__ after my graduation and would be able to organize a newspaper at your camp.

Finally, my neighbor, Ed Miller, sends his son to Camp Skylark, and he made me __7__ that you want to __8__ your nature program. I can help the campers to __9__ local birds and flowers, another one of my skills that might prove valuable if you hire me.

I would be __10__ if you called me at 212-400-5555 for an interview.

Sincerely,
Robert Kassel

Answer key, p. 197

F.   Words That Do Double Duty. Once again, as you did in Word Reviews #1 and 2, note the following words that appeared in Lessons 13–18. Each can serve as more than one part of speech:

rival (n., adj.)	pledge (v., n.)
brawl (v., n.)	appeal (v., n.)
duplicate (v., n.)	pedestrian (n., adj.)
thrust (v., n.)	budget (v., n.)
mature (v., adj.)	rave (v., adj.)

Make up two sentences for each of the above words, showing how it could be used as different parts of speech.

Examples: Jefferson H.S. was our long-time basketball *rival*. (n.)
            Harry was so jealous that he could *rival* (v.) Othello.

LESSON 19

"For one word a man is often deemed to be wise, and for one word he is often deemed to be foolish. We should be careful indeed what we say."

—Confucius, *Analects*

Words to Learn This Week

harvest
abundant
uneasy
calculate
absorb
estimate
morsel
quota
threat
ban
panic
appropriate

---

1. **harvest** (här' vist) gathering in of grain or other food crops
   a. This year's **harvest** was adequate* to feed all our people.
   b. The farmer decided to expand* his fields so that he would get a bigger **harvest**.
   c. If the **harvest** is poor, there is always the possibility of a famine.*

2. **abundant** (ə bun' dənt) more than enough; very plentiful
   a. It is urgent* that the hospital have an **abundant** supply of blood.
   b. An **abundant** harvest* was predicted* by the secretary of agriculture.
   c. In recent* years an **abundant** number of complaints have disturbed the telephone company.

3. **uneasy** (un ēz' ē) restless; disturbed; anxious
   a. Mrs. Spinner was **uneasy** about letting her son play in the vicinity* of the railroad tracks.
   b. The treasurer was **uneasy** about the company's budget.*
   c. Arnold felt **uneasy** about the meeting even though he tried to act in a casual* manner.

4. **calculate** (kal' kyə lāt) find out by adding, subtracting, multiplying, or dividing; figure
   a. The cook had to **calculate** the number of diners to see whether he could decrease* his order for meat.
   b. In order to see how expensive* the car was, the buyer **calculated** the tax and other charges.
   c. I used an abacus to **calculate** my average.

5. **absorb** (ab sôrb') take in or suck up (liquids); interest greatly.
   a. The sponge **absorbed** the beer which had leaked from the keg.*
   b. Our bodies must **absorb** those things which will nourish* them.
   c. I became **absorbed** in what the teacher was saying and did not hear the bell ring.

6. **estimate** (es' ta māt [v.], estə mət [n.]) form a judgment or opinion about; guess
   a. The driver **estimated** that the auto race would commence* at nine o'clock.
   b. I try to avoid* making **estimates** on things I know nothing about.
   c. In your **estimate,** who will be victorious* in this conflict?*

7. **morsel** (môr' sel) a small bite; mouthful; tiny amount
   a. When Reynaldo went into the restaurant, he pledged* to eat every **morsel** on his plate.
   b. Suzanne was reluctant* to try even a **morsel** of the lobster.
   c. If you had a **morsel** of intelligence, you would be uneasy,* too.

8. **quota** (kwō' tə) share of a total due from or to a particular state, district, person, etc.
   a. The company revealed* a **quota** of jobs reserved for college students.
   b. There was a **quota** placed on the number of people who could migrate* here from China.
   c. Lieutenant Dugan doubted* that a **quota** had been placed on the number of parking tickets each police officer was supposed to give out.

61

9. threat (thret) sign or cause of possible evil or harm
   a.   There is always the horrid* **threat** that my **job** will be abolished.*
   b.   It is absurd* to think that a tiny bug could be a **threat** to a person.
   c.   Our English teacher made a **threat** to take away our cell phones.

10. ban (ban) prohibit; forbid
   a.   The group unanimously* voted to **ban** all people who were under six feet.
   b.   Health officials are trying to expand* their field in order to **ban** cigarette advertising from newspapers and magazines.
   c.   I want to **ban** all outsiders from our discussion on security.*

11. panic (pan' ik) unreasoning fear; fear spreading through a group of people so that they lose control of themselves
   a. The leader of the lost group appealed* to them not to **panic**.
   b. When the danger was exaggerated,* a few people started to **panic**.
   c. The source* of **panic** in the crowd was a man with a gun.

12. appropriate (a prō' prē it) fit; set apart for some special use
   a. At an **appropriate** time, the chief promised to reveal* his plan.
   b. The lawn was an **appropriate** setting for Eileen's wedding.
   c. After some **appropriate** prayers, the dinner was served.

Words in Use

Read the following passage to see how the new words are used in it.

Protecting Our Health

Pick an apple, a tomato, a peach—no worms in the **harvest.** We are familiar with the **abundant** use of pesticides by farmers, but today's chemists are becoming **uneasy.** They **calculate** that there are 45,000 different pesticides, and all of them can be **absorbed by** the fruit on which they are sprayed. The chemists **estimate** that every **morsel** we eat in the future may contain a deadly **quota** of pesticide. The tragedy* will come slowly but the **threat** is real. These government chemists do not suggest that we **ban** pesticides. They are cautious* and do not easily **panic**. What is needed, they say, are **appropriate**, budgeted* doses that will not pollute* our food.

Picture It

Which of the words studied in this lesson is suggested by the picture?

Fill in the Blanks

Place one of the new words in each of the blanks below.

1. The committee recommended that we _____ all dangerous foods.
2. Dave had his _____ of cookies for the day.
3. You should always make sure that you have an _____ supply of gasoline for a long trip.
4. The rain was _____ into the concrete when it was dry.
5. Is this inexpensive* dress _____ for a formal wedding?
6. How much do you _____ that horse is worth?
7. Helen had an _____ feeling as she went on to the stage for the first time.
8. When you are in trouble the worst thing to do is to _____ .
9. The farmers had a good _____ of corn this year.
10. We _____ all the figures and came to one solid answer.
11. Every_____ the cook prepared was tasty.
12. The _____ of snow caused us to change our holiday plans.

Answer key, p. 197

Choose the Correct Word

Circle the word in parentheses that best fits the sense of the sentence.

1. When the food supply is (abundant, appropriate), there is no reason for anyone to go hungry.
2. Some people believe that the (threat, quota) of nuclear war is a very real danger of the twenty-first century.
3. If you feel (uneasy, appropriate) about being capable of doing this work, please let me help you get started.
4. It is important not to (panic, calculate) in emergency situations.
5. Farmers hope their labors will be rewarded with a plentiful (harvest, morsel).
6. To (calculate, absorb) whether I need an A or a B on my math final, I had to first figure my average to date.
7. It's difficult to believe that even today there are school boards that (ban, harvest) books such as *The Catcher in the Rye.*
8. The dish looked so strange and smelled so foul, that I found it difficult to taste a (morsel, quota) of the meal our host had prepared.
9. I can't possibly (absorb, ban) such an enormous* amount of information in just two hours.
10. Many countries have strict (quotas, threats) on the number of immigrants they admit each year.
11. If my (estimate, quota) is correct, the homes presently under construction will mean about 200 new elementary school students in the district next year.
12. The (appropriate, abundant) behavior for different situations is something we all learn as part of growing up.

Answer key, p. 197

Spotlight On

calculate—A Roman "taxi" driver used to charge his customers by figuring out, or calculating, the number of pebbles (Latin word–*calculus*) that dropped into a basket in a given time.

LESSON

20

Words to Learn This Week

emerge
jagged
linger
ambush
crafty
defiant
vigor
perish
fragile
captive
prosper
devour

1. **emerge** (i mėrj') come out; come up; come into view
    a. When the fight was over, the underdog* **emerged** the winner.
    b. You have to be nimble* to **emerge** from the narrow opening in five seconds.
    c. What **emerged** from the bottle was a blend* of fruit juices.

2. **jagged** (jag' id) with sharp points sticking out; unevenly cut or torn
    a. Being reckless,* Rudy didn't watch out for the **jagged** steel.
    b. It's an enormous* job to smooth the **jagged** edge of a fence.
    c. Leslie's hair was so **jagged** it was scarcely* possible to tell that it had just been cut.

3. **linger** (ling' gər) stay on; go slowly as if unwilling to leave
    a. The odor didn't vanish,* but **lingered** on for weeks.
    b. Some traditions* **linger** on long after they have lost their meanings.
    c. After the campus* closed for the summer, some students **lingered** on, reluctant* to go home.

4. **ambush** (am' bush) a trap in which soldiers or other enemies hide to make a surprise attack
    a. The **ambush** became a tragedy* for those who attempted it because they were all killed.
    b. General Taylor raved* about the ingenious* **ambush** he planned.
    c. The troops lay in **ambush** in the dense* woods all through the night.

5. **crafty** (kraf' tē) skillful in deceiving others; sly; tricky
    a. His **crafty** mind prepared a comprehensive* plan to defraud* his partners.
    b. Leo didn't use brutal* strength against his opponents,* but he used his **crafty** bag of tricks to beat them.
    c. The Indians did not fall for the **crafty** ambush.*

6. **defiant** (di fī' ənt) openly resisting; challenging*
    a. "I refuse to be manipulated,"* the **defiant** young woman told her father.
    b. Professor Carlyle was **defiant** of any attempt to disprove his theory.*
    c. **Defiant** of everyone, the addict* refused to be helped.

7. **vigor** (vig' ər) active strength or force
    a. Having a great deal of **vigor,** Jason was able to excel* in all sports.
    b. Tom Thumb made up for size by having more **vigor** than most people.
    c. Putting all her **vigor** into the argument, Patsy persuaded* me to let her drive.

8. **perish** (per' ish) be destroyed; die
    a. Unless the plant gets water for its roots to absorb,* it will **perish.**
    b. Custer and all his men **perished** at the Little Big Horn.
    c. We are trying to make sure that democracy will never **perish** from this earth.

9. **fragile** (fraj' əl) easily broken, damaged, or destroyed; delicate
    a. The expensive* glassware is very **fragile**.
    b. Things made out of plywood have a tendency* to be **fragile**.
    c. On the box was a label that read, "**Fragile**! Handle with care!"

10. captive (kap' tiv) prisoner
   a. The major was grateful* to be released after having been held **captive** for two years.
   b. Until the sheriff got them out, the two boys were held **captive** in the barn.
   c. Placido can hold an audience **captive** with his marvelous singing voice.

11. prosper (pros' pər) be successful; have good fortune
   a. Howard Hughes owned numerous* businesses and most of them **prospered**.
   b. No one should **prosper** from the misfortunes* of his or her friends.
   c. The annual* report showed that the new business was **prospering**.

12. devour (di vour') eat hungrily; absorb* completely; take in greedily*
   a. It was a horrid* sight to see the lion **devour** the lamb.
   b. The animal doctor was pleased to see the terrier **devour** the dog food.
   c. My aunt **devours** four or five mystery books each week.

Words in Use

Read the following passage to see how the new words are used in it.

A Home Where the Buffalo Roam

Even today in South Dakota a cowboy **emerges** from behind a **jagged** rock where he has **lingered** in **ambush** waiting for the **crafty** buffalo to appear. Although not wild—they are raised on vast* ranches—the gallant,* **defiant** bison need to be hunted with the same **vigor** cowboys showed a century* ago. For a while, Americans thought the buffalo would **perish** from the earth; fortunately* the buffalo is far from being such a **fragile** animal. Now more or less **captive**, the buffalo, an estimated* 10,000, are raised for profit by ranchers who **prosper** from the sale of buffalo meat. When did you **devour** your last morsel* of tasty buffalo burger?

Picture It

Which of the words studied in this lesson is suggested by the picture?

Fill in the Blanks

Place one of the new words in each of the blanks below.

1. If we do not do something about pollution,* we may _____ from this earth.
2. The _____ edge of that sheet of metal is very dangerous.
3. We were held _____ by the sinister* enemy for ten days.
4. The bank teller's _____ plan to steal a million dollars didn't succeed.
5. I like to _____ on until everyone else has left the theater.
6. My parents taught me not to be _____ of authority.
7. Did the _____ of the Lebanese soldiers fail?
8. Business persons can _____ if they are honest with their customers.
9. A new star has just _____ from the rock music world.
10. I can _____ a steak in two minutes when I am hungry.
11. With a surprising show of _____, the old woman swam up and down the pool six times!
12. A lack* of calcium in Tyrone's diet caused his bones to be quite _____ .

Answer key, p. 197

Antonyms (Opposites)

Circle the word that most nearly expresses the opposite meaning of the word printed in blue type.

1. **emerge**
   a. go back
   b. involve
   c. disturb
   d. ruin
   e. amuse

2. **captive**
   a. reluctant*
   b. free to leave
   c. active
   d. rapidly constructed
   e. solitary*

3. **ambush**
   a. openly attack
   b. readily remove
   c. secretly strive
   d. quickly determine
   e. water thoroughly

4. **fragile**
   a. demanding
   b. sturdy
   c. careful
   d. genuine
   e. shrewd

5. **devour**
   a. charge
   b. figure out
   c. nourish*
   d. leave untouched
   e. perish

6. **jagged**
   a. confusing
   b. smooth-edged
   c. linked together
   d. microscopic*
   e. unspoiled

7. **defiant**
   a. ready to act
   b. willing to obey
   c. reliable
   d. vulgar
   e. evasive

8. **linger**
   a. underestimate*
   b. exclude
   c. wither
   d. leave quickly
   e. neglect*

9. **vigor**
   a. lack of strength
   b. lack of funds
   c. lack of ability
   d. lack of understanding
   e. lack of tradition*

10. **crafty**
    a. honest
    b. wretched
    c. vulgar
    d. mystical
    e. absurd*

11. **prosper**
    a. be unsuccessful
    b. manipulate*
    c. penetrate*
    d. assemble*
    e. license

12. **perish**
    a. fight
    b. live
    c. ban*
    d. resent*
    e. molest*

Answer key, p. 197

Spotlight On

ambush—What kind of hiding place would best protect a person who wanted to ambush an enemy? The clue is in the word itself. Of course, the bushes or woods provided the greatest safety for the attacker. The bushes are better hidden in the word *ambuscade*, but the meaning is the same. Now you have gained two words in one stroke.

LESSON

21

1. **plea** (plē) request; appeal; that which is asked of another
   a. The employees* turned in a **plea** to their boss for higher pay.
   b. The president's **plea** to release the captives* was denied by the enemy.
   c. In court today, the judge consented* to the lawyer's **plea** for a light sentence.

Words to Learn This Week

plea
weary
collide
confirm
verify
anticipate
dilemma
detour
merit
transmit
relieve
baffle

---

2. **weary** (wēr' ē) tired
   a. I am **weary** of debating* the same topic* all day.
   b. The farmer grew **weary** of bringing in the harvest* every year for the past forty summers.
   c. Let me rest my **weary** bones here before the march commences.*

3. **collide** (kə līd') come together with force
   a. When the two autos **collided**, the people in the fragile* smaller car perished.*
   b. Committees are exploring* ways of keeping cars from **colliding**.
   c. In my estimate* the two bicycles **collided** at five o'clock.

4. **confirm** (kən fėrm') prove to be true or correct; make certain
   a. The way Victor talked back to his mother **confirmed** that he was defiant.*
   b. A probe* of the criminal's background **confirmed** that he had been in jail numerous* times.
   c. Years of research **confirmed** the theory* that smoking is harmful.

5. **verify** (ver' ə fī) prove to be true; confirm*
   a. A "yes man" is an employee* who will **verify** everything the boss says.
   b. I was there as a witness to **verify** the charges against the bus driver.
   c. The data* I turned in were **verified** by the clerks in our office.

6. **anticipate** (an tis' ə pāt) look forward to; expect
   a. We **anticipate** a panic* if the news is revealed* to the public.
   b. Harriet **anticipated** the approach* of the mailman with fright.
   c. With his weird* powers, Lonnie was able to **anticipate** the ringing of the telephone.

7. **dilemma** (də lem' ə) situation requiring a choice between two evils; a difficult choice
   a. It is sensible not to panic* in the face of a **dilemma**.
   b. Lottie faced the **dilemma** of whether to approve of the operation or not.
   c. In "The Lady or the Tiger," the hero had the **dilemma** of which door to open.

8. **detour** (dē' tōor) a roundabout way
   a. Pop was uneasy* about taking the **detour** in this strange town.
   b. In order to evade* city traffic, Anthony took a **detour**.
   c. The **detour** took us ten miles off our course.

9. **merit** (mer' it) goodness; worth; value
   a. There is little **merit** in lying to those you love.
   b. My brother was promoted because of **merit**, not because of friendship.
   c. I can't see any **merit** in your proposal.

10. transmit (trans mit') send over; pass on; pass along; let through
   a.   Garcia's message was **transmitted** to the appropriate* people.
   b.   Scientists can now **transmit** messages from space vessels* to earth.
   c.   Our local radio station does not **transmit** broadcasts after midnight.

11. relieve (ri lēv') make less; make easier; reduce the pain of; replace; release; free
   a.   The pills **relieved** the pain from the wound I received in the conflict.*
   b.   A majority* of the population* wanted to **relieve** the mayor of his duty.
   c.   The peace agreement **relieved** us of the threat* of an attack.

12. baffle (baf' əl) be too hard to understand or solve
   a.   How so mediocre* a player earned so much money **baffled** me.
   b.   The topic* of relativity is a **baffling** one.
   c.   Sherlock Holmes would undoubtedly* have been **baffled** by the way the crime was committed.

Words in Use

Read the following passage to see how the new words are used in it.

Safety in the Air

The most persistent* **plea** of **weary** pilots has always been for a machine that would warn them that they were about to **collide** with an oncoming airplane. Studies of landing patterns **confirm** that the number of collisions is increasing each year, and pilots **verify** hundreds of reports of near misses. Recently a system that would electronically **anticipate** oncoming airplanes was devised,* and the pilot's **dilemma** to dive or to climb, to **detour** to left or right, may be solved. The system has **merit,** though, only if every plane is equipped to **transmit** and receive a signal to and from an oncoming plane. But most aviation experts feel that only a system that watches every airplane in the sky will **relieve** a problem that tends to **baffle** every one who attempts to find a solution.

Picture It

Which of the words studied in this lesson is suggested by the picture?

Fill in the Blanks

Place one of the new words in each of the blanks below.

1. The first time a message was _____ over a telegraph was in 1840.
2. Can you _____ that this is your handwriting?
3. I took a _____ to avoid traffic.
4. We were all very _____ after the long trip.
5. There is _____ in being a good listener.
6. The judge listened to the burglar's _____ of not guilty.
7. The runner and catcher were about to _____ at home plate.
8. Tyrone was _____ that he didn't have any more work to do.
9. When you run a company you have at least one new _____ every day to solve.
10. Did you _____ our reservations at the hotel?
11. We were _____ as to who murdered the wretched* old man.
12. After having been married to Arthur for thirty years, Selma could _____ everything he was going to say.

    (NOTE: You might have used the same word in Sentences 2 and 10.)

    Answer key, p. 197

Word Detective

From the list of 12 new words that follows, choose the one that corresponds to each definition below.

plea	weary	collide	confirm
verify	anticipate	dilemma	detour
merit	transmit	relieve	baffle

1. a roundabout way   _____
2. that which is asked of another   _____
3. come together with force   _____
4. pass along   _____
5. be too hard to understand   _____
6. goodness; worth; value   _____
7. make easier; replace   _____
8. tired   _____
9. make certain   _____
10. a difficult choice   _____
11. prove to be true   _____
12. expect   _____

    (NOTE: The same words could be used for definitions 9 and 11.)

    Answer key, p. 197

Spotlight On

dilemma—The sport of bull fighting provides us with a vivid expression—being on the horns of a dilemma—to describe a situation in which we are faced with two choices, each equally unpleasant. It is as if we were asked to choose which horn of a bull we prefer to be gored by.

LESSON 22

"Words are like leaves, and where they most abound
Much fruit of sense beneath is rarely found."
—Alexander Pope, *Essay on Criticism*

Words to Learn This Week

warden
acknowledge
justice
delinquent
reject
deprive
spouse
vocation
unstable
homicide
penalize
beneficiary

1. **warden** (wôr' dən) keeper; guard; person in charge of a prison
   a. The **warden** found himself facing two hundred defiant* prisoners.
   b. A cautious* **warden** always has to anticipate* the possibility of an escape.
   c. When the journalists* asked to meet with **Warden** Thomas, he sent word that he was sick.

2. **acknowledge** (ak näl' ij) admit to be true
   a. The experts reluctantly* **acknowledged** that their estimate* of food costs was not accurate.*
   b. District Attorney Hogan got the man to **acknowledge** that he had lied in court.
   c. "I hate living alone," the bachelor* **acknowledged**.

3. **justice** (jus' tis) just conduct; fair dealing
   a. Daniel Webster abandoned* any hope for **justice** once he saw the jury.
   b. Our pledge* to the flag refers to "liberty and **justice** for all."
   c. The warden* acknowledged* that **justice** had not been served in my case.

4. **delinquent** (di ling' kwənt) an offender; criminal; behind time
   a. The youthful **delinquent** tried to avoid* going to jail.
   b. All **delinquents** are banned* from the Student Council at school.
   c. If you are **delinquent** in paying your dues, you will be dropped from membership in the club.

5. **reject** (ri jekt') refuse to take, use, believe, consider, grant, etc.
   a. When Sylvester tried to join the army, he was hoping the doctors would not **reject** him because of his eyesight.
   b. The reform* bill was unanimously* **rejected** by Congress.
   c. When his promotion was **rejected** by the newspaper owner, the editor* was thoroughly* bewildered.*

6. **deprive** (di prīv') take away from by force
   a. The poor man was **deprived** of a variety* of things that money could buy.
   b. We were **deprived** of a good harvest* because of the lack* of rain.
   c. Living in a rural* area, Betsy was **deprived** of concerts and plays.

7. **spouse** (spous) husband or wife
   a. When a husband prospers* in his business, his **spouse** benefits also.
   b. The woman and her **spouse** relieved* each other throughout the night at their child's bedside.
   c. "May I bring my **spouse** to the office party?" Dorinda asked.

8. **vocation** (vō kā' shən) occupation; business; profession; trade
   a. Red Smith's **vocation** was as a journalist* for the *Times*.
   b. Hiroko's **vocation** turned into his life's career.
   c. It is difficult to pick an appropriate* **vocation** when you are in elementary school.

9. **unstable** (un stā' bəl) not firmly fixed; easily moved or overthrown
   a. Some **unstable** people may panic* when they find themselves in trouble.
   b. I could detect* that the drinking glass was **unstable** and about to fall.
   c. Cathy's balance became **unstable** because she was very weary.*

10. **homicide** (häm' ə sīd) a killing of one human being by another; murder
    a. The police were baffled* as to who was responsible for the **homicide**.
    b. It took a crafty* person to get away with that **homicide**.
    c. News of the **homicide** quickly circulated* through our vicinity.*

11. **penalize** (pē' nə līz) declare punishable by law or rule; set a penalty for
    a. The Detroit Lions were **penalized** fifteen yards for their rough play.
    b. We were **penalized** for not following tradition.*
    c. Mrs. Robins **penalized** us for doing the math problem in ink.

12. **beneficiary** (ben ə fish' ē er ē or ben ə fish' ərē) person who receives benefit
    a. I was the **beneficiary** of $8,000 when my grandfather died.
    b. When the paintings were sold, the millionaire's niece was the **beneficiary**.
    c. My brother was the **beneficiary** of excellent advice from his guidance counselor.

Words in Use

Read the following passage to see how the new words are used in it.

A New Way to Treat Prisoners

The **warden** of a prison today will readily **acknowledge** the new trend in prison reform.* In an attempt to provide a different brand of **justice** for society's **delinquents,** officials now **reject** the idea that prison should completely **deprive** the convict of freedom. Thus, in some prisons inmates are allowed to leave the prison grounds to visit their spouses or to pursue* their **vocation.** Even the more **unstable** convict who may have committed **homicide** is not **penalized** as harshly* as before. The hope is that if persons emerge* from prison less defiant* than they do now, society will be the **beneficiary.**

Picture It

Which of the words studied in this lesson is suggested by the picture?

Fill in the Blanks

Place one of the new words in each of the blanks below.

1. Wayne's parents yelled at him because he was known as a _____ .
2. The courts will _____ you if you don't obey the law.
3. Are you satisfied with your _____ or are you thinking of getting a different job?
4. Five persons were being questioned by the police about the brutal* _____ .
5. I _____ the fact that I received the tapes.
6. When Steve asked his girlfriend to marry him, he did not anticipate* that she would _____ him.
7. The _____ of the prison set up stricter rules.
8. Mrs. Fried's _____ came home weary* after each day's work.
9. It is often _____ persons who commit serious crimes.
10. Clara felt as if she had been _____ of the better things in life.
11. _____ was served when the villain* was put behind bars.
12. Joseph was the _____ of large sums of money from his uncle's insurance policy.

Answer key, p. 197

Matching

Match the 12 new words in Column I with the definitions in Column II.

Column I	Column II
1. warden	a. murder
2. penalize	b. admit to be true
3. justice	c. person in charge of a prison
4. delinquent	d. not firmly fixed
5. vocation	e. take away from by force
6. spouse	f. a criminal
7. homicide	g. person who receives benefit
8. acknowledge	h. declare punishable by law or rule
9. unstable	i. husband or wife
10. beneficiary	j. occupation
11. reject	k. fair dealing
12. deprive	l. refuse to take, use, believe, grant, etc.

Answer key, p. 197

Spotlight On

beneficiary—Except for Benedict Arnold, who did not treat his country well, all other words beginning with *bene* speak only of good, for that is what this prefix (a letter or letters attached at the beginning of a word) means. Here is a list of such "good" words: benefactor, beneficent, beneficial, benefit, benevolent, benign. In your reading, have you come across the letters N.B. in front of certain passages? The author is telling you to "note it well" *(nota bene)*.

LESSON
23

"In words as fashions the same rule will hold,
Alike fantastic if too new or old;
Be not the first by whom the new are tried,
Nor yet the last to lay the old aside."

—Alexander Pope, *Essay on Criticism*

Words to Learn This Week

reptile
rarely
forbid
logical
exhibit
proceed
precaution
extract
prior
embrace
valiant
partial

1. **reptile** (rep' təl) a cold blooded animal that creeps or crawls; snakes, lizards, turtles, alligators, and crocodiles
   a. The lizard is a **reptile** with a very slender* body.
   b. **Reptiles** are kept in the museum's large hall.
   c. A crocodile is a **reptile** that is more nimble* in the water than out of it.

2. **rarely** (rãr' lē) seldom; not often
   a. You **rarely** hear adults raving* about a movie they just saw.
   b. People are **rarely** frank* with each other.
   c. I **rarely** attend the annual* meetings of our family circle.

3. **forbid** (fər bid') order someone not to do something; make a rule against
   a. Spitting on the floor is **forbidden** in public places.
   b. The law **forbids** drunken drivers to handle their autos.
   c. I **forbid** you to enter the dense* jungle because of the peril* that awaits you there.

4. **logical** (loj' ə kəl) reasonable; reasonably expected
   a. It is **logical** to spend a minimum* on needless things.
   b. In order to keep your car running well, it is only **logical** that you lubricate* it regularly.
   c. I used a **logical** argument to persuade* Lester to leave.

5. **exhibit** (eg zib' it) display; show
   a. A million-dollar microscope* is now on **exhibit** at our school.
   b. The bride and groom **exhibited** their many expensive* gifts.
   c. Kim frequently* **exhibited** her vast knowledge* of baseball before complete strangers.

6. **proceed** (prə sēd') go on after having stopped; move forward
   a. Only those with special cards can **proceed** into the pool area.
   b. When the actor was late, the show **proceeded** without him.
   c. The senator **proceeded** to denounce* those wholesalers* who would deprive* Americans of their quota* of beef.

7. **precaution** (prə kô' shən) measures taken beforehand; foresight
   a. Detectives used **precaution** before entering the bomb's vicinity.*
   b. We must take every **precaution** not to pollute* the air.
   c. Before igniting* the fire, the hunters took unusual **precaution**.

8. **extract** (eks trakt') pull out or draw out, usually with some effort
   a. Dr. Fogel **extracted** my tooth in an amateur* fashion.
   b. Chemists **extracted** the essential* vitamins from the grain.
   c. Spencer was ingenious* in **extracting** information from witnesses.

9. **prior** (prī' ər) coming before; earlier
   a. **Prior** to choosing his life's vocation,* Paul traveled to India.
   b. Myrna was unhappy **prior** to meeting her beau.
   c. President Obama had **prior** service as a senator.

10. embrace (em brās') hug one another; a hug
    a. After having been rivals* for years, the two men **embraced**.
    b. When Ellen's spouse* approached,* she slipped out of Doug's **embrace**.
    c. The young girl was bewildered* when the stranger **embraced** her.

11. valiant (val' yənt) brave; courageous
    a. Robin Hood was **valiant** and faced his opponents* without fear.
    b. The **valiant** paratroopers led the invasion.
    c. Grandma Joad had the ability* to be **valiant** when the need arose.

12. partial (pär' shəl) not complete; not total
    a. We made a **partial** listing of the urgently* needed supplies.
    b. Macy's had a sale on a **partial** selection of its winter clothes.
    c. Using only a **partial** amount of his great speed, Jim surpassed* all the other runners.

Words in Use

Read the following passage to see how the new words are used in it.

Handling Poisonous Snakes

How do the Indian snake charmers handle those live poisonous **reptiles** without being poisoned? Visitors to the Hopi Indians **rarely** leave the reservation without asking. Because Indians **forbid** any white person from taking part in such a ceremony, scientists could come to one **logical** answer: before the Indians **exhibit** the snakes, they **proceed** to remove the fangs. Yet some scientists verify* the fact that all the snakes have fangs. They have a different theory.* The Indians take an important **precaution:** they **extract** most of the poison **prior** to the snake dance. Now the Indian can **embrace** the snake without being poisoned. He will appear **valiant** because he knows that the snake has only a **partial** supply of its deadly poison.

Picture It

Which of the words studied in this lesson is suggested by the picture?

Fill in the Blanks

Place one of the new words in each of the blanks below.

1. I _____ my daughter when she came home from camp.
2. We _____ you to leave the area.
3. Did you _____ along the hall until you got to the room?
4. A turtle is a very common _____ .
5. We made a _____ listing of the people who owed the library books because it would take too long to copy all the names.
6. Betty Sue is always very _____ when she prepares her arguments for a debate.*
7. I _____ if ever go to the movies.
8. Have you seen the cave dweller _____ in the museum?
9. I went to high school _____ to entering the army.
10. Be sure to take the _____ not to swim after eating.
11. Sergeant York got a medal for being _____ in war.
12. Did you _____ the splinter from his foot?

Answer key, p. 197

Creativity Exercise

Now make up your own sentences, one for each of the new words you have just been taught.

1. _____

2. _____

3. _____

4. _____

5. _____

6. _____

7. _____

8. _____

9. _____

10. _____

11. _____

12. _____

Spotlight On

valiant—The famous Prince Valiant has appeared in the comics for many years as the ideal knight. Since English has so many synonyms for the quality of courage, he might have been called Prince Gallant, Intrepid, Audacious, Hardy, Resolute, Indomitable, Fearless, Dauntless, Chivalrous, or Heroic. Or was Prince Valiant just the right name?

"Words are the physicians of a mind diseased."

—Aeschylus, *Prometheus Bound*

1. **fierce** (fērs) savage; wild
   a. Barry was so **fiercely** angry that he thrust* his hand through the glass.
   b. One must take appropriate* precautions* when approaching* **fierce** dogs.
   c. He took one look at his **fierce** opponent* and ran.

2. **detest** (di test') dislike very much; hate
   a. The world **detests** people who aren't valiant.*
   b. Wally was certain that his girlfriend's parents would **detest** him because he had been a delinquent.*
   c. I **detest** Chinese food but I won't deprive* you of the chance to eat it.

3. **sneer** (snēr) show scorn or contempt by looks or words; a scornful look or remark
   a. The journalists* were cautious* about **sneering** at the Secretary of Defense.
   b. "Wipe that **sneer** off your face!" the dean told the delinquent.*
   c. When offered a dime as a tip, the taxi driver **sneered** at his rider.

4. **scowl** (skoul) look angry by lowering the eyebrows; frown
   a. Laverne **scowled** at her mother when she was prohibited* from going out.
   b. I dread* seeing my father **scowl** when he gets my report card.
   c. Because of a defect* in her vision,* it always appeared that Polly was **scowling**.

5. **encourage** (en ker' ij) give courage to; increase the confidence of
   a. We **encouraged** the coach to devise* a plan for beating Jefferson High.
   b. Some unstable* persons need to be **encouraged** to find a vocation.*
   c. A valiant* person rarely* needs to be **encouraged**.

6. **consider** (ken sid' ər) think about in order to decide
   a. Jon **considered** whether a comprehensive* report was necessary.
   b. Do you **consider** that dress to be a bargain at the wholesale* price?
   c. The wrestler was always **considered** to be the underdog* in every match.

7. **vermin** (ver' mən) small animals that are troublesome or destructive; fleas, bedbugs, lice, rats, and mice are vermin
   a. We should try to eliminate* all **vermin** from our house.
   b. Some reptiles* eat **vermin** as their food.
   c. Although **vermin** are not always visible,* they probably inhabit* every house in the city.

8. **wail** (wāl) cry loud and long because of grief or pain
   a. When tragedy* struck, the old people began to **wail**.
   b. In some countries the women are expected to **wail** loudly after their husbands die.
   c. When the Yankees lost the World Series, there was much **wailing** in New York.

**Words to Learn
This Week**

fierce

detest

sneer

scowl

encourage

consider

vermin

wail

symbol

authority

neutral

trifle

9. **symbol** (sim' bəl) something that stands for or represents something else
   a. The statue outside the court building is considered* a **symbol** of justice.*
   b. **Symbols** for God are prohibited* in their religion.
   c. An olive branch is a **symbol** of peace.

10. **authority** (ə thôr' ə tē) the right to command or enforce obedience; power delegated to another; an author or volume that may be appealed to in support of an action or belief
    a. No one should have the **authority** to dictate our career choice.
    b. Today a monarch* does not have the **authority** he once enjoyed.
    c. The Supreme Court is entrusted with the **authority** to interpret our Constitution.

11. **neutral** (no͞o' trəl) on neither side of a quarrel or war
    a. It is logical* to remain **neutral** in a violent* argument between spouses.*
    b. Switzerland was a **neutral** country in World War II.
    c. Adolph did not reject* the idea but remained **neutral** about it.

12. **trifle** (trī' fəl) a small amount; little bit; something of little value
    a. I ate a **trifle** for dinner rather than a vast* meal.
    b. Walter spends only a **trifle** of his time in studying French.
    c. At our meetings Alex always raises **trifling** objections to any new plan.

Words in Use

Read the following passage to see how the new words are used in it.

Punishment for Drug Abuse

A recent* attempt by New Jersey's attorney general to lessen the penalties* for use of marijuana has caused **fierce** arguments around the country. Those who **detest** the drug users **sneer** and **scowl** at the light treatment of offenders. They reject* the attorney general's recommendation as lacking a morsel* of sense, claiming it would only **encourage** more drug abuse. They **consider** the drug addict much like **vermin** that must be stamped out. Such citizens continually **wail** for stiffer penalties. Those in favor of a milder approach* to the drug problem point to the poor results achieved by prison terms. They feel addicts* should be given medical help. Also, in enforcing harsh* drug laws, police tend to be viewed as a **symbol** of unwelcome **authority**. The problem demands a solution. We cannot remain **neutral** or unconcerned, nor can we afford to muddle through with ineffective measures, for this is not a **trifling** matter.

Picture It

Which of the words studied in this lesson is suggested by the picture?

Fill in the Blanks

Place one of the new words in each of the blanks below.

1. I have it on the highest _____ that the lead in the play has been chosen.
2. I am going to _____ my brother to become a lawyer.
3. Uncle Sam is the well-known _____ of the United States.
4. We pay $5 a month to keep our house free from _____ .
5. When a country is _____ , it does not want to get involved in foreign conflict.*
6. What type of art work do you _____ to be beautiful?
7. The _____ lion clawed at the visitors to the zoo.
8. To hear the _____ of a person in sorrow is to hear a dismal* sound.
9. Only a _____ of Ivan's fortune was left to his human beneficiaries;* most of the money was given to his cats.
10. I _____ people who are jealous* of my success.
11. The unpleasant salesgirl always had a _____ on her face.
12. My father warned me not to _____ at our poor relatives.

Answer key, p. 197

Synonyms

Circle the word that most nearly expresses the meaning of the word printed in blue type.

1. **encourage**
   a. evade*
   b. approach*
   c. reassure
   d. cuddle

2. **neutral**
   a. impartial
   b. reckless
   c. abundant*
   d. bulky

3. **scowl**
   a. alter*
   b. forbid*
   c. frown
   d. complicate

4. **consider**
   a. think over
   b. assume responsibility
   c. issue orders
   d. accept a challenge*

5. **fierce**
   a. massive*
   b. sinister*
   c. savage
   d. coarse

6. **detest**
   a. abolish*
   b. hate
   c. baffle*
   d. ignore*

7. **authority**
   a. opinion
   b. valuable skill
   c. deciding factor
   d. power to act

8. **symbol**
   a. image
   b. concealed* evidence*
   c. absurdity*
   d. sacred* object

9. **trifle**
   a. fragile* glass
   b. flexible* hours
   c. small amount
   d. ignorant statement

10. **vermin**
    a. small and troublesome animals
    b. boring and disappointing movies
    c. curious readers
    d. crafty* clients*

11. **sneer**
    a. scornful look
    b. gallant* gesture
    c. sinister* act
    d. rude interruption

12. **wail**
    a. calm down
    b. cry loud and long
    c. go forward
    d. break even

Answer key, p. 197

Spotlight On

symbol—Our civilization is quite dependent upon symbols. Without them, the world would be drab and dull indeed. The very words we use are merely symbols for the things and ideas they represent. Symbols are used in language, writing, logic, mathematics, science, religion, trade, and sports. Find a symbol for each of the fields mentioned.

Word Review #4

These exercises are based on some of the words found in Lessons 19–24.

A. In each of the parentheses below there are two choices. Pick the one that fits better.

1. In order to help our own auto companies, the government set up (quotas, estimates) on the number of foreign cars it would allow to be sent here.
2. To make sure that our sauce is good, we hire workers to (harvest, reject) those tomatoes that are not ripe.
3. My hopes for visiting Canada this summer hang on a (fragile, logical) thread.
4. Try to (extract, acknowledge) every ounce of juice you can get from these oranges.
5. When I need help with a (dilemma, trifle), I turn to my father, who always gives me good advice.
6. Since you have made (partial, abundant) payment for your bicycle, you still owe quite a few dollars.
7. If you (linger, proceed) too long over your breakfast, you will be late for school.
8. I didn't want to get mixed up in the fight between Luke and Pete, so I took a (neutral, defiant) position.
9. Once I had (calculated, exhibited) how long it would take to do the jobs, I knew what to charge.
10. After the facts were (confirmed, relieved), the editor* printed the story.

Answer key, p. 197

B. **Opposites.** In Column I are ten words from Lessons 19–24. Match them correctly with their *opposite* meanings in Column II.

Column I	Column II
1. detest	a. huge piece
2. perish	b. hide
3. valiant	c. wide awake
4. emerge	d. afraid
5. unstable	e. afterwards
6. weary	f. be fond of
7. scowl	g. often
8. prior	h. live
9. morsel	i. smile
10. rarely	j. steady

Answer key, p. 197

C. Which of the vocabulary choices in parentheses fits best in these newspaper headlines?

1. **Egyptian Art _____ to Open at Local Museum** (Quota, Exhibit, Extract, Symbol)
2. **Middle East Countries to Test _____ Peace**   (Fragile, Appropriate, Prior, Neutral)
3. **Trucks _____ in Highway Accident**   (Proceed, Linger, Collide, Detour)
4. **Ask Retired Judge to Solve _____**   (Threat, Panic, Plea, Dilemma)
5. **Slum Houses to Be Rid of _____**   (Vermin, Merit, Reptiles, Vigor)
6. **Police _____ Arrest of Jewelry Thief**   (Transmit, Merit, Extract, Confirm)
7. **New Arrivals Hope to _____ in America**   (Prosper, Verify, Emerge, Ban)
8. **Family Pets _____ in Four-Alarm Fire**   (Partial, Perish, Scowl, Devour)
9. **"Must Meet _____," Salesmen Are Told**   (Beneficiary, Quota, Threat, Merit)
10. **Farmers Pleased with _____ Crop**   (Logical, Uneasy, Abundant, Jagged)

Answer key, p. 197

D. From the list of words below choose the word that means:

wail	precaution	symbol	collide	merit	absorb
quota	beneficiary	baffle	verify	jagged	devour
proceed	acknowledge	prior	ambush	crafty	trifle
penalize	appropriate	deprive	panic	prosper	warden
harvest	transmit	plea	anticipate	defiant	vigor

1 a trap from which to make a surprise attack *and* is a simpler word for *ambuscade*
2 the person to be paid money from an insurance policy *and* begins with the prefix meaning "good"
3 a letter, character, mark, sign, or abbreviation *that* represents an idea or quality
4 the end product of a farmer's work *but also* refers to the product of any toil or effort
5 alarm *and* is derived from the name of the Greek god who brought fear whenever he appeared
6 succeed *and also* attain one's desires
7 defeat *as well as* perplex or puzzle
8 the chief officer of a prison *and also* a guardian or a superintendent

9. taking care beforehand *as well as* provision for an emergency
10. something of little value or importance *and also* to play with or treat lightly someone's feelings

Answer key, p. 197

E. **Letter Writing.** The following business letter uses ten words that appeared in lessons 19–24. Fill in the blanks with those words selected from the group below:

abundant	confirm	encourage	merit	quota
acknowledge	consider	forbid	precaution	rarely
anticipate	detour	fragile	prior	reject
appropriate	emerge	linger	proceed	reptiles

Bluefish Inn
Route 2435
Telluride, CO 79865
March 15, 2011

Mr. Douglas Milleridge
9123 Willow Wick Drive
Baltimore, MD 43671

Dear Mr. Milleridge:

Thank you for your recent inquiry about Bluefish Inn.

Our resort overlooks Bluefish Lake from a beautiful wooded setting at the north end of the lake. The inn was built in 1930 of native pine logs and is one of the most impressive log structures in Colorado. Many travelers make a __1__ just to see the inn. Recently remodeled, the inn is __2__ for family reunions, company outings, and business meetings.

At 8,700 feet above sea level, Bluefish Lake, five miles long and two miles wide, is a unique mountain lake because of its deep, clear waters and surrounding pine forest. The area around the lake is free of mosquitos, and hikers __3__ see dangerous __4__ . In the summer the lake offers a refreshing change of climate from the hot city. During the winter months, Bluefish Lake is accessible by car, and that is the time to take advantage of excellent ice fishing and skiing. It can be quite cold, so as a __5__ , bring warm clothes. Fall at the lake is peaceful and spectacular. The forests that surround the lake are brilliant when the fall colors __6__ .

Although many species of fish are caught, Bluefish Lake is especially famous for its __7__ deep water lake trout, that often weigh over 20 pounds. If you fish, you can __8__ catching a record breaking trout.

We hope you will __9__ vacationing with us. Write soon so we can __10__ your reservation. Please feel free to call our toll-free number if you have any questions.

Yours truly,
Richard Constanza
Manager

Answer key, p. 197

F. **Words That Do Double Duty.** Once again, as you did in the previous Word Reviews, note the following words, which appeared in Lessons 19–24. Each can serve as more than one part of speech:

exhibit (v., n.)	detour (v., n.)
harvest (v., n.)	delinquent (n., adj.)
panic (v., n.)	reject (v., n.)
ambush (v., n.)	sneer (v., n.)
plea (v., n.)	scowl (v., n.)

Make up two sentences for each of the above words, showing how it could be used as two different parts of speech.

Examples: The talented students in the art class will *exhibit* their paintings on Open School Night.
    Last week my friends and I visited the arts and crafts *exhibit* at the fair.

LESSON
25

1. **architect** (är' ke təkt) a person who makes plans for buildings and other structures; a maker; a creator
   a. The famous **architect**, Frank Lloyd Wright, designed his buildings to blend* with their surroundings.
   b. An **architect** must have a knowledge of the materials that will be used in his structures.
   c. General Eisenhower was the **architect** of victory over the Nazis in World War II.

2. **matrimony** (mat' rə mō' nē) married life; ceremony of marriage
   a. Though **matrimony** is a holy state, our local governments still collect a fee for the marriage license.
   b. Because of lack of money, the sweetness of their **matrimony** turned sour.
   c. Some bachelors* find it very difficult to give up their freedom for the blessings of **matrimony**.

3. **baggage** (bag' ij) the trunks and suitcases a person takes when he or she travels; an army's equipment
   a. When Walt unpacked his **baggage**, he found he had forgotten his radio.
   b. Mrs. Montez checked her **baggage** at the station and took the children for a walk.
   c. The modern army cannot afford to be slowed up with heavy **baggage**.

4. **squander** (skwän' dər) spend foolishly; waste
   a. Do not **squander** your money by buying what you cannot use.
   b. Because Freddy **squandered** his time watching television, he could not catch up on his homework.
   c. In his will, Mr. Larson warned his children not to **squander** their inheritance.

5. **abroad** (a brôd') outside one's country; going around; far and wide
   a. More people are going **abroad** for vacations.
   b. Is there any truth to the rumor **abroad** that school will be open all summer?
   c. The news of the president's illness spread **abroad**.

6. **fugitive** (fyoo' jə tiv) a runaway
   a. Paul was a **fugitive** from the slums, abandoned* by all his friends.
   b. After escaping from prison, Tom led an unhappy life as a **fugitive** from the law.
   c. The **fugitives** from the unsuccessful revolution were captured.

7. **calamity** (kə lam' ə tē) a great misfortune; serious trouble
   a. Failure in one test should not be regarded as a **calamity**.
   b. The death of her husband was a **calamity** that left Mrs. Marlowe numb.*
   c. What is more dismal* than one **calamity** following upon the heels of another?

8. **pauper** (pô' pər) a very poor person
   a. The fire that destroyed his factory made Mr. Bloomson a **pauper**.
   b. The richest man is a **pauper** if he has no friends.
   c. Since he was once a **pauper** himself, Max is willing to help the needy whenever he can.

Words to Learn This Week

architect
matrimony
baggage
squander
abroad
fugitive
calamity
pauper
envy
collapse
prosecute
bigamy

9. **envy** (en' vē) jealousy; the object of jealousy; to feel jealous
   a. Marilyn's selection as Prom Queen made her the **envy** of every senior.
   b. My parents taught me not to **envy** anyone else's wealth.
   c. Our **envy** of Nora's skating ability is foolish because with practice all of us could do as well.

10. **collapse** (kə laps') a breakdown; to fall in; break down; fail suddenly; fold together
    a. A heavy flood caused the bridge to **collapse**.
    b. His failure in chemistry meant the **collapse** of Bob's summer plans.
    c. **Collapse** the trays and store them in the closet.

11. **prosecute** (präs' ə ko͞ot) bring before a court; follow up; carry on
    a. Drunken drivers should be **prosecuted**.
    b. The district attorney refused to **prosecute** the case for lack of evidence.
    c. The general **prosecuted** the war with vigor.*

12. **bigamy** (big' ə mē) having two wives or two husbands at the same time
    a. Some people look upon **bigamy** as double trouble.
    b. Mr. Winkle, looking at his wife, thought **bigamy** was one crime he would never be guilty of.
    c. Some religious groups are in favor of **bigamy** even though it is against the law of the land.

Words in Use

Read the following passage to see how the new words are used in it.

Love and Marriage

The famous **architect** Melville Fenton grew tired of **matrimony** and devised* a scheme to free himself of his spouse.* He told her he had been engaged by an American company to design its new office building in Paris. Packing his **baggage**, he left his home and proceeded* to cut all his ties with his former life. He changed his name, secured a new job, and quickly forgot his faithful wife.

Not having any responsibilities, he began to **squander** his money and energy. He married another woman, believing he was safe from the law. But his first wife had grown suspicious and resentful.*

She learned from his employer that he had not gone **abroad**, that in fact he had left the firm altogether. With a little detective work, she soon discovered her husband's whereabouts. He had become a **fugitive** from justice* and one **calamity** after another overtook him. He lost his job, became a **pauper** and was no longer the **envy** of his acquaintances. Then his second wife grew ill and died.

After the **collapse** of his plans, there was only one logical* step for Melville to take. He embraced* his wife and asked for her forgiveness. Much to his relief, she decided not to **prosecute** him for **bigamy**.

Fill in the Blanks

Place one of the new words in each of the blanks below.

1. The _____ compartment of the plane was inspected for bombs.
2. A storm on the night of the prom meant _____ for the senior class plans.
3. Good government would assure that there are no more _____ in the land.
4. The strain of the three-hour examination almost brought Leslie to a state of _____ .
5. Now that the quintuplets have come along, we are calling on an _____ to devise* plans for an extension to our home.
6. The hungry man was _____ for stealing a loaf of bread.
7. Bringing expensive* toys to newborn infants is just another way to _____ your money.
8. Bloodhounds were brought in to hunt for the _____ in the dense* forest.
9. When it was learned that Mr. Smythe had failed to divorce his first wife, he was charged with _____ .
10. Traveling _____ is an educational experience.
11. What is there to _____ in a high mark that was not honestly achieved?
12. Everyone can see that _____ has brought Jim and Stella great happiness.

Answer key, p. 197

Creativity Exercise

Now make up your own sentences, one for each of the new words you have just been taught.

1. _____

2. _____

3. _____

4. _____

5. _____

6. _____

7. _____

8. _____

9. _____

10. _____

11. _____

12. _____

Picture It

Which of the words studied in this lesson is suggested by the picture?

Spotlight On

architect—The architect is only the first of many workers needed before a building is completed. Some others are engineers, bulldozer operators, welders, carpenters, masons, lathers, plumbers, electricians, roofers, painters, plasterers, tilers, glaziers. Of course, you might simply hire a contractor who would then have all the headaches.

LESSON
26

"What do you read, my Lord?" "Words, words, words."

—Shakespeare, *Hamlet*

Words to Learn This Week

possible
compel
awkward
venture
awesome
guide
quench
betray
utter
pacify
respond
beckon

1. **possible** (päs' ə bl) able to be, be done, or happen; able to be true; able to be done or chosen properly
   a. Call me tomorrow evening if **possible**.
   b. It is now **possible** for man to walk on the moon.
   c. Considering* Melissa's weakness in writing, it is not **possible** for her to help you with your composition.

2. **compel** (kəm pel') force; get by force
   a. It is not possible* to **compel** a person to love his fellow man.
   b. Heavy floods **compelled** us to stop.
   c. Mr. Gorlin is a teacher who does not have to **compel** me to behave.

3. **awkward** (ô' kwərd) clumsy; not well-suited to use; not easily managed; embarrassing
   a. Sally is very **awkward** in speaking to the class but quite relaxed with her own group of friends.
   b. The handle of this bulky* suitcase has an **awkward** shape.
   c. Slow down because this is an **awkward** corner to turn.

4. **venture** (ven' chər) a daring undertaking; an attempt to make money by taking business risks; to dare; to expose to risk
   a. Ulysses was a man who would not reject* any **venture,** no matter how dangerous.
   b. John Jacob Astor made his fortune by a lucky **venture** in animal furs.
   c. Medics **venture** their lives to save wounded soldiers.

5. **awesome** (ô' səm) causing or showing great fear, wonder, or respect
   a. The towering mountains, covered with snow, are an **awesome** sight.
   b. Connie had such an **awesome** amount of work to complete before graduation she doubted* she would have everything ready in time.
   c. The atom bomb is an **awesome** achievement for mankind.

6. **guide** (gīd) a person who shows the way; to direct; to manage
   a. Tourists often hire **guides**.
   b. The Indian **guided** the hunters through the forest.
   c. Use the suggestions in the handbook as a study **guide**.

7. **quench** (kwench) put an end to; drown or put out
   a. Foam will **quench** an oil fire.
   b. Only iced tea will **quench** my thirst on such a hot day.
   c. He reads and reads and reads to **quench** his thirst for knowledge.

8. **betray** (bitrā') give away to the enemy; be unfaithful; mislead; show
   a. Nick's awkward* motions **betrayed** his nervousness.
   b. Without realizing what he was doing, the talkative soldier **betrayed** his unit's plans.
   c. The child's eyes **betrayed** his fear of the fierce* dog.

9. **utter** (ut' ər) speak; make known; express
   a. When Violet accidentally stepped on the nail, she **uttered** a sharp cry of pain.
   b. Seth was surprised when he was told that he had **uttered** Joan's name in his sleep.
   c. When Mr. Fuller saw that his house had not been damaged in the fire, he **uttered** a sigh of relief.*

10. pacify (pas' ə fī) make calm; quiet down; bring peace to
    a. This toy should **pacify** that screaming baby.
    b. We tried to **pacify** the woman who was angry at having to wait so long in line.
    c. Soldiers were sent to **pacify** the countryside.

11. respond (ri spänd') answer; react
    a. Greg **responded** quickly to the question.
    b. My dog **responds** to every command I give him.
    c. Mrs. Cole **responded** to the medicine so well that she was better in two days.

12. beckon (bek' ən) signal by a motion of the hand or head; attract
    a. Jack **beckoned** to me to follow him.
    b. The delicious smell of fresh bread **beckoned** the hungry boy.
    c. The sea **beckons** us to adventure.

Words in Use

Read the following passage to see how the new words are used in it.

Some Tall Tales

Do you think it is **possible** to defeat an opponent so fierce* that a glance* at her turns one to stone? This was the fate of anyone who looked upon the Medusa, a dreaded* monster whose hair was made of hissing serpents. The brave Perseus undertook to fight the Medusa, but he was **compelled** to do battle in a most **awkward** manner. To help Perseus in his **venture,** the goddess Minerva had lent him her bright shield, and the god Mercury had given him winged shoes. Cautiously he approached the **awesome** monster. Using the image of the Medusa in his shield as a **guide,** he succeeded in cutting off her head and fixing it to the center of Minerva's shield.

Perseus then flew to the realm of King Atlas whose chief pride was his garden filled with golden fruit. Thirsty and near collapse,* he pleaded with the king for water to **quench** his thirst and for a place to rest. But Atlas feared that he would be **betrayed** into losing his golden apples. He **uttered** just one word, "Begone!" Perseus, finding that he could not **pacify** Atlas, **responded** by **beckoning** him to look upon Medusa's head. Atlas was changed immediately into stone. His head and hair became forests, his body increased in bulk and became cliffs, and the gods ruled that the heaven with all its stars should rest upon his shoulders. Can there be a worse calamity* than that which befell Atlas?

Picture It

Which of the words studied in this lesson is suggested by the picture?

Fill in the Blanks

Place one of the new words in each of the blanks below.

1. History has shown us that tyranny* cannot _____ the human desire for freedom.
2. The sailors used the North Star to _____ them to their destination.
3. Our eyes _____ to sudden light by blinking.
4. The coach _____ to the pitcher to watch for a bunt.
5. Little Benjy was foolish enough to _____ out on the thin ice.
6. If we are _____ to vote without hearing all sides of the issue, we could make a serious mistake.
7. Power in the hands of the ignorant is an _____ responsibility.
8. Benedict Arnold _____ his country.
9. The only _____ excuse for Barry's failure is his lack* of effort.
10. It was not possible* to _____the excited woman after she was fined for jaywalking.
11. The last words _____ by the dying soldier were, "We must hold the fort."
12. Ralph found himself in an _____ situation when his blind date turned out to be a foot taller than he.

Answer key, p. 198

True or False

Based on the way the new word is used, write T (true) or F (false) next to the sentence.

1. An **awkward** person is very graceful.
2. An **awesome** sight is one that causes great wonder and respect.
3. If someone tells you it's **possible** to do something, that means the thing cannot be done.
4. To **beckon** is to signal by a motion of the hand or head to call someone over to you.
5. A person who shows you the way is a **guide.**
6. To **utter** is to remain silent.
7. To quiet an angry mob is to **pacify** the crowd.
8. If you are **compelled** to do something, you are forced to do it.
9. A person who undertakes a **venture** is afraid to take risks of any kind.
10. If I **respond** to your suggestion, I react to it.
11. To **quench** something is to renew it.
12. To **betray** someone is to be unfaithful or misleading.

Answer key, p. 198

Spotlight On

respond—The next time you receive an invitation to a party, the host or hostess may want to be sure you are coming so that adequate preparations can be made. In that case, he or she will write R.S.V.P. on the invitation to tell you in simple French *(répondez s'il vous plaît)* to please respond.

"My words fly up, my thoughts remain below: Words without thoughts never to heaven go."

—Shakespeare, *Hamlet*

Words to Learn This Week

despite
disrupt
rash
rapid
exhaust
severity
feeble
unite
cease
thrifty
miserly
monarch

1. **despite** (di spīt') in spite of
   a. The player continued in the game **despite** his injuries.
   b. **Despite** being shy, Ted signed up to audition on *American Idol*.
   c. We won the game by a shutout **despite** the fact that our team got only three hits.

2. **disrupt** (dis rupt') upset; cause to break down
   a. Pam's clowning **disrupted** the class every day.
   b. The storm **disrupted** the telephone lines throughout the area.
   c. The collapse* of the government **disrupted** the services we took for granted, such as mail delivery.

3. **rash** (rash) a breaking out with many small red spots on the skin; outbreak of many instances within a short time: too hasty or careless
   a. The report of a **rash** of burglaries in the neighborhood was exaggerated.*
   b. Poison ivy causes a **rash**.
   c. It is **rash** to threaten an action you cannot carry out.

4. **rapid** (ra' pid) very quick; swift
   a. We took a **rapid** walk around the camp before breakfast.
   b. If you work **rapidly** you can complete the test in twenty minutes.
   c. The response* to the surprise attack was a **rapid** retreat.

5. **exhaust** (ig zôst') empty completely; use up; tire out
   a. To **exhaust** the city's water supply would be a calamity.*
   b. The long climb to the top of the mountain **exhausted** our strength.
   c. If we continue to squander* our money recklessly,* our treasury will soon be **exhausted**.

6. **severity** (sə ver' ə tē) strictness; harshness; plainness; violence
   a. The **severity** of the teacher was not appreciated by the pupils until they reached the final examinations.
   b. The **severity** of the Black Plague can be imagined from the fact that thirty percent of the population* died.
   c. Rosita complained to the principal about the **severity** of the punishment that the Student Court gave to her.

7. **feeble** (fē' bl) weak
   a. We heard a **feeble** cry from the exhausted* child.
   b. The guide* made a **feeble** attempt to explain why he had taken the wrong turn.
   c. The **feeble** old man collapsed* on the sidewalk.

8. **unite** (yu̇ nīt') join together; become one
   a. The thirteen colonies **united** to form one country.
   b. Matrimony* **united** two famous Virginia families.
   c. America and Russia were **united** against a common enemy in World War II.

9. **cease** (sēs) stop
   a. **Cease** trying to do more than you can.
   b. The whispering in the audience **ceased** when the curtain went up.
   c. When you **cease** making war, you can then begin to pacify* the small villages the enemy controls.

10. thrifty (thrif' tē) saving; careful in spending; thriving
  a. By being **thrifty,** Miss Benson managed to get along on her small income.
  b. A **thrifty** person knows that squandering* money can lead to financial* calamity.*
  c. By **thrifty** use of their supplies, the shipwrecked sailors were able to survive* for weeks.

11. miserly (mī' zər lē) stingy; like a miser
  a. Being **miserly** with our natural resources will help us to live longer on this earth.
  b. A **miserly** person rarely* has any friends.
  c. Silas Marner abandoned* his **miserly** habits when Eppie came into his life.

12. monarch (män' ərk) king or queen; ruler
  a. There are few modern nations that are governed by **monarchs**.
  b. The **monarchs** of ancient Rome considered themselves descendants* of the gods.
  c. Men sometimes believe that they are **monarchs** in their own homes.

Words in Use

Read the following passage to see how the new words are used in it.

Problems We Face

Despite wars, disease, and natural disasters,* our world is experiencing a population explosion (boom) that threatens* to change or **disrupt** life as we have known it. Vast* numbers of people must be fed and housed, and in the process a whole **rash** of problems has descended* upon the human race.

First has been the pollution* of the air and the contamination* of the water supply. Second has been the **rapid exhaustion** of fuels, minerals, and other natural resources. The response* to this situation has ranged from utter* disbelief to exaggerated* concern.

Since scientists themselves disagree on the **severity** of the problem, our **feeble** knowledge is surely unable to suggest the correct course of action. But we cannot stand still because there is too much at stake. We are, therefore, compelled* to **unite** in our efforts to insure that human life on this planet does not **cease**. We must learn to be **thrifty**, even **miserly**, with the gifts of nature that we have formerly taken for granted. If our past reveals* a reckless* squandering* of our natural possessions, we must now find an intelligent guide* to their use so that we may remain **monarchs** of a world that has peace and plenty.

Picture It

Which of the words studied in this lesson is suggested by the picture?

Fill in the Blanks

Place one of the new words in each of the blanks below.

1. The dying soldier made a last _____ effort to rise.
2. Though the victim's breathing had _____, the fireman continued giving oxygen.
3. We often regret a _____ statement made in the heat of an argument.
4. Now that you have _____ all your excuses, tell us the truth.
5. The bout was fought to determine who would be the _____ of the ring.
6. An increase in pollution* will _____ our normal ways of life.
7. Macy's Department Store always says, "It pays to be _____ ."
8. I have learned to read Spanish _____, but I cannot speak it so well.
9. The _____ of the pain compelled* Frank to call the doctor in the middle of the night.
10. Under certain conditions, oxygen will _____ with hydrogen to form water.
11. _____ a warning glance from the teacher, Harold continued to annoy the girl next to him.
12. It is best to be neither too _____ nor too careless about one's money.

Answer key, p. 198

Creativity Exercise

Now make up your own sentences, one for each of the new words you have just been taught.

1. _____
2. _____
3. _____
4. _____
5. _____
6. _____
7. _____
8. _____
9. _____
10. _____
11. _____
12. _____

Spotlight On

thrifty—If a person is very thrifty with money, would you describe him or her as economical or stingy, careful or miserly, frugal or greedy? Though the trait is the same in each case, the word describing it has a different value judgment. The word you choose really depends upon what you think of the person.

LESSON
28

1. **outlaw** (out' lô) an exile; an outcast; a criminal; to declare unlawful
   a. Congress has **outlawed** the sale of certain drugs.
   b. The best-known **outlaw** of the American West was Jesse James.
   c. An animal that is cast out by the rest of the pack is known as an **outlaw**.

Words to Learn This Week

outlaw
promote
undernourished
illustrate
disclose
excessive
disaster
censor
culprit
juvenile
bait
insist

2. **promote** (prə mōt') raise in rank or importance; help to grow and develop; help to organize
   a. Students who pass the test will be **promoted** to the next grade.
   b. An accurate* knowledge of other cultures will **promote** good will among people of different backgrounds.
   c. Several bankers invested an enormous* sum of money to **promote** the idea.

3. **undernourished** (un' dər ner' isht) not sufficiently fed
   a. The **undernourished** child was so feeble* he could hardly walk.
   b. There is evidence* that even wealthy people are **undernourished** because they do not eat sufficient quantities* of healthful foods.
   c. An infant who drinks enough milk will not be **undernourished.**

4. **illustrate** (il' əs trāt or i lus' trat) make clear or explain by stories, examples, comparisons, or other means; serve as an example
   a. To **illustrate** how the heart sends blood around the body, the teacher described how a pump works.
   b. This exhibit* will **illustrate** the many uses of atomic energy.
   c. These stories **illustrate** Mark Twain's serious side.

5. **disclose** (dis klōz') uncover; make known
   a. The lifting of the curtain **disclosed** a beautiful winter scene.
   b. This letter **discloses** the source* of his fortune.
   c. Samson, reclining* in the arms of Delilah, **disclosed** that the secret of his strength was in his long hair.

6. **excessive** (ek ses' iv) too much; too great; extreme
   a. Pollution* of the atmosphere is an **excessive** price to pay for so-called progress.
   b. Numerous* attempts have been made to outlaw* jet planes that make **excessive** noise.
   c. The inhabitants* of Arizona are unaccustomed* to **excessive** rain.

7. **disaster** (də zas' tər) an event that causes much suffering or loss; a great misfortune
   a. The hurricane's violent* winds brought **disaster** to the coastal town.
   b. The San Francisco earthquake and the Chicago fire are two of the greatest **disasters** in American history.
   c. The coach considered* the captain's injury a **disaster** for the team.

8. **censor** (sen' sər) person who tells others how they ought to behave; one who changes books, plays and other works so as to make them acceptable to the government; to make changes in
   a. Some governments, national and local, **censor** books.
   b. The **censor** felt that fiction* as well as other books should receive the stamp of approval before they were put on sale.
   c. Any mention of the former prime minister was outlawed* by the **censor.**

9. **culprit** (kul' prit) offender; person guilty of a fault or crime
   a. Who is the **culprit** who has eaten all the strawberries?
   b. The police caught the **culprit** with the stolen articles in his car.
   c. In the Sherlock Holmes story, the **culprit** turned out to be a snake.

10. **juvenile** (jōō' və nīl or jōō' və nl) young; youthful; of or for boys and girls; a young person
   a. My sister is known in the family as a **juvenile** delinquent.*
   b. Paula is still young enough to wear **juvenile** fashions.
   c. Ellen used to devour* "Cinderella" and other stories for **juveniles.**

11. **bait** (bāt) anything, especially food, used to attract fish or other animals so that they may be caught; anything used to tempt or attract a person to begin something he or she does not wish to do; to put bait on (a hook) or in (a trap); torment by unkind or annoying remarks
   a. The secret of successful trout fishing is finding the right **bait.**
   b. How can you expect to **bait** Mike into running for the class presidency when he has already refused every appeal?*
   c. Eddie is a good hunter because he knows the merit* of each kind of **bait** for the different animals.

12. **insist** (in sist') keep firmly to some demand, statement, or position
   a. Mother **insists** that we do our homework before we start sending e-mails.
   b. She **insisted** that Sal was not jealous* of his twin brother.
   c. The doctor **insisted** that Marian get plenty of rest after the operation.

Words in Use

Read the following passage to see how the new words are used in it.

What Did You Have for Breakfast?

A parents' organization to protect children's health appealed* to a Senate committee to **outlaw** television commercials that **promote** the purchase of sugary products. Too much advertising urges the young child to eat caramels, chocolate, cookies, and pastries. This results in poor eating habits and leaves youngsters **undernourished** and subject to rapid* tooth decay and other diseases.

To **illustrate** the extent of the problem, a recent survey of one typical* day of CBS's Channel 7 in Boston between 7 A.M. and 2 P.M. **disclosed** 67 commercials for sweet-tasting products. Several witnesses said that many children's cereals contained more than 50 percent sugar, that children often forced their parents to buy the cereals, and

that **excessive** use of sugar from cereals, soft drinks and snack foods is a national **disaster.** Dr. Jean Mayer, professor of nutrition at Harvard University, recommended **censoring** the **culprits** in advertising for **juvenile** viewers. Recognizing the powerful opponents* in the food industry who will resist* control, Dr. Mayer said that no feeble* efforts will do. "Sugar-coated nothings," he added, "must cease* to be the standard diet of the American child."

Other witnesses pointed out that many cereal boxes, as **bait** for the children, used offers of dolls, balloons, airplane or car models, magic kits, monster cutouts and similar trifles,* but the cereal inside the box, they **insisted**, had no more food value than the container it came in.

Fill in the Blanks

Place one of the new words in each of the blanks below.

1. Many Americans can be considered* _____ because they deprive* their body of proper foods in favor of rich, fatty foods.
2. Though he was threatened* with imprisonment, Martin would not _____ the whereabouts of the treasure.
3. When the report of the airplane _____ reached us, many people pledged* their help in locating* survivors.*
4. The only hope for the world is to _____ war.
5. The police were reluctant* to use _____ force, even to preserve* order.
6. This is a court of justice* for the _____ and the innocent alike.

7. Certain foods that _____ tooth decay should be banned* from the market.

8. An artist was hired to _____ a book on the birds of this vicinity.*

9. If you _____ on shouting, I shall be compelled* to leave.

10. It would be a disaster* for freedom of the press if the_____were permitted to tell us what we can read.

11. James has just about exhausted* his father's patience with his _____ behavior.

12. Only a brutal* person would _____ someone who is disabled.

Answer key, p. 198

Word Detective

From the list of 12 new words that follows, choose the one that corresponds to each definition below.

outlaw	promote	undernourished	juvenile
illustrate	disclose	excessive	bait
disaster	censor	culprit	insist

1. something used to attract or lure   _____

2. to raise in rank or importance; help to organize   _____

3. a person guilty of a fault or crime   _____

4. to keep firmly to some demand or position   _____

5. to declare unlawful   _____

6. a young person   _____

7. a person who tells others how they should behave   _____

8. to uncover; make known   _____

9. too much; too great; extreme   _____

10. an event that causes much suffering or loss   _____

11. make clear or explain by stories, examples, or other means   _____

12. not sufficiently fed   _____

Answer key, p. 198

Spotlight On

disaster—Shakespeare tells us that Romeo and Juliet were star-crossed lovers; that is, they were under the influence of an evil star *(dis-aster)*. This belief is not far removed from that of people who follow the horoscopes and those who are concerned about the sign of the zodiac they were born under.

Picture It

Which of the words studied in this lesson is suggested by the picture?

LESSON
29

---

1. toil (toil) hard work; to work hard; move with difficulty
   a. The feeble* old man **toiled** up the hill.
   b. After years of **toil**, scientists disclosed* that they had made progress in controlling the dreaded* disease.
   c. Despite* all his **toil**, Fred never succeeded in reaching his goal.

2. blunder (blun' dər) stupid mistake; to make a stupid mistake; stumble; say clumsily
   a. The exhausted* boy **blundered** through the woods.
   b. Bert's awkward* apology* could not make up for his serious **blunder**.
   c. The general's **blunder** forced his army to a rapid* retreat.

3. daze (dāz) confuse
   a. The severity* of the blow **dazed** the fighter and led to his defeat.
   b. When he ventured* out of the house at night, the child was **dazed** by the noise and the lights.
   c. **Dazed** by the flashlight, Maria blundered* down the steps.

4. mourn (môrn) grieve; feel or show sorrow for
   a. Sandra did not cease* to **mourn** for John Lennon.
   b. The entire city **mourned** for the people lost in the calamity.*
   c. We need not **mourn** over trifles.*

5. subside (səb sīd') sink to a lower level; grow less
   a. After the excessive* rains stopped, the flood waters **subsided.**
   b. The waves **subsided** when the winds ceased* to blow.
   c. Danny's anger **subsided** when the culprit* apologized.*

6. maim (mām) cripple; disable; cause to lose an arm, leg, or other part of the body
   a. Auto accidents **maim** many persons each year.
   b. Though he went through an awesome* experience in the crash, Fred was not seriously **maimed**.
   c. Car manufacturers insist* that seat belts can prevent the **maiming** of passengers in the event of a crash.

7. comprehend (käm' pri hend') understand
   a. If you can use a word correctly, there is a good chance that you **comprehend** it.
   b. You need not be a pauper* to **comprehend** fully what hunger is.
   c. My parents say that they cannot **comprehend** today's music.

8. commend (kə mend') praise; hand over for safekeeping
   a. Everyone **commended** the mayor's thrifty* suggestion.
   b. Florence **commended** the baby to her aunt's care.
   c. The truth is that we all like to be **commended** for good work.

9. final (fī' nal) coming last; deciding
   a. The **final** week of the term is rapidly* approaching.
   b. Jose was commended* for his improvement in the **final** test.
   c. The **final** censor* of our actions is our own conscience.

10. exempt (eg zempt') make free from; freed from
   a. Our school **exempts** bright pupils from final* exams.
   b. School property is **exempt** from most taxes.
   c. Juvenile* offenders are not **exempt** from punishment.

Words to Learn This Week
toil
blunder
daze
mourn
subside
maim
comprehend
commend
final
exempt
vain
repetition

11. vain (vān) having too much pride in one's ability, looks, etc.; of no use
  a.   Josephine is quite **vain** about her beauty.
  b.   To be perfectly frank, I do not see what she has to be **vain** about.
  c.   Brian made numerous* **vain** attempts to reach the doctor by telephone.

12. repetition (rep' ə tish' ən) act of doing or saying again
  a.   The **repetition** of new words in this book will help you to learn them.
  b.   Any **repetition** of such unruly* behavior will be punished.
  c.   After a **repetition** of his costly mistake, Jerry was fired from his job.

Picture It
Which of the words studied in this lesson is suggested by the picture?

Words in Use
Read the following passage to see how the new words are used in it.

Camp Safety

For years a furniture salesman from Connecticut, Mitch Kurman, has **toiled** ceaselessly* for the passage of a youth summer camp safety bill. Why? Because his son David was drowned when his canoe overturned in the raging* waters of the Penobscot River. The camp counselors leading the trip were inexperienced, had **blundered** into dangerous waters, and had no life jackets for the canoers.

Mr. Kurman was naturally **dazed** by the tragedy.* But rather than merely **mourn** his loss and wait for the painful memory to **subside**, he began a campaign that took him on hundreds of journeys to speak to governors, senators, and congressmen. He had learned that 250,000 children are injured or **maimed** annually* in camp accidents. It was hard for him to **comprehend** why we have laws that outlaw* mistreatment of alligators, coyotes, birds and bobcats, but we have no law to prevent disasters* to children in summer camps.

Wherever he went, Mr. Kurman was **commended** for his efforts, but he received only trifling* support from the lawmakers. One bill, requiring people to put on life preservers when they took to the water, died in the **final** reading. Another such bill **exempted** private ponds and lakes, exactly the waters where most summer camps are located.* Even a bill calling for a survey of camp safety conditions was at first defeated. Mr. Kurman's struggle so far has been in **vain**, but he continues his battle to avoid* a **repetition** of the accident that took his son's life.

Fill in the Blanks

Place one of the new words in each of the blanks below.

1. There is a tendency* to _____ politicians from keeping campaign promises.
2. A _____ of such a blunder* could be disastrous.
3. The guide* was compelled* to admit he had _____ far from the intended route.
4. A miserly* person cannot _____ the joy of sharing.
5. Though doctors _____ to cure the undernourished* child, he never regained his full health.
6. Three workers were _____ when the ladder collapsed.*
7. The policeman was _____ for his bravery in capturing the armed outlaw.*
8. The perfect attendance of our class illustrated* the importance of this _____ exam.
9. Friend and foe united* in _____ the death of the leader, for she was respected by all.
10. The drowning man's cries were uttered* in _____, because no one was near to hear them.
11. Miguel's fever _____ after he took the medicine.
12. My brother was in such a _____ over the tragedy* that he could hardly respond* to questions.

Answer key, p. 198

Matching

Match the 12 new words in Column I with the definitions in Column II.

Column I	Column II
1. comprehend	a. grieve
2. repetition	b. hard work
3. exempt	c. sink to a lower level
4. vain	d. coming last
5. commend	e. stupid mistake
6. maim	f. act of doing or saying again
7. toil	g. praise
8. final	h. make free from
9. blunder	i. understand
10. mourn	j. disable; cripple
11. daze	k. confuse
12. subside	l. having too much pride in one's ability, looks, etc.

Answer key, p. 198

Spotlight On

maim—When you buy a car, read the insurance policy carefully. Insurance companies don't use words like *maim* carelessly, because this word has a very specific meaning. *Maim* suggests the loss or destruction of an arm or leg or both; to be *maimed* a person would have to suffer permanent injury. Would the insurance company use the word *mutilate*?

LESSON
30

"You cram these words into mine ears against
The stomach of my sense."

—Shakespeare, *The Tempest*

---

1. **depict** (di pikt') represent by drawing or painting; describe
   a. The artist and the author both tried to **depict** the sunset's beauty.
   b. Mr. Salinger **depicted** the juvenile* character with great accuracy.*
   c. Al Pacino said he would **depict** a different kind of Shylock.

2. **mortal** (môr' tl) sure to die sometime; pertaining to man; deadly; pertaining to or causing death
   a. We must live with the knowledge that all living creatures are **mortal**.
   b. His rash* venture* brought him to a **mortal** illness.
   c. The two monarchs* were **mortal** enemies.

3. **novel** (näv' l) new; strange; a long story with characters and plot
   a. The architect* created a **novel** design that pleased everyone.
   b. The **novel** plan caused some unforeseen* problems.
   c. Robert was commended* by his teacher for the excellent report on the American **novel**, *The Grapes of Wrath*.

4. **occupant** (äk' yə pent) person in possession of a house, office, or position
   a. A feeble* old woman was the only **occupant** of the shack.
   b. The will disclosed* that the **occupant** of the estate was penniless.
   c. The **occupant** of the car beckoned* us to follow him.

5. **appoint** (ə point') decide on; set a time or place; choose for a position; equip or furnish
   a. The library was **appointed** as the best place for the urgent* meeting.
   b. Though Mr. Thompson was **appointed** to a high position, he did not neglect* his old friends.
   c. The occupant* of the well-**appointed** guest room considered* himself quite fortunate.*

6. **quarter** (kwôr' tər) region; section; (quarters) a place to live; to provide a place to live
   a. The large family was unaccustomed* to such small **quarters**.
   b. Ellen moved to the French **Quarter** of our city.
   c. The city **quartered** the paupers* in an old school.

7. **site** (sīt) position or place (of anything)
   a. The agent insisted* that the house had one of the best **sites** in town.
   b. We were informed by our guide* that a monument would be built on the **site** of the historic battle.
   c. For the **site** of the new school, the committee preferred an urban* location.*

8. **quote** (kwōt) repeat exactly the words of another or a passage from a book; that is, something that is repeated exactly; give the price of; a quotation
   a. She often **quotes** her spouse* to prove a point.
   b. The stockbroker **quoted** gold at a dollar off yesterday's closing price.
   c. Biblical **quotes** offer a unique* opportunity for study.

9. **verse** (vers) a short division of a chapter in the Bible; a single line or a group of lines of poetry
   a. The **verse** from the Bible that my father quoted* most frequently* was, "Love thy neighbor as thyself."
   b. Several **verses** of a religious nature were contained in the document.*
   c. Though it is not always easy to comprehend,* Shakespeare's **verse** has merit* that is worth the toil.*

10. **morality** (mə ral' ə te) the right or wrong of an action; virtue; a set of rules or principles of conduct
   a. The editor* spoke on the **morality** of "bugging" the quarters* of a political opponent.*
   b. We rarely consider* the **morality** of our daily actions, though that should occupy* a high position in our thinking.
   c. Kenny's unruly* behavior has nothing to do with his lack* of **morality**.

11. **roam** (rōm) wander; go about with no special plan or aim
   a. In the days of the Wild West, outlaws* **roamed** the country.
   b. A variety* of animals once **roamed** our land.
   c. The bachelor* promised his girlfriend that he would **roam** no more.

12. **attract** (a trakt') draw to oneself; win the attention and liking of
   a. The magnet **attracted** the iron particles.
   b. Adventure was the thrill that **attracted** the famous mountain climber to the jagged* peak.
   c. A glimpse* into the brightly colored room **attracted** the children's attention.

Words in Use

Read the following passage to see how the new words are used in it.

Bible Zoo

One of the most popular* tales of the Bible **depicts** the great flood that destroyed every **mortal** except Noah and his family and the animals on his ark. Should there be a repetition* of that disaster,* there is one place where all the biblical animals are already gathered. The man to be commended* for this **novel** collection is Professor Aharon Shulov, a zoologist at Hebrew University in Jerusalem, Israel.

Professor Shulov **appointed** himself a committee of one to search out the 130 creatures mentioned in the Old Testament. Among the **occupants** of this zoo are crocodiles, camels, apes, peacocks, deer, foxes, and sheep, some of whom had to be imported from other lands. They are settled in suitable **quarters** on a twenty-five acre **site** in Jerusalem.

Visitors to the zoo not only get to view and feed the animals, but they are also treated to **quotes** from Bible **verses** that encourage* the study of the Good Book and teach **morality** amidst the waddling of the ducks and the wailing* of the wolves. Not surprisingly, the children have the final* word at a special corner of the zoo, called the Garden of Eden, where animal cubs **roam** freely, **attracting** the attention of hundreds of youngsters who visit daily.

Fill in the Blanks

Place one of the new words in each of the blanks below.

1. The judge _____ to this case must be a person of justice* and honesty.
2. I knew that the culprit* was in _____ terror of being caught.
3. The _____ of the collapsed* building were dazed* by the tragedy.*
4. How can you _____ in a favorable light a person who betrayed* his country?
5. Let us explore* another _____ for the hospital where the population* is not so dense.*
6. A good line of _____ is thrifty* with words and bursting with feeling.
7. Troops were_____in the city in a vain* attempt to keep order.
8. The price he_____for the car was essentially* the same as that of his competitor.*
9. Seeing the movie based on the _____ does not exempt* you from reading the book.
10. The death of the millionaire _____ a bewildering* number* of hopeful beneficiaries.*
11. The new _____ has not won unanimous* acceptance; there are those who prefer the traditional* ways.
12. When I _____ abroad,* I come across many historic sites* and structures.

Answer key, p. 198

Creativity Exercise

Now make up your own sentences, one for each of the new words you have just been taught.

1. _____

2. _____

3. _____

4. _____

5. _____

6. _____

7. _____

8. _____

9. _____

10. _____

11. _____

12. _____

Spotlight On

mortal—The main part of this word, *mort-*, comes from the Latin and means "to die." Some words you have heard contain this same root—*mortgage, mortify,* and *mortuary*. How are they related to the meaning "to die"? In detective stories, watch for the words "rigor mortis."

Picture It

Which of the words studied in this lesson is suggested by the picture?

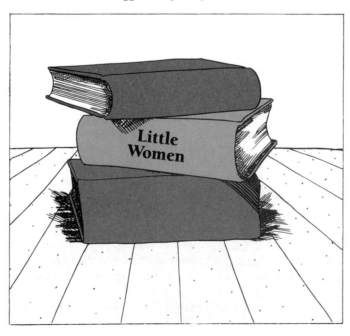

Word Review #5
These exercises are based on some of the words found in Lessons 25–30.

A. In each of the parentheses below there are two choices. Pick the one that fits better.

1. Will storekeepers be (proscecuted, pacified) for raising prices without government permission?
2. With a few strokes of his brush, Norman Rockwell could (depict, commend) beautiful scenes.
3. Eric's serious (toil, blunder) caused him to lose the card game.
4. It is useless to (mourn, maim) over spilt milk.
5. Through his love of racing cars, Trevor (squandered, subsided) all the money he had inherited.
6. Although she was very unhappy, Dora refused to (utter, comprehend) one word of complaint.
7. At each step of the way, signs have been placed to (guide, attract) you through the winding caves.
8. The bachelor* met a lovely girl and decided to enter into (matrimony, bigamy).
9. Willie Mays had a (mortal, novel) way of catching a fly ball that most fans had never seen.
10. I tried to (unite, disrupt) the angry cousins but they would not let me make peace between them.

Answer key, p. 198

B. Opposites. In Column I are ten words from Lessons 25–30. Match them correctly with their *opposite* meanings in Column II.

Column I	Column II
1. roam	a. well-fed
2. undernourished	b. strong
3. disclose	c. start
4. rapid	d. could not happen
5. pauper	e. not enough
6. possible	f. stay at home
7. feeble	g. careful
8. cease	h. rich person
9. excessive	i. hide
10. rash	j. slow

Answer key, p. 198

C. Which of the vocabulary choices in parentheses fits best in these newspaper headlines?
1. **Flood Waters _____ as Emergency Ends**   (Collapse, Subside, Quench, Respond)
2. **12-Year-Old Mugger Protected by_____ Law**   (Final, Rash, Juvenile, Fugitive)
3. **Diplomat Sent to _____ Angry Canadians**   (Pacify, Prosecute, Betray, Disrupt)
4. **Hundreds at Church _____ for Accident Victims**   (Beckon, Mourn, Respond, Venture)
5. **_____ Fire Expected in Lebanese War**   (Cease, Squander, Compel, Commend)
6. **Former_____ Does Not Miss Royal Luxury**   (Guide, Monarch, Architect, Censor)
7. **Merger Effort Will _____ the Two Companies** (Daze, Betray, Depict, Unite)
8. **Painter Aims to _____ Life in Haiti**   (Outlaw, Depict, Exhaust, Utter)
9. **Bank Rewards _____ Depositors**   (Rash, Pauper, Excessive, Thrifty)
10. **"Forgetful" Husband Accused of _____**   (Morality, Bigamy, Toil, Severity)

Answer key, p. 198

D. From the list of words below choose the word that means:

occupant	disrupt	calamity	morality	utter	pacify
site	venture	beckon	toil	subside	commend
promote	verse	mortal	culprit	commend	fugitive
quench	exempt	maim	compel	architect	monarch
censor	quarter	awesome	bigamist	thrifty	disaster

1. subject to death *and* has the same root as *mortgage*
2. lose a bodily part *and therefore* be crippled or disabled
3. a great misfortune *and* suggests one is under the influence of "an unlucky star"
4. economical or stingy *but also* could describe someone who is prosperous because of hard work and good management
5. one who draws plans for a house *but also* refers to the creator of any plan or idea
6. a person with two wives or two husbands *and* is derived from the Greek word for "two weddings"
7. put out, as a fire, *and also* satisfy, as one's thirst
8. a ruler, rare in modern times *and also* master
9. an official with the power to remove objectionable material from a book or film *as well as* a person who reads mail in wartime, to remove information that might be useful to the enemy
10. provide lodgings *as well as* a particular district or section

Answer key, p. 198

E. Letter Writing. The following letter to the editor of a school newspaper uses ten words that appeared in Lessons 25–30. Fill in the blanks with those words selected from the group below:

architect	comprehend	excessive	rapid	site
attract	despite	occupant	rash	squander
awesome	disclose	possible	repetition	thrifty
awkward	envy	promote	respond	undernourished

2794 Houston Street
New York, NY 10047
October 9, 2011

The Student Voice
Eastside High School
New York, NY 10036

Dear Editor:

I am writing in response to the article in the school newspaper, "Cafeteria Needs More Customers."

If the new cafeteria is to __1__ more students, I believe the menu should be changed. It would be a good idea to avoid the __2__ of the same old sandwiches, soups, and desserts. I think it might be __3__ to offer some ethnic foods like pizza, tacos, and bagels. Students also enjoy eating rice dishes and curries. The dietician could __4__ good eating habits for __5__ students by serving milk instead of soft drinks. I will admit the low prices allow the students to be __6__ .

I find that the cafeteria is an __7__ place in which to eat. __8__ the large size of the room, the __9__ has designed a very low ceiling. As a result, the noise level is __10__ , so it is difficult to have relaxing conversation.

I hope the school authorities will make the cafeteria more inviting to the students.

Yours truly,
Jun Ihara

Answer key, p. 198

F. Words That Do Double Duty. Once again, as you did in the previous Word Reviews, note the following words, which appeared in Lessons 25–30. Each can serve as more than one part of speech:

outlaw (v., n.)	toil (v., n.)
venture (v., n.)	blunder (v., n.)
guide (v., n.)	rash (n., adj.)
censor (v., n.)	novel (n., adj.)
bait (v., n.)	quarter (v., n.)

Make up two sentences for each of the above words, showing how it could be used as two different parts of speech.

Examples: Television stations agreed to *outlaw* cigarette advertisements.
          In the famous movie, *High Noon,* a group of *outlaws* plan to kill the sheriff.

LESSON
31

—Shakespeare, *Sonnet lxxvi*

Words to Learn This Week

commuter
confine
idle
idol
jest
patriotic
dispute
valor
lunatic
vein
uneventful
fertile

1. **commuter** (kə mūt' ər) one who travels regularly, especially over a considerable distance, between home and work
   a. The average **commuter** would welcome a chance to live in the vicinity* of his or her work.
   b. Have your **commuter's** ticket verified* by the conductor.
   c. A novel* educational program gives college credit to **commuters** who listen to a lecture while they are traveling to work.

2. **confine** (kən fīn') keep in; hold in
   a. The fugitive* was caught and **confined** to jail for another two years.
   b. A virus that was circulating* in the area **confined** Al to his house.
   c. Polio **confined** President Roosevelt to a wheelchair.

3. **idle** (ī' dl) not doing anything; not busy; lazy; without any good reason or cause; to waste (time)
   a. Any attempt to study was abandoned* by the student, who **idled** away the morning.
   b. The **idle** hours of a holiday frequently* provide the best time to take stock.
   c. Do not deceive* yourself into thinking that these are just **idle** rumors.

4. **idol** (ī' dl) a thing, usually an image, that is worshiped; a person or thing that is loved very much
   a. This small metal **idol** illustrates* the art of ancient Rome.
   b. John Wayne was the **idol** of many young people who liked cowboy movies.
   c. Scientists are still trying to identify* this **idol** found in the ruins.

5. **jest** (jest) joke; fun; mockery; thing to be laughed at; to joke; poke fun
   a. Though he spoke in **jest**, Mark was undoubtedly* giving us a message.
   b. Do not **jest** about matters of morality.*
   c. In some quarters,* honesty and hard work have become subjects of **jest**.

6. **patriotic** (pā trē ät' ik) loving one's country; showing love and loyal support for one's country
   a. It is **patriotic** to accept your responsibilities to your country.
   b. The **patriotic** attitude of the captive* led him to refuse to cooperate with the enemy.
   c. Nathan Hale's **patriotic** statement has often been quoted:* "I regret that I have but one life to give for my country."

7. **dispute** (dis pūt') disagree; oppose; try to win; a debate or disagreement
   a. Our patriotic* soldiers **disputed** every inch of ground during the battle.
   b. The losing team **disputed** the contest up until the final* minute of play.
   c. Many occupants* of the building were attracted* by the noisy **dispute**.

8. **valor** (val' ər) bravery; courage
   a. The **valor** of the Vietnam veterans deserves the highest commendation.*
   b. No one will dispute* the **valor** of Washington's men at Valley Forge.
   c. The fireman's **valor** in rushing into the flaming house saved the occupants* from a horrid* fate.

9. **lunatic** (lōō' nə tik) crazy person; insane; extremely foolish
   a. Only a **lunatic** would willingly descend* into the monster's cave.
   b. Certain **lunatic** ideas persist* even though they have been rejected* by all logical* minds.
   c. My roommate has some **lunatic** ideas about changing the world.

10. **vein** (vān) mood; a blood vessel that carries blood to the heart; a crack or seam
    in a rock filled with a different mineral
    a. A **vein** of lunacy* seemed to run in the family.
    b. Mario's wrist was severely* cut by the rock, causing his **vein** to bleed heavily.
    c. Explorations disclosed* the rich **vein** of copper in the mountain.

11. **uneventful** (un' i vent' fəl) without important or striking happenings
    a. After the variety* of bewildering* experiences at the start of our trip, we were happy that the
       rest of the journey was **uneventful**.
    b. Our annual* class outing proved quite **uneventful**.
    c. The meeting seemed **uneventful** but expert observers realized that important decisions were
       being made.

12. **fertile** (fir' tl) bearing seeds or fruit; producing much of anything
    a. Chicks hatch from **fertile** eggs.
    b. The loss of their **fertile** lands threw the farmers into a panic.*
    c. A **fertile** mind need never be uneasy* about finding life uneventful.*

Words in Use

Read the following passage to see how the new words are used in it.

Record Holders

The *Guinness Book of World Records* is full of fascinating facts. For example, the champion **commuter** is Bruno Leuthardt of Germany, who traveled 370 miles each day for ten years to his teaching job and was late only once because of a flood. The record for being buried alive is held by Emma Smith of Ravenshead, England. She was **confined** in a coffin for 100 days. What a way to spend the **idle** hours! Peter Clark of London collected 1276 autographed pictures of famous men and women. Obviously* not all were his **idols**, but he did set a record.

What drives people to these unusual practices? Some are simply done in **jest,** some for **patriotic** reasons. Certainly no one would **dispute** the **valor** of the "record-makers," even if the records themselves may be no more lasting than a popular* song. While one need not be a **lunatic**, he must have a **vein** of recklessness* to participate in such activities as bungee-jumping, high diving, or parachute jumping.

If you are tired of leading a dull, **uneventful** life, remember the mortais* whose **fertile** imaginations have found novel* ways to add excitement to their lives.

Fill in the Blanks

Place one of the new words in each of the blanks below.

1. Celia was left _____ after working so hard all her life.
2. I would _____ that claim if I did not know you were jesting.*
3. This site* will attract many home buyers because of the advantages for the _____ .
4. The early pioneers exhibited* great _____ in braving the hardships* of the new frontiers.
5. A _____ of caution* helped Mr. Samler to avoid* the obvious* risks in his new job.
6. It is no misfortune* to spend a few _____ days without excitement and conflict.*
7. The _____ element of society ignores* the warnings about the dangers of drugs.
8. Since the statement was made in _____ it is not a valid* point to argue.
9. I asked my opponent* in the debate* to _____ his remarks to the subject under discussion.
10. How can we transmit* a healthy _____ view to the next generation?
11. People have always wanted to inhabit* the land where the soil is most _____ .
12. People still worship the _____ of greed* and power.

Answer key, p. 198

Creativity Exercise

Now make up your own sentences, one for each of the new words you have just been taught.

1. _____
2. _____
3. _____
4. _____
5. _____
6. _____
7. _____
8. _____
9. _____
10. _____
11. _____
12. _____

Picture It

Which of the words studied in this lesson is suggested by the picture?

Spotlight On

lunatic—Here's an old word for an old idea; the Romans believed that our minds are affected by the moon—*luna* means "moon" in Latin—and that *lunatics* grew more crazy as the moon became fuller. In primitive civilizations, fear of the full moon was not unusual.

LESSON 32

"Out, idle words, servants to shallow fools!
Unprofitable sounds, weak arbitrators!"

—Shakespeare, *The Rape of Lucrece*

Words to Learn This Week

refer
distress
diminish
maximum
flee
vulnerable
signify
mythology
provide
colleague
torment
loyalty

1. **refer** (ri fir') hand over; send, direct, or turn for information, help, or action; (refer to) direct attention to or speak about; assign to or think of as caused by
   a. Let us **refer** the dispute* to the dean.
   b. Our teacher **referred** us to the dictionary for the meanings of the difficult words in the novel.*
   c. The speaker **referred** to a verse in the Bible to support his theory.*

2. **distress** (dis tres') great pain or sorrow; misfortune; dangerous or difficult situation; to cause pain or make unhappy
   a. The family was in great **distress** over the accident that maimed* Kenny.
   b. My teacher was **distressed** by the dismal performance of our class on the final* examination.
   c. Long, unscheduled delays at the station cause **distress** to commuters.*

3. **diminish** (də min' ish) make or become smaller in size, amount or importance
   a. The excessive* heat **diminished** as the sun went down.
   b. Our **diminishing** supply of food was carefully wrapped and placed with the baggage.*
   c. The latest news from the battlefront confirms* the report of **diminishing** military activity.

4. **maximum** (mak' sə məm) greatest amount; greatest possible
   a. Chris acknowledged* that the **maximum** he had ever walked in one day was fifteen miles.
   b. We would like to exhibit* this rare* collection to the **maximum** number of visitors.
   c. The committee anticipated* the **maximum** attendance of the first day of the performance.

5. **flee** (flē) run away; go quickly
   a. The **fleeing** outlaws* were pursued* by the police.
   b. One could clearly see the clouds **fleeing** before the wind.
   c. The majority* of students understand that they cannot **flee** from their responsibilities.

6. **vulnerable** (vul' ner ə bl) capable of being injured; open to attack, sensitive to criticism, influences, etc.
   a. Achilles was **vulnerable** only in his heel.
   b. The investigator's nimble* mind quickly located the **vulnerable** spot in the defendant's alibi.
   c. A **vulnerable** target for thieves is a solitary* traveler.

7. **signify** (sig' nə fī) mean; be a sign of; make known by signs, words, or actions; have importance
   a. "Oh!" **signifies** surprise.
   b. A gift of such value **signifies** more than a casual* relationship.
   c. The word "fragile"* stamped on a carton **signifies** that it must be handled with caution.*

8. **mythology** (mi thäl' e jē) legends or stories that usually attempt to explain something in nature
   a. The story of Proserpina and Ceres explaining the seasons is typical* of Greek **mythology**.
   b. From a study of **mythology** we can conclude* that the ancients were concerned with the wonders of nature.
   c. Ancient **mythology** survives* to this day in popular* expressions such as "Herculean task" or "Apollo Project."

9. **colleague** (käl' ēg) associate; fellow worker
   a. The captain gave credit for the victory to his valiant* **colleagues.**
   b. Who would have predicted* that our pedestrian* **colleague** would one day win the Nobel Prize for medicine?
   c. We must rescue our **colleagues** from their wretched* condition.

10. **torment** (tôr ment' or tôr' ment) cause very great pain to; worry or annoy very much; cause of very great pain; very great pain
    a. Persistent* headaches **tormented** him.
    b. The illustrations* in our history text show the **torments** suffered by the victims of the French Revolution.
    c. The logical* way to end the **torment** of doubt over the examination is to spend adequate* time in study.

11. **provide** (pro vīd') to supply; to state as a condition; to prepare for or against some situation
    a. How can we **provide** job opportunities for all our graduates?
    b. Hal said he would bring the ball **provided** he would be allowed to pitch.
    c. The government is obligated, among other things, to **provide** for the common welfare and secure the blessings of peace for all citizens.

12. **loyalty** (loi' əl tē) faithfulness to a person, government, idea, custom, or the like
    a. The monarch* referred* to his knights' **loyalty** with pride.
    b. Nothing is so important to transmit* to the youth as the sacredness* of **loyalty** to one's country.
    c. Out of a sense of **loyalty** to his friends, Michael was willing to suffer torments,* and he therefore refused to identify* his colleagues* in the plot.

Words in Use

Read the following passage to see how the new words are used in it.

How Our Language Grows

Many popular* expressions in our language have interesting backgrounds. When we **refer** to a person's weak spot as his *Achilles heel,* we are recalling the story of the mighty Greek hero of the Trojan War, Achilles, a warrior of unusual strength and valor.* The mother of Achilles, in whose veins* flowed the blood of the gods, was warned at his birth that her son would die in battle. In great **distress,** she sought to save her son. In order to **diminish** his chances of being hurt and to give him **maximum** protection* in combat, she dipped the infant in the river Styx. The magic waters touched every part of the child's body except the heel that she held in her hand. Thus it happened many years later that as Achilles started to **flee** from an attack, a poisoned arrow struck him in the heel, the only spot where he was **vulnerable.**

Today, the meaning of *Achilles heel* is not confined* to a weak spot in the body but it also **signifies** a weakness in the character of an individual, or in the defenses of a nation, or in the structure of a system.

American politics, rather than **mythology,** provides the explanation for the word *bunk.* This word came into the language in 1820 when Felix Walker, the representative from Buncombe County, North Carolina, formed the habit of making long, unnecessary speeches in Congress. When his **colleagues** asked him why he was **tormenting** them so, he **apologized** by saying it was his patriotic* duty to put those speeches in the record out of **loyalty** to his supporters at home. The word "Buncombe" was shortened to "bunk" and came to mean any thought that has little or no worth.

Fill in the Blanks

Place one of the new words in each of the blanks below.

1. The uneventful* flow of news was interrupted by a report of a ship in _____ .
2. Our temperature for the day dropped from a _____ of 85 degrees to a minimum* of 70 degrees.
3. The dishonest employee* planned to _____ with several thousand dollars of the company's money.
4. It was easy to see that the club members resented* Phil's _____ them with silly questions.
5. Colonel Bishop's deep sense of _____ to his men signifies* an honest and honorable nature.

6. Elizabeth was finally* persuaded* to _____ for her remark and to pledge* to be more careful in the future.
7. What I admire in Marty is that he never abandoned* his _____ in their time of need.
8. Mr. Harris' manipulation* of the bank funds _____ his greed.*
9. Debra had a tendency* to _____ all her questions to the librarian instead of looking them up herself.
10. The registration for this course has _____ to the point where we must consider* eliminating* it from the curriculum.
11. The names of the days of the week are based on the names of the gods and goddesses of Norse _____ .
12. The distressing* fact is that we are all _____ to natural disasters.*

Answer key, p. 198

Word Detective

From the list of 12 new words that follows, choose the one that corresponds to each definition below.

refer	distress	diminish	maximum
flee	vulnerable	signify	mythology
colleague	torment	apologize	loyalty

 1. be a sign of   _____
 2. run away   _____
 3. great pain or sorrow   _____
 4. greatest amount   _____
 5. direct, send, or turn for information, help, or action _____
 6. faithfulness   _____
 7. associate; fellow worker   _____
 8. legends or stories   _____
 9. capable of being injured   _____
10. cause very great pain to   _____
11. become smaller in size   _____
12. express regret   _____

Answer key, p. 198

Spotlight On

colleague—You may hear people use this word, but most writers find it difficult to spell. The word follows no rules and the only way to learn it is to memorize it once and for all. On the other hand, you can probably get along quite well with "associate," but that's not easy to spell either.

Picture It

Which of the words studied in this lesson is suggested by the picture?

LESSON 33

**"I understand a fury in your words,
But not the words."**

—Shakespeare, *Othello*

Words to Learn This Week

volunteer
prejudice
shrill
jolly
witty
hinder
lecture
abuse
mumble
mute
wad
retain

1. **volunteer** (väl ən ter') person who enters any service of his or her own free will; to offer one's services
   a. The draft has been abolished* and replaced by a **volunteer** army.
   b. Terry did not hesitate* to **volunteer** for the most difficult jobs.
   c. The boys were reluctant* to **volunteer** their services to help clean up after the dance.

2. **prejudice** (prej' ə dis) an opinion formed without taking time and care to judge fairly; to harm or injure
   a. **Prejudice** against minority* groups will linger* on as long as people ignore* the facts.
   b. Eliminating* **prejudice** should be among the first concerns of a democracy.
   c. The witness's weird* behavior **prejudiced** Nancy's case.

3. **shrill** (shril) having a high pitch; high and sharp in sound; piercing
   a. Despite* their small size, crickets make very **shrill** noises.
   b. The **shrill** whistle of the policeman was warning enough for the fugitive* to stop in his tracks.
   c. A **shrill** torrent* of insults poured from the mouth of the shrieking* woman.

4. **jolly** (jäl' ē) merry; full of fun
   a. The **jolly** old man, an admitted bigamist,* had forgotten to mention his first wife to his new spouse.*
   b. When the **jolly** laughter subsided,* the pirates began the serious business of dividing the gold.
   c. Are you aware* that a red-suited gentleman with a **jolly** twinkle in his eyes is stuck in the chimney?

5. **witty** (wit' ē) cleverly amusing
   a. Mr. Carlson's **witty** introduction qualifies* him as a first-rate speaker.
   b. Fay is too slow to appreciate such **witty** remarks.
   c. The lawyer tried to prosecute* the case by being **witty** and thereby entertaining the jury.

6. **hinder** (hin' dər) hold back; make hard to do
   a. Deep mud **hindered** travel in urban* centers.
   b. The storm **hindered** the pursuit* of the fleeing* prisoners.
   c. Mona's gloomy* nature **hinders** her relationships with other people.

7. **lecture** (lek' chər) speech or planned talk; a scolding; to scold
   a. Rarely* have I heard a **lecture** with such clear illustrations.*
   b. Henry's father **lectured** him on the awesome* perils* of drug addiction.*
   c. A famous journalist* delivered a **lecture** on prejudice* in the press.

8. **abuse** (ə būz' or ə būs') make bad use of; use wrongly; treat badly; scold very severely; bad or wrong use; bad treatment
   a. Those who **abuse** the privileges of the honor system will be penalized.*
   b. The editor* apologized* for the **abuse** we had suffered as a result of his article.
   c. Brutal* **abuse** of children in the orphanage was disclosed* by the investigation.

9. **mumble** (mum' bl) speak indistinctly
   a. Ricky **mumbled** his awkward* apology.*
   b. This speech course will encourage* you to stop **mumbling** and to speak more distinctly.
   c. When the witness continued to **mumble**, the judge asked him to speak up.

10. **mute** (mūt) silent; unable to speak
    a. The usually defiant* child stood **mute** before the principal.
    b. People are no longer willing to remain **mute** on the subject of abuse* of gun control.
    c. The horror of the famine* left the inhabitants* of the land **mute** with their tragic* memories.

11. **wad** (wäd) small, soft mass; to roll or crush into a small mass
    a. To decrease* the effects of the pressure, the diver put **wads** of cotton in his ears.
    b. The officer challenged* George to explain the **wad** of fifty dollars which he had in his pocket.
    c. Because the automatic firing mechanism was defective,* the hunter had to **wad** the powder into the gun by hand.

12. **retain** (ri tān') keep; remember; employ by payment of a fee
    a. Despite* her lack* of funds Mrs. Reilly **retained** a detective* to follow her spouse*
    b. China dishes have the unique* quality* of **retaining** heat longer than metal pans.
    c. Like the majority* of people, I can **retain** the tune but not the words of a song.

Words in Use

Read the following passage to see how the new words are used in it.

Don't Look over My Shoulder!

The kibitzer is a person who **volunteers** useless information, especially in card games, causing the players to be **prejudiced** against him. The name comes from a Yiddish word which originally referred* to a certain bird whose **shrill** cry scared the animals away upon the approach* of the hunters. Though the kibitzer may think he is being **jolly** or **witty,** his advice often **hinders** more than it helps. We may scowl* at him or **lecture** him for his **abuse** of our friendship, but he still continues to **mumble** his unwelcome remarks. The serious player may even wish he could make the kibitzer **mute** by sticking a **wad** of cotton in his mouth. The kibitzer, however, may not realize that he is causing torment* or distress* to his colleagues.* Thus we may have to resign* ourselves to his annoying habit if we wish to **retain** him as a friend.

Picture It

Which of the words studied in this lesson is suggested by the picture?

Fill in the Blanks

Place one of the new words in each of the blanks below.

1. The culprit* _____ his oath* in court as if his tongue were numb.*
2. The _____ of material stuffed under Mr. Marlowe's shirt made him look bulky* enough to play the part of Santa.
3. With the evidence* mounting* against him, Dr. Parkman was persuaded* to _____ the best lawyer in the state.
4. In a fine showing of loyalty,* many _____ responded* to the fire.
5. Our party was a _____ blend* of good fellowship, song, and dance.
6. The defense attorney made a desperate plea* to the jury not to allow the hazy* evidence* to _____ them against his client.*
7. Edith's fierce* loyalty* has _____ the investigation of the crime.
8. Flynn was usually talkative but the accident left him _____ .
9. There were visible* signs that the child had been severely* _____ .
10. The _____ screams of the jet planes lead many people to envy* the quiet country life.
11. Father gave Steve a _____ for neglecting* to wash the car.
12. A _____ line in Shakespeare's plays may not get a chuckle in our century.*

Answer key, p. 198

Creativity Exercise

Now make up your own sentences, one for each of the new words you have just been taught.

1. _____
2. _____
3. _____
4. _____
5. _____
6. _____
7. _____
8. _____
9. _____
10. _____
11. _____
12. _____

Spotlight On

prejudice—Even a newcomer to this word might be able to figure out its meaning from the parts of the word itself; *pre* means "before" and *judge* means "decide." So a person who "decides before" thinking out a problem is *prejudiced*.

"His words are a very fantastical banquet, just so many strange dishes."
—Shakespeare, *Much Ado About Nothing*

1. **candidate** (kan' də dāt) person who is proposed for some office or honor
   a. We can have a maximum* of four **candidates** for the office of president.
   b. Each **candidate** for mayor seemed confident* he would be victorious.*
   c. Derek Jeter is a **candidate** for baseball's Hall of Fame.

2. **precede** (prē sēd') go before; come before; be higher in rank or importance
   a. Lyndon Johnson **preceded** Richard Nixon as president.
   b. In a gallant* gesture, Ronnie allowed Amanda's name to **precede** his in the program listing.
   c. A prominent* speaker **preceded** the ceremony of the granting of the diplomas.

3. **adolescent** (ad' ə les' nt) growing up to manhood or womanhood; youthful; a person from about 13 to 22 years of age
   a. In his **adolescent** years, the candidate* claimed, he had undergone many hardships.*
   b. There is a fiction* abroad* that every **adolescent** is opposed to tradition.*
   c. Our annual rock festival attracts* thousands of **adolescents**.

4. **coeducational** (kō ej' e ka' shən l) having to do with educating both sexes in the same school
   a. There has been a massive* shift to **coeducational** schools.
   b. **Coeducational** institutions, once thought to have a disruptive* effect, have been found to be beneficial.*
   c. In choosing a college, Ned leans toward schools that are **coeducational**.

5. **radical** (rad' ə kl) going to the root; fundamental; extreme; person with extreme opinions
   a. The tendency* to be vicious* and cruel is a **radical** fault.
   b. We observe that the interest in **radical** views is beginning to subside.*
   c. Because Richard was a **radical**, the Conservative Party would not accept him as a candidate.*

6. **spontaneous** (spon ta' nē əs) of one's own free will; natural; on the spur of the moment; without rehearsal
   a. The vast* crowd burst into **spontaneous** cheering at the skillful play.
   b. Be cautious* with these oily rags because they can break out in **spontaneous** flame.
   c. William's **spontaneous** resentment* at the mention of his sister was noted by the observant* teacher.

7. **skim** (skim) remove from the top; move lightly (over); glide along; read hastily or carelessly
   a. This soup will be more nourishing* if you **skim** off the fat.
   b. I caught a glimpse* of Mark and Marge **skimming** over the ice.
   c. Detective Corby, assigned to the homicide,* was **skimming** through the victim's book of addresses.

8. **vaccinate** (vak' sə nāt) inoculate with vaccine as a protection against smallpox and other diseases
   a. There has been a radical* decline in polio since doctors began to **vaccinate** children with the Salk vaccine.
   b. The general population* has accepted the need to **vaccinate** children against the once-dreaded* disease.
   c. Numerous* examples persist* of people who have neglected* to have their infants **vaccinated**.

9. **untidy** (un tī' dē) not neat; not in order
   a. The bachelor's* quarters* were most **untidy**.
   b. We must start a cleanup campaign to keep the campus* from being so **untidy**.
   c. Finding the house in such an **untidy** condition baffled* us.

10. **utensil** (ū ten' səl) container or tool used for practical purposes
    a. Several **utensils** were untidily* tossed about the kitchen.
    b. Edward's baggage* contained all the **utensils** he would need on the camping trip.
    c. Some people are so old-fashioned that they reject* the use of any modern **utensil**.

11. **sensitive** (sen' sə tiv) receiving impressions readily; easily affected or influenced; easily hurt or offended
    a. The eye is **sensitive** to light.
    b. From the experiment we may conclude* that mercury in a thermometer is **sensitive** to changes in temperature.
    c. James is **sensitive** about his wretched* handwriting.

12. **temperate** (tem' pər it) not very hot and not very cold; moderate
    a. The United States is mostly in the North **Temperate** Zone
    b. All students received the appeal* to be **temperate** and not to jump to conclusions* in judging the new grading system.
    c. Mrs. Rollins commended* her class for their **temperate** attitude when she announced the extra assignment.

Words in Use

Read the following passage to see how the new words are used in it.

A Course for Parents

A course entitled "The Responsibilities of Parenthood" sounds as if it should be offered to students who are immediate **candidates** for parenthood. Not according to Dr. Lee Salk, who feels that teaching children about parenthood should **precede** the **adolescent** years. Dr. Salk, of the New York Hospital, teaches a volunteer* **coeducational** class of junior high school youngsters what it means to be a parent. He does not lecture* or present **radical** views. Rather, he conducts **spontaneous** discussions by encouraging* students to imagine that they are parents and asking them such questions as "What would you do if you found your child smoking?" or "How would you prepare your child for the first day of school?" The lessons **skim** over such topics as the need to **vaccinate** children against diseases or to teach them not to be **untidy** or to use **utensils** properly. The class is more concerned with preparing students emotionally to become better parents some day and with making children **sensitive** to the responsibilities of parenthood.

The class members often express **temperate** and mature views. One girl said she would not approve of having a nurse bring up her child. Another felt that money earned through baby-sitting or other jobs should be shared with parents. When asked how his students rate, Dr. Salk retained* a hopeful outlook. "They are ready for this information," he declared. "I think they'll be honest parents."

Fill in the Blanks

Place one of the new words in each of the blanks below.

1. It is to Mitchell's credit that he gained a harvest* of friends in his _____ years.
2. The _____ who gets the job must have an adequate* knowledge* of journalism.*
3. Detective Wayne threatened* to take _____ action if the outlaws* did not surrender.

4. You can scarcely* call Jay's hour-long acceptance speech a _____ response* to his victory.
5. If you consent* to have yourself _____ against the Asiatic flu, you will be relieved* of further tension or worry.
6. Brad identified* the _____ as a miniature* radiation gauge.
7. Kim is _____ about her poor grades, yet she rejects* offers of help.
8. The warden* tried to soothe* the violent* men by speaking to them in a _____ manner.
9. From the piles of rubbish it is obvious* that the occupant* of this room was an _____ person.
10. The data* show that _____ classes tend to encourage* greater competition* in learning.
11. A rise in the wholesale* prices _____ the sharp increase on the retail level.
12. In the hazy* sunlight, we watched the swallows _____ over the water.

Answer key, p. 198

Matching

Match the 12 new words in Column I with the definitions in Column II.

Column I	Column II
1. sensitive	a. not very hot and not very cold
2. coeducational	b. of one's own free will
3. vaccinate	c. youthful
4. spontaneous	d. inoculate
5. untidy	e. having to do with education of both sexes at the same school
6. precede	f. remove from the top
7. adolescent	g. extreme
8. radical	h. person who is proposed for some office
9. utensil	i. go before
10. candidate	j. not neat
11. temperate	k. receiving impressions readily
12. skim	l. container or tool used for practical purposes

Answer key, p. 198

Picture It

Which of the words studied in this lesson is suggested by the picture?

Spotlight On

vaccinate—The first vaccines designed to protect us from disease were discovered by Louis Pasteur in France in 1885. He prepared a serum from cows (*vache* is the word for cow in French) and injected it into his patients. These patients did not contract smallpox, a dreaded disease that was conquered with the first vaccine.

"Thou weigh'st thy words before thou givest them breath."
—Shakespeare, *Othello*

Words to Learn This Week

vague
elevate
lottery
finance
obtain
cinema
event
discard
soar
subsequent
relate
stationary

1. **vague** (vāg) not definite; not clear; not distinct
   a. Joe's position was **vague** because he wanted to remain neutral* in the dispute.*
   b. When asked her opinion, Gladys was tactful* enough to give a **vague** answer that did not hurt anyone.
   c. The **vague** shape in the distance proved to be nothing more weird* than a group of trees.

2. **elevate** (el' ə vāt) raise; lift up
   a. Private Carbo was **elevated** to higher rank for his valor.*
   b. Reading a variety* of good books **elevates** the mind.
   c. The candidate* spoke from an **elevated** platform.

3. **lottery** (lot' ər ē) a scheme for distributing prizes by lot or chance
   a. The merit* of a **lottery** is that everyone has an equal chance.
   b. We thought that a **lottery** was an absurd* way of deciding who should be the team captain.
   c. The rash* young man claimed the **lottery** prize only to find he had misread his number.

4. **finance** (fə nans') money matters; to provide money for
   a. The new employee* boasted of his skill in **finance.**
   b. Frank circulated* the rumor that his uncle would **finance** his way through college.
   c. Mrs. Giles retained* a lawyer to handle her **finances.**

5. **obtain** (əb tān') get; be in use
   a. An adolescent* is finding it increasingly difficult to **obtain** a good job without a diploma.
   b. David **obtained** accurate* information about college from his guidance counselor.
   c. Because this is a coeducational* school, different rules **obtain** here.

6. **cinema** (sin' ə mə) moving picture
   a. Censors* have developed a rating system for the **cinema.**
   b. Today's **cinema** is full of homicides* and violence.*
   c. A best-seller is often the source* of **cinema** stories.

7. **event** (i vent') happening; important happening; result or outcome; one item in a program of sports
   a. The greatest **event** in Ellie's life was winning the $1,000,000 lottery.*
   b. We chose our seat carefully and then awaited the shot put **event**.
   c. There is merit* in gaining wisdom even after the **event**.

8. **discard** (dis kärd') throw aside
   a. Anna casually* **discarded** one boyfriend after another.
   b. Confident* that he held a winning hand, Slim refused to **discard** anything.
   c. Asked why he had **discarded** his family traditions,* Mr. Menzel remained mute.*

9. **soar** (sôr) fly upward or at a great height; aspire
   a. We watched the **soaring** eagle skim* over the mountain peak.
   b. An ordinary man cannot comprehend* such **soaring** ambition.
   c. The senator's hopes for victory **soared** after his television appearance.

10. **subsequent** (sub' sə kwənt) later; following; coming after
    a. **Subsequent** events* proved that Sloan was right.
    b. Further explanations will be presented in **subsequent** lectures.*
    c. Though the enemy forces resisted* at first, they **subsequently** learned that their efforts were in vain.*

11. **relate** (rə lāt') tell; give an account of; connect in thought or meaning
    a. The traveler **related** his adventures with some exaggeration.*
    b. After viewing the cinema's* latest show, the observant* student was able to **relate** every detail.
    c. Would you say that misfortune* is **related** to carelessness?

12. **stationary** (stā' shən er' ē) having a fixed station or place; standing still; not moving; not changing in size, number or activity
    a. A factory engine is **stationary.**
    b. The population* of our town has been **stationary** for a decade.*
    c. Caught in the middle of traffic, the frightened pedestrian* remained **stationary** in the busy street.

Words in Use

Read the following passage to see how the new words are used in it.

Summer Travel

If you are tired of making **vague** excuses for another dull summer at home, here is a thought to **elevate** your spirits. You do not need anything so radical* as winning a **lottery** to **finance** a trip to Europe. A student identity card that can be **obtained** for a few dollars from the Council on International Educational Exchange entitles you to discount tickets on certain charter flights to London and Paris, as well as reduced admission to many museums, **cinemas**, and musical **events**.

Once in Europe, you can stretch your budget by staying at approved* youth hostels for about ten dollars a night. So don't **discard** your hopes of becoming an international traveler. Soon you can be **soaring** into the skies or skimming* over the waves to new adventures that you will **subsequently** relate to your **stationary** friends.

Picture It

Which of the words studied in this lesson is suggested by the picture?

Fill in the Blanks

Place one of the new words in each of the blanks below.

1. Our club consented* to hold a _____ as a means of raising money.
2. If you want to _____ data* on employment opportunities, a good source* is the Bulletin of the Department of Labor.
3. Some call it a _____ but I call it a movie.
4. Our team excelled* in the last _____ of the track meet.
5. As I watched the huge jet _____ into the sky, I wished that I were on board.
6. Since Margaret has become his neighbor, Bud's progress in school has been practically _____ .
7. _____ to his phone call, I received a confirmation* in the mail.
8. We are compelled* to _____ this outdated theory.*
9. How does that evidence* _____ to the case?
10. Tim's argument may be logical* but it is too _____ to be convincing.
11. With no one to _____ the project, the entire scheme collapsed.*
12. This feeble* speech will do little to _____ the spirits of the audience.

Answer key, p. 198

Word Detective

From the list of 12 new words that follows, choose the one that corresponds to each definition below.

elevate	obtain	soar	vague
relate	stationary	lottery	discard
cinema	subsequent	finance	event

1. raise; lift up   _____
2. later; following; coming after   _____
3. moving picture   _____
4. important happening   _____
5. fly upward or at a great height; aspire   _____
6. not definite; not clear; not distinct   _____
7. not moving   _____
8. a scheme for distributing prizes by lot or chance   _____
9. tell; connect in thought or meaning   _____
10. get; be in use   _____
11. money matters; to provide money for   _____
12. throw aside   _____

Answer key, p. 198

Spotlight On

cinema—French words like *cinema* are common in English, and the French have adopted many of our words as well. Our words *weekend* and *drugstore* are heard every day in France. In our country French words are often used to imply high quality. When you pay eight dollars, you go to the *cinema,* not the movies.

LESSON 36

"Here are a few of the unpleasant'st words
That ever blotted paper."

—Shakespeare, *The Merchant of Venice*

Words to Learn This Week

prompt
hasty
scorch
tempest
soothe
sympathetic
redeem
resume
harmony
refrain
illegal
narcotic

1. **prompt** (prämpt) quick; on time; done at once; to cause (someone) to do something; remind (someone) of the words or actions needed
   a. Be **prompt** in assembling* your baggage.*
   b. Terry's caution* **prompted** him to ask many questions before he consented.*
   c. Larry was confident* he knew his lines well enough not to need any **prompting**.

2. **hasty** (hās' tē) quick; hurried; not well thought out
   a. A **hasty** glance* convinced him that he was being followed.
   b. Rather than make a **hasty** decision, Mr. Torres rejected* the offer.
   c. Myra apologized* for the **hasty** visit.

3. **scorch** (skôrch) burn slightly; dry up; criticize sharply
   a. The hot iron **scorched** the tablecloth.
   b. Farmers reported that their wheat was being **scorched** by the fierce* rays of the sun.
   c. Mr. Regan gave the class a **scorching** lecture* on proper behavior in the cafeteria.

4. **tempest** (tem' pist) violent* storm with much wind; a violent disturbance
   a. The **tempest** drove the ship on the rocks.
   b. Following the weather report of the approaching* **tempest**, we were prompted* to seek immediate shelter.
   c. When Mr. Couche saw that a **tempest** was brewing over the issue, he hastily* called a meeting.

5. **soothe** (sooth) quiet; calm; comfort
   a. With an embrace,* the mother **soothed** the hurt child.
   b. Heat **soothes** some aches; cold **soothes** others.
   c. Rosalie's nerves were **soothed** by the soft music.

6. **sympathetic** (sim' pə thet' ik) having or showing kind feelings toward others; approving; enjoying the same things and getting along well together
   a. Judge Cruz was **sympathetic** to the lawyer's plea* for mercy.
   b. Father was fortunately* **sympathetic** to my request to use the car on weekends.
   c. We were all **sympathetic** to Suzanne over her recent* misfortune.*

7. **redeem** (ri dəm') buy back; pay off; carry out; set free; make up for
   a. The property on which money has been lent is **redeemed** when the loan is paid back.
   b. My family was relieved* to hear that the mortgage had been **redeemed**.
   c. Mr. Franklin promptly* **redeemed** his promise to help us in time of need.

8. **resume** (rə zoom') begin again; go on; take again
   a. **Resume** reading where we left off.
   b. Those standing may **resume** their seats.
   c. The violinist **resumed** playing after the intermission.

116

9. **harmony** (här' mə nē) situation of getting on well together or going well together; sweet or musical sound
   a. We hoped the incident would not disrupt* the **harmony** that existed between the brothers.
   b. I am sympathetic* to Warren because his plans are in **harmony** with mine.
   c. We responded* to the **harmony** of the song by humming along.

10. **refrain** (ri frān') hold back
    a. **Refrain** from making hasty* promises.
    b. Milo could not **refrain** from laughing at the jest.*
    c. If you want to be heard, you must **refrain** from mumbling.*

11. **illegal** (i lē' gl) not lawful; against the law
    a. It is **illegal** to reveal* the names of juvenile* delinquents.*
    b. Bigamy* is **illegal** in the United States.
    c. Mr. Worthington's **illegal** stock manipulations* led to his jail sentence.

12. **narcotic** (när kät' ik) drug that produces drowsiness, sleep, dullness, or an insensible condition, and lessens pain by dulling the nerves
    a. Opium is a powerful **narcotic**.
    b. We do not have adequate* knowledge of the **narcotic** properties of these substances.
    c. The doctor prescribed a **narcotic** medicine to soothe* the patient's suffering.

Words in Use

Read the following passage to see how the new words are used in it.

A Helping Hand

Youth workers Bill Nash and Jim Boyle are house-hunters, not so much for a house as for a concerned family willing to house and feed troubled youngsters temporarily. They try to give **prompt** attention to those who cannot or will not live at home.

For some, leaving home may have been the result of a **hasty** decision, based on a **scorching** remark and the subsequent* **tempest** within the family. The cooling-off period away from the family is a time to **soothe** feelings. With **sympathetic** outsiders, youngsters have a chance to **redeem** them-selves. The hope, of course, is that they will learn to relate* to adults again and quickly **resume** a normal life of **harmony** with their own families.

Some people **refrain** from offering their homes, expressing vague* fears of the harmful effects on their own children. But this has not been the case, even when the problem of the "visitor" was the **illegal** use of **narcotics**. One parent remarked, "With us it worked the other way. The horror of drugs became real to my own son. We got a lot more than we gave."

Fill in the Blanks

Place one of the new words in each of the blanks below.

1. I insist* on a _____ answer to my question.
2. Harriet's anger was subsequently* _____ by the apology.*
3. The minister said those who are not _____ from sin will perish.*
4. Joseph could not _____ from embracing* his long-lost brother.
5. My cat and dog, though traditionally* enemies, have lived in perfect _____ for years.
6. Because he liked to be prompt,* Sal ate only a _____ meal.
7. The farmers were grateful* that the _____ had not destroyed their harvest.*
8. Jenny picked up the hot iron just as it was about to _____ my shirt.
9. The couple seemed so _____ that the breakup baffled* us.
10. Chris Pollaro _____ his former position with the company.
11. It is _____ to own firearms without a license.
12. It is impossible* to estimate* the harm caused by the illegal* use of _____ .

Answer key, p. 198

Creativity Exercise

Now make up your own sentences, one for each of the new words you have just been taught.

1. _____

2. _____

3. _____

4. _____

5. _____

6. _____

7. _____

8. _____

9. _____

10. _____

11. _____

12. _____

Spotlight On

narcotics—The age of a word can often give us a clue as to the age of the substance it describes. It seems that *narcotics* are indeed ageless. The word itself has been traced back to an ancient language called Indo-European, but we are certain it was used in the Golden Age of Greece. In those times, as now, *narcotics* were used to reduce pain.

Picture It

Which of the words studied in this lesson is suggested by the picture?

Word Review #6

These exercises are based on some of the words found in Lessons 31–36.

A. In each of the parentheses below there are two choices. Pick the one that fits better.

1. When he was asked to (relate, confine) his story to the judge, Mr. Parsons grew very nervous.
2. I was surprised to get such a (prompt, shrill) answer to my letter since I had only mailed it on Tuesday.
3. After drinking for three hours, Corky had only a (subsequent, vague) memory of what had taken place at the party.
4. Because my father works in the post office, he can (redeem, obtain) the new stamps that come out each month.
5. Mrs. Sykes stopped her daughter's piano lessons in June but will (resume, refrain) them in September.
6. We could see that the cook was (distressed, soothed) by his wild looks and his violent curses.
7. The cowboys knew that if they lit a fire they would be (vulnerable, temperate) to attack by the outlaws.*
8. Everyone agreed that the Wright brothers' idea about flying was a (radical, sensitive) one.
9. It was an (uneventful, idol) week for us because no one telephoned and no one came to visit.
10. Gina gave (maximum, stationary) attention to her little sister after their mother died.

Answer key, p. 198

B. **Opposites.** In Column I are ten words taught in Lessons 31–36. Match them correctly with their *opposite* meanings, which you will find in Column II.

Column I	Column II
1. hasty	a. remain
2. idle	b. lower
3. flee	c. talkative
4. mumble	d. neat
5. jolly	e. sad
6. elevate	f. grow larger
7. discard	g. slow
8. mute	h. keep
9. diminish	i. speak clearly
10. untidy	j. busy

Answer key, p. 198

C. Which of the vocabulary choices in parentheses fits best in these newspaper headlines?

1. **Health Department to _____ Kindergartners**   (Diminish, Retain, Vaccinate, Sooth)
2. **Closing of Factory Causes 450 to Be _____**   (Idol, Temperate, Idle, Sympathetic)
3. **Giants' Chances Are _____ with Loss to Phils**   (Resumed, Elevated, Fertile, Diminished)
4. **Divers to _____ Search for Sunken Vessel**   (Resume, Redeem, Precede, Signify)
5. **Deny _____ Against Older Workers**   (Distress, Prejudice, Dispute, Loyalty)
6. **_____ Professors Speak Out Against Nuclear Plant**   (Illegal, Sympathetic, Radical, Adolescent)
7. **Teenage _____ to Sing in Rock Musical**   (Colleague, Idol, Mute, Jest)
8. **Our Shoreline _____ to Erosion**   (Confined, Related, Vulnerable, Retained)
9. **Frat Members Spend _____ Night in Cemetery**   (Uneventful, Vague, Hasty, Prompt)
10. **_____ Refuses to Pay Until Trains Are Cleaned**   (Colleague, Commuter, Volunteer, Jest)

Answer key, p. 198

D. From the list of words below choose the word that means:

harmony	candidate	subsequent	hinder	diminish	confine
soothe	tempest	utensil	abuse	signify	idol
radical	soar	temperate	lunatic	loyalty	vaccinate
cinema	mute	shrill	lottery	commuter	discard
redeem	spontaneous	prejudice	retain	colleague	fertile

1. insane *and* is related to the Latin word for "moon"
2. a fellow worker *and* sounds like (and is in fact derived from the same source as) *college*
3. unreasonable opinion *and* indicates a closed mind
4. protect against disease *and* is based on the French word for "cow"
5. a motion picture *and* is the first element of _____ tography and _____ scope
6. unable to speak *and also* may refer to the softening of colors and tones as well as sounds
7. occurring naturally *and* appears in phrases like "_____ applause" and "_____ generation"

8. having your number picked *and* a _____ are related to games of chance.
9. reject or throw away *and* would be appropriate in a poker game
10. save from sin *as well as* recover ownership

Answer key, p. 198

E. Letter Writing. The following business letter uses 10 words that appeared in Lessons 31–36. Fill in the blanks with those words, selected from the group below:

confine	elevate	provide	retain	temperate
diminish	fertile	radical	signified	torment
dispute	harmony	referred	spontaneous	utensil
distress	hinder	relate	sympathetic	vein

38 Grand Avenue
Rockaway Park, NY
October 24, 2011

President
Toshiba Corporation
4724 Oak Drive
Sacramento, CA 53895

Dear Sir:

As president of the Toshiba Corporation, you are perhaps my last resort in helping to solve a problem that has caused me great ___1___. Let me ___2___ to you the relevant facts.

On September 20, 1995 I purchased a Toshiba T1960CS 4860X2 50 Mhz Computer from B and G Computer World at Kings Plaza, Brooklyn, NY. I was very pleased with my acquisition for the first few days. Then I ran into difficulties. I went to B and G and exchanged the Intel modem for a Megahertz modem. The computer worked for a few hours, and then the problem returned. I was ___3___ to Randy's Computer, a computer repair service. Five times I brought my computer in for repairs, all to no avail.

Finally, in complete frustration, I called Toshiba in California and asked for a replacement computer since it appeared that the one I had purchased was not functioning and no one knew how to set it right. The Toshiba representative was ___4___ but only offered the suggestion that I contact Toshiba's regional manager in New Jersey. This I did and was told that all of Toshiba's products are handled by Ingram Distributors and there are as many as five intermediate companies including them and Toshiba. He did not ___5___ that there were ___6___ grounds for complaint, but he ___7___ that he could not ___8___ me with a new computer because "There would be too much paperwork."

I loved the machine for the short time it was working properly. Unfortunately, it has a ___9___ fault that no one can find and correct. I have lost many precious hours trying to ___10___ the computer I originally purchased, but all my efforts have been in vain.

Now I ask for your cooperation. If it is true that your company has a policy not to replace a defective piece of equipment, maybe you can make an exception in my case. The aggravation I have endured is really not fair. I had so much faith in the Toshiba. Please don't let that trust go to waste.

Sincerely,
Michael Neuman

Answer key, p. 198

F. Words That Do Double Duty. The following words in Lessons 31–36 are capable of serving as more than one part of speech:

idle (n., adj., v.)	refrain (n., v.)	prompt (v., adj.)
jest (n., v.)	finance (n., v.)	abuse (n., v.)
lunatic (n., adj.)	mute (n., v.)	
volunteer (n., v.)	torment (n., v.)	

Make up two sentences for each of the above words, showing how it could be used as two different parts of speech.

Examples: Surely you *jest* (v.) when you say that you are not planning to go to college.
Many a word said in *jest* (n.) has an element of truth.

LESSON 37

*"Zounds! I was never so bethump'd with words
Since I first call'd my brother's father dad."*

—Shakespeare, *King John*

Words to Learn This Week

heir
majestic
dwindle
surplus
traitor
deliberate
vandal
drought
abide
unify
summit
heed

---

1. **heir** ($\tilde{a}$ r) person who has a right to someone's property after that one dies; person who inherits anything
   a. Though Mr. Sloane is the **heir** to a gold mine, he lives like a miser.*
   b. The monarch* died before he could name an **heir** to the throne.
   c. It is essential* that we locate the rightful **heir** at once.

2. **majestic** (mə jes' tik) grand; noble; dignified; kingly
   a. The lion is the most **majestic** creature of the jungle.
   b. In Greek mythology,* Mt. Olympus was the **majestic** home of the gods.
   c. The graduates marched into the auditorium to the music of the **majestic** symphony.

3. **dwindle** (dwin' dl) become smaller and smaller; shrink
   a. Our supply of unpolluted* water has **dwindled**.
   b. With no visible* signs of their ship, hopes for the men's safety **dwindled** with each passing hour.
   c. After the furious tempest,* the **dwindling** chances of finding the raft vanished* entirely.

4. **surplus** (sir' pləs) amount over and above what is needed; excess, extra
   a. The bank keeps a large **surplus** of money in reserve.
   b. **Surplus** wheat, cotton, and soybeans are shipped abroad.*
   c. No mortal* ever considers* that he has a **surplus** of good things.

5. **traitor** (trā' ter) person who betrays his or her country, a friend, duty, etc.
   a. The patriot* sneered* when asked to stand on the same platform with the man who was accused of being a **traitor**.
   b. No villain* is worse than a **traitor** who betrays* his country.
   c. Do not call him a **traitor** unless you can verify* the charge.

6. **deliberate** (di lib' ər āt or di lib' ər it) to consider carefully; intended; done on purpose; slow and careful, as though allowing time to decide what to do
   a. Rico's excuse was a **deliberate** lie.
   b. My grandfather walks with **deliberate** steps.
   c. Judge Sirica **deliberated** for a week before making his decision known.

7. **vandal** (van' dl) person who willfully or ignorantly destroys or damages beautiful things
   a. Adolescent* **vandals** wrecked the cafeteria.
   b. The **vandals** deliberately* ripped the paintings from the wall.
   c. We could scarcely* believe the damage caused by the **vandals**.

8. **drought** (drout) long period of dry weather; lack of rain; lack of water; dryness
   a. Because of the **drought**, some farmers began to migrate* to more fertile* regions.
   b. In time of **drought,** the crops become scorched.*
   c. As the **drought** wore on, people began to grumble against those who had squandered* water when it was more plentiful.

9. **abide** (ə bīd') accept and follow out; remain faithful to; dwell; endure
   a. The team decided unanimously* to **abide** by the captain's ruling.

    b.   Senator Ervin **abided** by his promise not to allow demonstrations in the committee room.

    c.   My mother cannot **abide** dirt and vermin.*

10. unify (ū′ n ə f ī) unite; make or form into one

    a.   The novel* traces the developments that **unified** the family.

    b.   After the Civil War our country became **unified** more strongly.

    c.   It takes a great deal of training to **unify** all these recruits into an efficient fighting machine.

11. summit (sum′ it) highest point; top

    a.   We estimated* the **summit** of the mountain to be twenty thousand feet.

    b.   Do not underestimate* Ruth's ambition to reach the **summit** of the acting profession.

    c.   The **summit** meeting of world leaders diminished* the threat* of war.

12. heed (hēd) give careful attention to; take notice of; careful attention

    a.   I demand that you **heed** what I say.

    b.   Florence pays no **heed** to what the signs say.

    c.   Take **heed** and be on guard against those who try to deceive* you.

Picture It

Which of the words studied in this lesson is suggested by the picture?

Words in Use

Read the following passage to see how the new words are used in it.

Listen to Smokey the Bear

At one time the United States was **heir** to great riches, for more than half of our country was covered with forests. Now the **majestic** woodlands have **dwindled** to the point where we have no **surplus** of trees. Of course, only a **traitor** to the beauties of nature would **deliberately** set a forest fire, but careless citizens are the **vandals** who are responsible for much of the destruction. In time of **drought** especially, scorching* fires started by careless smokers can reduce a beautiful forest to acres of blackened stumps.

Theodore Roosevelt understood that we cannot **abide** the continual loss of our precious forests but we must learn to live in harmony* with nature. In 1905 he appointed* Gifford Pinchot to head the Forest Service which promptly* began to **unify** efforts in caring for our national forests. The modern forest rangers, from the "lookouts" stationed on mountain **summits** to the "smoke-jumpers" who parachute from airplanes to fight fires, ask us to **heed** the advice of Smokey the Bear, who has become their symbol.* Smokey says, "Only *you* can prevent forest fires."

Fill in the Blanks

Place one of the new words in each of the blanks below.

1. The exhausted* regiment _____ down to a few troops.
2. Secret documents* listed the _____ to the large fortune.
3. Iris made a _____ attempt to ignore* their biting comments.
4. The _____ of waste materials has polluted* our rivers.
5. Charles blundered* off in the wrong direction without _____ my warning cries.
6. Lincoln tried in vain* to keep the North and South _____ .
7. It did not take long before the unruly* crowd turned into a mob of howling _____ .
8. The confirmed* bachelor* could not _____ having anyone touch a single utensil* in his home.
9. If the _____ does not end soon, I can predict* a famine.*
10. The population* rise will reach its _____ in a few years and then it will level off.
11. Lt. Jenkins lost every morsel* of self-respect and became a _____ to his flag.
12. The loyal* captain, _____ in defeat, won the sympathy* of the people.

Answer key, p. 198

Antonyms (Opposites)

Circle the word that most nearly expresses the opposite meaning of the word printed in blue type.

1. **vandal**
   a. repairer
   b. arsonist
   c. captive*
   d. adolescent*
   e. informer

2. **abide**
   a. discard*
   b. dispute*
   c. deprive*
   d. provide
   e. summon

3. **summit**
   a. tempest*
   b. beneficiary
   c. duplicate*
   d. base
   e. finance*

4. **surplus**
   a. scarceness*
   b. harmony*
   c. hindrance
   d. assistance
   e. rejection

5. **majestic**
   a. fertile*
   b. theatrical
   c. courteous
   d. harsh
   e. ordinary

6. **drought**
   a. ambush*
   b. flood
   c. hardship*
   d. earthquake
   e. windstorm

7. **unify**
   a. separate
   b. redeem*
   c. abuse*
   d. confine*
   e. compress

8. **deliberate**
   a. unintentional
   b. subsequent*
   c. reassuring
   d. comprehensive*
   e. ingenious*

9. **traitor**
   a. addict*
   b. amateur*
   c. bachelor*
   d. patriot*
   e. lunatic*

10. **heed**
    a. abuse*
    b. ignore*
    c. hinder*
    d. discard*
    e. vaccinate*

11. **heir**
    a. evil sinner
    b. accurate reporter
    c. double dealer
    d. fair judge
    e. disinherited son

12. **dwindle**
    a. ignore*
    b. illustrate*
    c. arrest
    d. mumble
    e. increase

Answer key, p. 198

Spotlight On

drought—Yes, the *gh* is silent as in "might" and several other English words. Why? Well, *drought* was an old English word with the *gh* sound pronounced. When the French invaded and conquered England, they brought (there it is again) their language and it had no *gh* sound in it. Eventually their influence was so great that English words containing *gh* took on French pronunciation.

"Believe my words
For they are certain and unfallible."

—Shakespeare, *I Henry VI*

---

1. **biography** (bī äg' rə fē) the written story of a person's life; the part of literature that consists of biographies
   a. Our teacher recommended* the **biography** of the architect* Frank Lloyd Wright.
   b. The reading of a **biography** gives a knowledge of people and events* that cannot always be obtained* from history books.
   c. The **biography** of Malcolm X is a popular* book in our school.

2. **drench** (drench) wet thoroughly; soak
   a. A heavy rain **drenched** the campus,* and the students had to dry out their wet clothing.
   b. The **drenching** rains resumed* after only one day of sunshine.
   c. His fraternity friends tried to **drench** him but he was too clever for them.

3. **swarm** (swôrm) group of insects flying or moving about together; crowd or great number; to fly or move about in great numbers
   a. As darkness approached,* the **swarms** of children playing in the park dwindled* to a handful.
   b. The mosquitoes **swarmed** out of the swamp.
   c. Our campus* **swarmed** with new students in September.

4. **wobble** (wäb' l) move unsteadily from side to side
   a. Little Perry thrust* his feet into the oversized shoes and **wobbled** over to the table.
   b. A baby **wobbles** when it begins to walk alone.
   c. Lacking experience on the high wire, the clown **wobbled** along until he reached the safety of the platform.

5. **tumult** (tu' mūlt or tōō' mult) noise; uproar; violent* disturbance or disorder
   a. The sailors' voices were too feeble* to be heard above the **tumult** of the storm
   b. There was such a **tumult** in the halls we concluded* an accident had occurred.
   c. The dreaded* cry of "Fire!" caused a **tumult** in the theater.

6. **kneel** (nēl) go down on one's knees; remain on the knees
   a. Myra **knelt** down to pull a weed from the drenched* flower bed.
   b. The condemned* man **knelt** before the monarch* and pleaded* for mercy.
   c. **Kneeling** over the still figure, the lifeguard tried to revive* him.

7. **dejected** (di jek' tid) in low spirits; sad
   a. His biography* related* that Edison was not **dejected** by failure.
   b. The defeated candidate* felt **dejected** and scowled* when asked for an interview.
   c. There is no reason to be **dejected** because we did not get any volunteers.*

8. **obedient** (ō bē' dē ənt) doing what one is told.; willing to obey
   a. The **obedient** dog came when his master beckoned.*
   b. **Obedient** to his father's wishes, Guy did not explore* any further.
   c. When parents make reasonable requests of them, the majority* of my friends are **obedient**.

Words to Learn This Week

biography
drench
swarm
wobble
tumult
kneel
dejected
obedient
recede
tyrant
charity
verdict

9. **recede** (ri sēd') go back; move back; slope backward; withdraw
   a. As you ride past in a train, you have the unique* feeling that houses and trees are **receding**.
   b. Mr. Ranford's beard conceals* his **receding** chin.
   c. Always cautious,* Mr. Camhi **receded** from his former opinion.

10. **tyrant** (tī' rənt) cruel or unjust ruler; cruel master; absolute ruler
    a. Some **tyrants** of Greek cities were mild and fair rulers.
    b. The **tyrant** demanded loyalty* and obedience* from his subjects.
    c. Though Ella was a **tyrant** as director of the play, the whole cast was grateful* to her when the final curtain came down.

11. **charity** (char' ə tē) generous giving to the poor; institutions for helping the sick, the poor, or the helpless; kindness in judging people's faults
    a. A free hospital is a noble **charity**.
    b. The entire community is the beneficiary* of Henry's **charity**.
    c. The hired hand was too proud to accept help or **charity**.

12. **verdict** (vėr' dikt) decision of a jury; judgment
    a. The jury returned a **verdict** of guilty for the traitor.*
    b. We were cautioned* not to base our **verdict** on prejudice.*
    c. Baffled* by the **verdict**, the prosecutor* felt that the evidence* had been ignored.*

Words in Use

Read the following passage to see how the new words are used in it.

Gulliver's Travels

Jonathan Swift tried to show the smallness of people by writing the **biography** of Dr. Lemuel Gulliver. In one of his strangest adventures, Gulliver was shipwrecked. **Drenched** and weary,* he fell asleep on the shore. In the morning, he found himself tied to pegs in the ground, and **swarming** over him were hundreds of little people six inches high.

After a time he was allowed to stand, though he began to **wobble** from being bound so long. He was then marched through the streets, naturally causing a **tumult** wherever he went. Even the palace was not big enough for him to enter, nor could he **kneel** before the king and queen. But he did show his respect for them in another way.

The king was **dejected** because he feared an invasion of Lilliput by Blefuscu, the enemy across the ocean. The reason for the war between the two tiny peoples would seem small and foolish to us. The rebels of Blefuscu were originally Lilliputians who would not abide* by the royal decision to crack their eggs on the small end instead of on the larger end. Gulliver, **obedient** to the king's command, waded out into the water when the tide **receded**, and sticking a little iron hook into each of fifty warships, he pulled the entire enemy fleet to Lilliput. Gulliver later escaped from Lilliput when he realized the tiny king was really a **tyrant** with no **charity** in his heart.

Oddly enough, the **verdict** of generations of readers has taken no heed* of the author's intention in *Gulliver's Travels*. Instead, while Lilliputians are still the symbol* of small, narrow-minded people, Swift's savage attack upon humankind has become one of the best-loved children's classics.

Fill in the Blanks

Place one of the new words in each of the blanks below.

1. The principal probed* the cause of the _____ in the cafeteria.
2. A _____ of insects descended* on the picnic food.
3. When asked for their _____ on the agreement, the members gave their approval spontaneously.*
4. The first project in our creative writing class was a _____ of a close friend or relative.
5. Until the flood waters _____ , the authorities prohibited* anyone from returning to the vicinity.*
6. Mr. Finley was redeemed* in the eyes of his employees* by his _____ in overlooking their costly error.
7. The grateful* traveler would _____ in prayer every night.

8. Mother is an expert at soothing* our _____ spirits.
9. It is absurd* to surrender your rights to a _____ when you have abundant* reason to remain free.
10. We faced the dilemma* of being _____ in the downpour while we covered our boat or having to bail the water out of the boat after the rain had ceased.*
11. Melinda shrieked* as the unstable* pedestrian* _____ into the path of the oncoming car.
12. A glance* from the mother was enough of a reminder to bring the _____ child back to her side.

Answer key, p. 198

True or False

Based on the way the new word is used, write T (true) or F (false) next to the sentence.

1. A **swarm** is a small group.
2. To be **obedient** is to do what you are told; to be willing to obey.
3. A painting of a woman **kneeling** shows the woman walking with a parasol.
4. A **biography** is the written story of a person's life.
5. When reporters describe the **tumult** in the streets, they are referring to the noisy mob.
6. To **recede** is to go forward.
7. If you get **drenched,** you'll be soaking wet.
8. The jury's decision is called the **verdict.**
9. I was **dejected** to learn that I had won the lottery.
10. A **tyrant** is a just and kind ruler.
11. To **wobble** is to move unsteadily from side to side.
12. To show **charity** in judging others is to be kind and lenient in judging their faults.

Answer key, p. 198

Spotlight On

biography—This is a good time to settle an easy question. A *biography* is a book written about a person's life. The author may write of someone else's life or his or her own; however, when a book is written about one's own life, it's more accurately labeled an *auto*biography.

Picture It
Which of the words studied in this lesson is suggested by the picture?

"Ah, kill me with thy weapon, not with words!"
—Shakespeare, *III Henry VI*

---

1. **unearth** (un ėrth') dig up; discover; find out
   a. The digging of the scientists **unearthed** a buried city.
   b. A plot to defraud* the investors was **unearthed** by the F.B.I.
   c. The museum exhibited* the vase that had been **unearthed** in Greece.

2. **depart** (di pärt') go away; leave; turn away (from); change; die
   a. We arrived in the village in the morning and **departed** that night.
   b. Stan was vague* about **departing** from his usual manner of choosing a partner.
   c. Vera was reluctant* to mention that her uncle had long since **departed**.

3. **coincide** (kō' in sīd') occupy the same place in space; occupy the same time; correspond exactly; agree
   a. If these triangles were placed one on top of the other, they would **coincide.**
   b. Because Pete's and Jim's working hours **coincide,** and they live in the same vicinity,* they depart* from their homes at the same time.
   c. My verdict* on the film **coincides** with Adele's.

4. **cancel** (kan' sl) cross out; mark so that it cannot be used; wipe out; call off
   a. The stamp was only partially* **canceled**.
   b. Because the first shipment contained defective* parts, Mr. Zweben **canceled** the rest of the order.
   c. Having found just the right man for the job, Captain Mellides **canceled** all further interviews.

5. **debtor** (det' ər) person who owes something to another
   a. If I borrow a dollar from you, I am your **debtor**.
   b. As a **debtor** who had received many favors from the banker, Mr. Mertz was reluctant* to testify against him.
   c. A gloomy* **debtor's** prison was once the fate of those who could not repay their loans.

6. **legible** (lej' ə bl) able to be read; easy to read; plain and clear
   a. Julia's handwriting is beautiful and **legible**.
   b. Nancy hesitated* in her reading because the words were scarcely* **legible**.
   c. Our teacher penalizes* us for compositions that are not **legible**.

7. **placard** (plak' ärd) a notice to be posted in a public place; poster
   a. Colorful **placards** announced an urgent* meeting.
   b. **Placards** were placed throughout the neighborhood by rival* groups.
   c. Numerous* **placards** appeared around the city calling for volunteers.*

8. **contagious** (kan tāj' əs) spreading by contact, easily spreading from one to another
   a. Scarlet fever is **contagious**.
   b. I find that yawning is often **contagious**.
   c. Interest in the project was **contagious**, and soon all opposition to it collapsed.*

9. **clergy** (kler' jē) persons prepared for religious work; clergymen as a group
   a. We try never to hinder* the **clergy** as they perform their sacred* tasks.

    b.   Friar Tuck was a member of the **clergy** who loved a jolly* jest.*

    c.   The majority* of the **clergy** felt the new morality* was a menace* to society.

10. **customary** (kus' tǝm er' ē) usual

    a.   It was **customary** for wealthy Romans to recline* while they were dining.

    b.   The Robin Williams movie received the **customary** rave* reviews from the critics.

    c.   The traitor* rejected* the **customary** blindfold for the execution.

11. **transparent** (trans par' ǝnt) easily seen through; clear

    a.   Window glass is **transparent.**

    b.   Colonel Thomas is a man of **transparent** honesty and loyalty.*

    c.   The homicide* was a **transparent** case of jealousy* that got out of hand.

12. **scald** (skôld) pour boiling liquid over; burn with hot liquid or steam; heat almost to the boiling point

    a.   Do not neglect* to **scald** the dishes before drying them.

    b.   The **scalding** lava pouring from the mountain placed everyone in peril.

    c.   By being hasty,* Stella **scalded** her hand.

Picture It

Which of the words studied in this lesson is suggested by the picture?

Words in Use

Read the following passage to see how the new words are used in it.

Roast Beef on Rye

A little digging will **unearth** the roots of our language and habits. For instance, our word "sandwich" is derived from the Earl of Sandwich, who lived in the time of George III. This gentleman would not **depart** from the gambling table for hours on end. If his play happened to **coincide** with dinner, he would **cancel** his regular meal and order a slice of meat to be served to him between two pieces of bread. The biography* of the Earl claims that we are his **debtors** for his discovery of the sandwich. Charles Dickens later used the phrase "sandwich man" to describe someone who walks about with a clearly **legible** message on **placards** hung on his chest and back.

An example of a superstition is the fear of walking under a ladder. This must have been a **contagious** fear for it seems to have started with the ancient belief that spirits lived in trees or wood. "Knocking on wood" was a way of calling up the friendly spirit to protect one from harm. Today a member of the **clergy** might sneer* at this custom, expecting that by this time such superstitions would have receded* into the past with witches and ghosts.

Another expression, "giving someone the cold shoulder," has been traced to the Middle Ages, when a host would serve his guests a cold shoulder of mutton or beef instead of the **customary** hot food. This was a **transparent** attempt to show the guest he was no longer welcome. The host had thus found a more charitable* yet effective way of expressing his feelings without using a **scalding** remark.

Fill in the Blanks

Place one of the new words in each of the blanks below.

1. After several hours, Raoul abandoned* his search to _____ for home.
2. The police department _____ all leaves until the dangerous lunatic* was captured.
3. The _____ helped to advertise the circus.
4. Since the disease is so _____ , it is essential* to identify* the carrier.
5. It was fortunate* that the journalist* had _____ the sinister* plan to assassinate the president.
6. It was _____ for the victorious* general to ride at the head of a parade.
7. When she slipped in the shower, Myra was _____ by the hot water.
8. Through the _____ curtain, the entire scene was visible.*
9. Only a portion of the scrolls found in the cave were _____ , but their value should not be underestimated.*
10. The duties of the _____ are not confined* to religious matters.
11. The _____ was brought to court for having deceived* the bank with a false statement of his finances.*
12. Since their interests do not _____ there is still a lingering* doubt in my mind if they should enter into matrimony.*

Answer key, p. 199

Matching

Match the 12 new words in Column I with the definitions in Column II.

Column I	**Column II**
1. contagious	a. dig up; discover
2. scald	b. able to be read
3. clergy	c. a notice to be posted
4. cancel	d. usual
5. transparent	e. cross out; call off
6. depart	f. easily spread from one to another
7. unearth	g. pour boiling water over
8. customary	h. easily seen through
9. debtor	i. going away
10. coincide	j. persons prepared for religious work
11. legible	k. person who owes something to another
12. placard	l. correspond exactly

Answer key, p. 199

Spotlight On

legible—An important idea in vocabulary can be learned with this word. A clear handwriting is described as *legible*—here the word is used *literally*, that is, in its exact, real meaning. When Thomas Wolfe wrote "murder sweltered in his heart and was *legible* upon his face," he used the word *figuratively*, that is, in an imaginative, unusual sense. Many words can be used either literally or figuratively.

LESSON 40

"He hath heard that men of few words are the best men."
—Shakespeare, *Henry V*

1. **epidemic** (ep ə dem' ik) an outbreak of a disease that spreads rapidly* so that many people have it at the same time; widespread
   a. All of the schools in the city were closed during the **epidemic**.
   b. The depiction* of violence* in the movies has reached **epidemic** proportions.
   c. During the **epidemic** we were forbidden* to drink water unless it had been boiled.

2. **obesity** (ō bēs' ə tē) extreme fatness
   a. **Obesity** is considered* a serious disease.
   b. The salesman tactfully* referred* to Jack's **obesity** as "stoutness."
   c. At the medical convention the topic* discussed was the prevention of childhood **obesity**.

3. **magnify** (mag' nə fī) cause to look larger than it really is; make too much of; go beyond the truth in telling
   a. A microscope* is a **magnifying** glass.
   b. It seems that Mr. Steinmetz **magnified** the importance of the document* in his possession.
   c. Some people have a tendency* to **magnify** every minor* fault in others.

4. **chiropractor** (kī' rə prak' tər) a person who treats ailments by massage and manipulation of the vertebrae and other forms of therapy on the theory* that disease results from interference with the normal functioning of the nervous system
   a. The **chiropractor** tried to relieve* the pain by manipulating* the spinal column.
   b. Mrs. Lehrer confirmed* that a **chiropractor** had been treating her.
   c. The **chiropractor** recommended hot baths between treatments.

5. **obstacle** (äb' sti kal) anything that gets in the way or hinders; impediment; obstruction
   a. The soldiers were compelled* to get over such **obstacles** as ditches and barbed wire.
   b. Ignorance* is an **obstacle** to progress.
   c. Prejudice* is often an **obstacle** to harmony* among people.

6. **ventilate** (ven' tl āt) change the air in; purify by fresh air; discuss openly
   a. We **ventilated** the kitchen by opening the windows.
   b. The lungs **ventilate** the blood.
   c. There is merit* in **ventilating** the topic* of the prom before the entire senior class.

7. **jeopardize** (jep' ər dīz) risk; endanger
   a. Soldiers **jeopardize** their lives in war.
   b. Mr. Marcos revised* his opinion of police officers after two of them had **jeopardized** their lives to save his drowning child.
   c. Though it **jeopardized** his chance for a promotion,* Mr. Rafael ventured* to criticize his boss.

8. **negative** (neg' ə tiv) saying no; minus; showing the lights and shadows reversed
   a. The captain gave a **negative** response* to the request for a leave.
   b. Three below zero is a **negative** quantity.*
   c. A **negative** image is used to print a positive picture.

9. **pension** (pen' shən) regular payment that is not wages; to make such a payment
   a.   **Pensions** are often paid because of long service, special merit,* or injuries received.
   b.   The **pension** is calculated* on the basis of your last year's income.
   c.   Mrs. Colby **pensioned** off her employee after thirty years of loyal* service.

10. **vital** (vī' tl) having to do with life; necessary to life; causing death, failure or ruin; lively
    a.   We must preserve* and protect our **vital** resources.
    b.   Eating is a **vital** function, the obese* man reminded me.
    c.   The valiant* soldier died of a **vital** wound in Iraq.

11. **municipal** (mū nis' əpl) of a city or state; having something to do in the affairs of a city or town
    a.   The state police assisted the **municipal** police in putting down the riot.
    b.   There was only a mediocre* turnout for the **municipal** elections.
    c.   The **municipal** government placed a ban* on parking during business hours.

12. **oral** (ô' rəl) spoken; using speech; of the mouth
    a.   An **oral** agreement is not enough; we must have a written promise.
    b.   **Oral** surgery is necessary to penetrate* to the diseased root.
    c.   His unique* **oral** powers made Lincoln a man to remember.

Words in Use

Read the following passage to see how the new words are used in it.

Weight-watchers

Judging from the popularity* of books on dieting, one would think an **epidemic** of **obesity** is sweeping the nation. Although being fat is not contagious,* it is a condition not to be sneered* at since it affects one-fourth of all Americans. Without **magnifying** the problem, professionals concerned* with the nation's health, from **chiropractors** to medical specialists, agree that being overweight is a major **obstacle** to good health. They point out that people will readily see the need to **ventilate** their homes for fresh air to get rid of vermin* that may cause disease, but they **jeopardize** their health by eating the wrong foods or the wrong amount of foods.

Coincidentally,* a recent survey of employment agencies showed that obesity* has a **negative** effect on a person's chances of landing a job. While the job-seeker is asking about salary and **pensions,** the employer is thinking about the worker's health—and weight is a **vital** consideration when it comes to injuries, disease, and absenteeism.

Some **municipal** jobs, in fact, do require an applicant to be within normal weight range, and one New York bank insists on an **oral** understanding that applicants will take off excess weight. As the *Wall Street Journal* put it, "Fat people often find slim pickings in the job market."

Fill in the Blanks

Place one of the new words in each of the blanks below.

1. Intemperate* eating habits can lead to _____ .
2. To avoid* an _____, the Surgeon-General ordered a thorough* study of the situation.
3. At a recent* meeting of _____, a new treatment for arthritis was discussed.
4. The humid* air in this room must be _____ .
5. One thousand angry voters loudly signified* an _____ objection to the motion.
6. The frightened man tormented* himself by _____ every unpleasant experience into a calamity.*
7. If used as a precedent,* this verdict* will prove to be an _____ to justice.*
8. Without the _____ he had confidently* expected, Mr. Halcroft faced hardships* in his retirement.
9. The sale of the vacant* lot for construction of an office building will _____ the residential character of the neighborhood.
10. Preserve* the _____ in case we need more prints.
11. We should all attend the meeting at the _____ center, for the issues are of vital* concern to every citizen.
12. The heart and the brain are considered* the most _____ organs in the human body.

Answer key, p. 199

Picture It

Which of the words studied in this lesson is suggested by the picture?

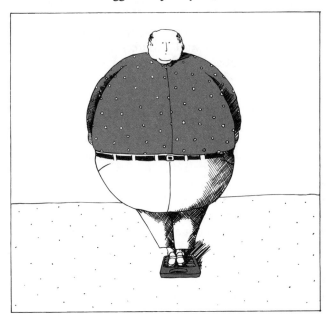

Creativity Exercise

Now make up your own sentences, one for each of the new words you have just been taught.

1.

2.

3.

4.

5.

6.

7.

8.

9.

10.

11.

12.

Spotlight On

obesity—Be careful when you refer to your friend's *obesity* that you don't use a word that causes embarrassment. If you call your friend *obese* you'll be using correct medical terminology; however, avoid calling him or her "fat," "chubby," or "corpulent"—words that convey the same idea but in an unpleasant manner.

LESSON
41

"What care I for words? yet words do well
When he that speaks them pleases those that hear."

—Shakespeare, *As You Like It*

Words to Learn This Week

complacent
wasp
rehabilitate
parole
vertical
multitude
nominate
potential
morgue
preoccupied
upholstery
indifference

---

1. **complacent** (kəm plā' s'nt) pleased with oneself; self-satisifed
   a. Senator Troy denounced* the **complacent** attitude of the polluters* of our air.
   b. How can you be **complacent** about such a menace?*
   c. I was surprised that Martin was so **complacent** about his brief part in the play.

2. **wasp** (wäsp) an insect with a slender* body and powerful sting
   a. When the **wasps** descended* on the picnic, we ran in all directions.
   b. A swarm* of **wasps** attacked us as we were reclining* on the porch.
   c. The piercing* sting of a **wasp** can be very painful.

3. **rehabilitate** (rē hə bil' ə tāt) restore to good condition; make over in a new form; restore to former standing, rank, reputation, etc.
   a. The old house was **rehabilitated** at enormous* expense.
   b. The former criminal completely **rehabilitated** himself and was respected by all.
   c. This wing of the house must be **rehabilitated** promptly,* as there is a danger it will collapse.*

4. **parole** (pə rōl') word of honor; conditional freedom; to free (a prisoner) under certain conditions
   a. The judge **paroled** the juvenile* offenders on condition that they report to him every three months.
   b. Since the prisoner has been rehabilitated,* his family is exploring* the possibility* of having him **paroled**.
   c. The fugitive* gave his **parole** not to try to escape again.

5. **vertical** (ver' tə kl) straight up and down with reference to the horizon, for example, a vertical line
   a. It wasn't easy to get the drunken man into a **vertical** position.
   b. The way to vote for your candidate* is to pull the lever from the horizontal position to the **vertical** position.
   c. A circle surrounding a **vertical** line that ends in an inverted V is the well-known peace symbol.*

6. **multitude** (mul' tə tood) a great number; a crowd
   a. A **multitude** of letters kept pouring in to the movie idol.*
   b. The fleeing* culprit* was pursued* by a fierce* **multitude**.
   c. Flood victims were aided by a **multitude** of volunteers.*

7. **nominate** (näm' ə nāt) name as a candidate for office; appoint to an office
   a. Three times Bryant was **nominated** for office but he was never elected.
   b. The president **nominated** him for Secretary of State.
   c. Though Danny was **nominated** last, he emerged* as the strongest candidate.*

8. **potential** (pə ten' shəl) possibility* as opposed to actuality; capability of coming into being or action
   a. Mark has the **potential** of being completely rehabilitated.*
   b. The coach felt his team had the **potential** to reach the finals.*
   c. Destroying nuclear weapons reduces a **potential** threat* to human survival.*

9. **morgue** (môrg) place where bodies of unknown persons found dead are kept; the reference library of a newspaper office

a.   There is a slender* chance that we can identify* the body in the **morgue**.
b.   Bodies in the **morgue** are preserved* by low temperatures.
c.   In the **morgue** of the *New York Times* there are biographies* of most famous people.

10. preoccupied (prē äk' yu pīd) took up all the attention
a.   Getting to school in time for the test **preoccupied** Judy's mind.
b.   My boss is always **preoccupied** with ways of cutting down on the workers' lateness.
c.   Charity* cases **preoccupied** Mrs. Reynaldo's attention.

11. upholstery (up hō l' stər ē) coverings and cushions for furniture
a.   Our old sofa was given new velvet **upholstery**.
b.   The Browns' **upholstery** was so new that we were wary* about visiting them with the children.
c.   One hundred eighty-five dollars was the estimate* for changing the **upholstery** on the dining-room chairs.

12. indifference (in dif' ər əns) lack of interest, care, or attention
a.   Allen's **indifference** to his schoolwork worried his parents.
b.   It was a matter of **indifference** to Bernie whether the story circulating* about his engagement was true or not.
c.   My father could not refrain* from commenting on Linda's **indifference** toward her brother's tears.

Picture It

Which of the words studied in this lesson is suggested by the picture?

Words in Use

Read the following passage to see how the new words are used in it.

Where Do We Go from Here?

When we grow too **complacent** with ourselves, along come writers who, **wasp**-like, sting us with reminders of the many problems we face—from **rehabilitating** former prisoners on **parole** to feeding the world's hungry population. Those authors do not see civilization rising almost **vertically** to greater and greater heights. Though a **multitude** of problems beset America, they **nominate** the large urban centers as **potentially** the most dangerous and requiring the most immediate attention. They see the cities as the **morgues** of dead hopes and lost ideals.

We are **preoccupied** with trifles* like the **upholstery** in our homes or personal matters like pension* and benefits, but now we are called upon to contribute to our community on every vital* level—moral,* political, economic. We are not being urged to give up our beloved possessions, but our civilization can be saved only if we overcome the epidemic* of **indifference**. We must begin to live with a new openness to others and a determination to become the best of which we are capable.

Fill in the Blanks

Place one of the new words in each of the blanks below.

1. The children shrieked* with fear as the _____ flew over them.
2. It is illegal* to _____ prisoners until they have served a minimum* sentence.
3. The municipal* council voted to _____ the run-down section of the city and to make it a model residential area.
4. Mike Pavonna was the unanimous* choice of the _____ for the office of mayor.
5. With all this equipment, we have the _____ to survive* for weeks in the most frigid* climate.
6. The worn _____ betrayed* the poverty of the family.
7. His family was distressed at Frank's _____ to the normal adolescent* activities.
8. Unfortunately,* Carmen was too _____ with dates to devote much time to her studies.
9. To start the air circulating,* turn the button to a _____ position.
10. Bob was pleased to be _____ for the presidency, but he gallantly* declined in favor of Carole.
11. When the security* leak was discovered, the editor called the newspaper _____ to check if there was any precedent* for such a case.
12. The winner's _____ smile annoyed some of the members of the audience.

Answer key, p. 199

Synonym Search

Circle the word that most nearly expresses the meaning of the word printed in blue type.

1. stung by a **wasp**
   (a) remark   (b) lunatic*   (c) tragedy*   (d) traitor*   (e) insect
2. voters who are too **complacent** to change
   (a) self-satisfied   (b) assertive   (c) bewildered*   (d) distressed*   (e) juvenile*
3. the candidate **nominated** for office
   (a) encouraged*   (b) underestimated*   (c) designated   (d) employed   (e) motivated
4. furniture **upholstery**
   (a) material   (b) antiques   (c) wax   (d) style   (e) comfort
5. **rehabilitate** a drug user
   (a) punish*   (b) unearth*   (c) locate*   (d) restore   (e) upset
6. **vertical** lines
   (a) curved   (b) jagged*   (c) hidden   (d) lengthwise   (e) sideways
7. **preoccupied** with thoughts of the work ahead of him
   (a) absorbed   (b) affected   (c) amused   (d) covered   (e) lost
8. a **multitude** of sins
   (a) great number   (b) thorough* review   (c) total destruction   (d) valid* criticism
   (e) strong conviction
9. **potential** earnings
   (a) easily financed*   (b) economical* and instant   (c) possible as opposed to actual
   (d) miserly*   (e) repeatedly jeopardized*
10. bodies kept in the **morgue** for identification
    (a) undertaker's establishment   (b) camp grounds   (c) office building   (d) rooming house
    (e) health resort
11. **indifference** to pain
    (a) inattention   (b) sympathy   (c) vulnerability*   (d) tendency*   (e) prejudice
12. out on **parole**
    (a) appeal*   (b) conditional freedom   (c) conflicting evidence   (d) confinement
    (e) reduced sentence

Answer key, p. 199

Spotlight On

wasp—Newspaper writers enjoy taking the first letters of titles or expressions and constructing a word from them. While a *wasp* is certainly an insect, it also, when spelled *W.A.S.P.*, stands for Women's Air Service Pilots or White-Anglo-Saxon-Protestant. Since a *wasp* is not regarded by most people with affection, you can imagine that the acronym (a word made up of first letters of a phrase) was not meant as a compliment to Protestants.

LESSON
42

"By my troth, captain, these are very bitter words."
—Shakespeare, *II Henry IV*

---

1. **maintain** (mān tān') keep; keep up; carry on; uphold; support; declare to be true
    a. Angelo **maintained** his hold on the jagged* rock though his fingers were becoming numb.*
    b. The judge **maintained** his opinion that the verdict* was fair.
    c. The pauper* was unable to **maintain** his family without the help of charity.*

2. **snub** (snub) treat coldly, scornfully, or with contempt; cold treatment
    a. Darryl later apologized* to Sally for **snubbing** her at the dance.
    b. Sandra was tormented* by the thought that she might be **snubbed** by her classmates.
    c. I considered* it a rude **snub** when I was not invited to the party.

3. **endure** (en dyur' or en door') last; keep on; undergo; bear; stand
    a. How can you **endure** such disrespect?
    b. The valiant* officer **endured** serious burns on September 11th.
    c. Dr. Hardy was confident* he could **endure** the hardships* of space travel.

4. **wrath** (rath) very great anger; rage
    a. Anticipating* Father's **wrath,** we tried to give him the news slowly.
    b. There is no rage* like the **wrath** of an angry bear.
    c. After Ernie's **wrath** subsided,* we were able to tell him what happened.

5. **expose** (eks pōz') lay open; uncover; leave unprotected; show openly
    a. Soldiers in an open field are **exposed** to the enemy's gunfire.
    b. Foolish actions **expose** a person to the sneers* of others.
    c. The article **exposed** the vital* document* as a forgery.

6. **legend** (lej' ənd) story coming from the past, which many people have believed; what is written on a coin or below a picture
    a. Stories about King Arthur and his knights are popular* **legends**.
    b. **Legend** has exaggerated* the size of Paul Bunyan.
    c. The **legend** on the rare coin was scarcely* legible.*

7. **ponder** (pän' dər) consider carefully
    a. Not wishing to act hastily,* the governor **pondered** the problem for days.
    b. After **pondering** the question, the board decided to grant the parole.*
    c. The villagers, faced with a famine,* **pondered** their next move.

8. **resign** (ri zīn') give up; yield; submit
    a. Vito **resigned** his position as editor* of the school paper.
    b. Upon hearing the news of the defeat, the football coach promptly* **resigned.**
    c. Upon examining the injury, the chiropractor* told Jim he had better **resign** himself to a week in bed.

9. **drastic** (dras' tik) acting with force or violence*
    a. The police took **drastic** measures to end the crime wave.
    b. The most **drastic** changes in centuries* have taken place during our lifetime.
    c. In the interests of justice,* **drastic** action must be taken.

Words to Learn This Week
maintain
snub
endure
wrath
expose
legend
ponder
resign
drastic
wharf
amend
ballot

10. wharf (hwôrf) platform built on the shore or out from the shore beside which ships can load or unload
   a.   We watched the exhausted* laborers unloading the cargo on the **wharf.**
   b.   The lawyer insisted* that his client* was never seen near the **wharf** where the crime had taken place.
   c.   Waiting at the **wharf** for the supply ships to unload was a starving multitude* of people.

11. amend (ə mend') change for the better; correct; change
   a.   It is time you **amended** your ways.
   b.   Each time they **amended** the plan, they made it worse.
   c.   Rather than **amend** the club's constitution again, let us discard* it and start afresh.

12. ballot (bal' ət) piece of paper used in voting; the whole number of votes cast; the method of secret voting; to vote or decide by using ballots
   a.   Clyde, confident* of victory, dropped his **ballot** into the box.
   b.   After we counted the **ballots** a second time, Leo's victory was confirmed.*
   c.   To avoid embarrassing the candidates,* we **ballot** instead of showing hands.

Words in Use

Read the following passage to see how the new words are used in it.

A Time for Decision

Carl Brown walked wearily* from the bus stop, his thoughts preoccupied* with the day's events. He had become accustomed to receiving the blame for his colleagues'* mistakes. He could remain complacent* when less deserving workers were promoted* ahead of him. He could even **maintain** an air of indifference* when the young man he had trained now **snubbed** him. What he could not **endure** was the ridicule of his fellow employees.* His **wrath** flamed at the thought that his secret had been **exposed**. The **legend** of his honesty had died.

Carl Brown **pondered** his next move. Should he **resign** or take even more **drastic** measures? His steps led past the **wharf** where the ships were unloading their cargoes of fruit. He looked into the dark waters and took a deep breath. No, this was not a sin that could be erased. He heaved a sigh and determined to **amend** his ways. Never again would he sign his **ballot** "Carl Smith."

Picture It

Which of the words studied in this lesson is suggested by the picture?

Fill in the Blanks

Place one of the new words in each of the blanks below.

1. When the third person she approached turned away from her, Marilyn had a vague* feeling she was being _____ .
2. Achilles' _____ did not cease* until he had taken revenge on the slayer of his friend.
3. As the captain _____ their situation, he realized that resistance* was in vain.*
4. Father _____ that all forms of gambling should be declared illegal.*
5. The prophet warned that the land cannot _____ such violations of morality.*
6. To diminish* the chances of raising weaklings, the ancient Spartans used to_____ to the elements the babies that they did not want.
7. The Robin Hood stories are a good illustration* of a _____ from the Middle Ages.
8. The _____ is the symbol* of the democratic way of choosing leaders.
9. Because of the secret nature of the cargo, visits to the _____ area were prohibited.*
10. The patriot* was _____ dying for his deed.
11. We are trying to persuade* the sponsors of the bill to _____ it in order to improve its chances for passage.
12. The guinea pigs could not put up with _____ changes in their diet.

Answer key, p. 199

Creativity Exercise

Now make up your own sentences, one for each of the new words you have just been taught.

1. _____
2. _____
3. _____
4. _____
5. _____
6. _____
7. _____
8. _____
9. _____
10. _____
11. _____
12. _____

Spotlight On

ballot—This method of voting derives its name from the small balls (or stones) that were placed secretly in a box, a practice that is still used in some organizations even today. In city, state, and national elections, voting machines seem to be used in densely populated areas, but in farm towns and small cities, voters still drop their *ballots* (paper) in a box.

Word Review #7

These exercises are based on some of the words found in Lessons 37–42.

A. In each of the parentheses below there are two choices. Pick the one that fits better.

1. It was (legible, customary) for Mrs. Thorpe to leave her baby at our house when she went shopping.
2. Only a (drastic, deliberate) change in the weather can save our city from the flood.
3. Don't (jeopardize, rehabilitate) your future by doing something now that you may be sorry for later.
4. After the (parole, tumult) died down, the prisoners went back to their cells quietly.
5. Lucille thought that she could (ponder, endure) great pain, but a visit to the dentist changed her mind.
6. While walking across the lawn, I got (drenched, scalded) by the cold water sprinkler.
7. After the waters (receded, abided), we walked up and down the beach looking for interesting shells.
8. Our chances for success (dwindled, coincided) with each passing day.
9. When Sheldon reached the (summit, potential) of the mountain, he rested before trying to come down.
10. I was too (resigned, preoccupied) with my work to pay attention to the television set.

Answer key, p. 199

B. **Opposites.** In Column I are ten words from Lessons 37–42. Match them correctly with their *opposite* meanings in Column II.

Column I	Column II
1. surplus	a. shortage
2. heed	b. bury
3. unearth	c. written
4. magnify	d. refuse to listen
5. amend	e. leave the same
6. oral	f. arrive
7. depart	g. split up
8. unify	h. happiness
9. wrath	i. stand up straight
10. kneel	j. make smaller

Answer key, p. 199

C. Which of the vocabulary choices in parentheses fits best in these newspaper headlines?

1. **Search Is on for _____ to Millionaire's Fortune**   (Verdict, Heir, Obstacle, Surplus)
2. **False "Arabs" _____ Member of Congress**   (Heed, Expose, Endure, Ponder)
3. **_____ of Measles Breaks Out in County**   (Summit, Swarm, Potential, Epidemic)
4. **Accused of _____ Attempt to Sell Secrets**   (Legible, Customary, Majestic, Deliberate)
5. **_____ History of Tribe to Be Tape-Recorded**   (Oral, Drastic, Complacent, Negative)
6. **Bad Economic News Causes _____ at Stock Market**   (Charity, Multitude, Verdict, Tumult)
7. **Major Refuses to _____ by Previous Agreement**   (Unify, Abide, Recede, Snub)
8. **Forced to _____ Tonight's Show, Apologizes Producer**   (Magnify, Cancel, Unify, Nominate)
9. **Prisons Fail to _____ , Charges Social Work Expert**   (Rehabilitate, Jeopardize, Amend, Dwindle)
10. **Tells Life Story of Michael Jackson _____**   (Clergy, Ballot, Biography, Indifference)

Answer key, p. 199

D. From the list of words below choose the word that means:

vandal	wobble	indifference	endure	placard	rehabilitate
legend	coincide	swarm	tumult	resign	municipal
complacent	drench	maintain	transparent	verdict	wasp
abide	nominate	snub	legible	pension	contagious
multitude	potential	dwindle	obesity	ballot	surplus

1. the exercise of a democratic privilege *and* may be done by sophisticated machinery or simply by a piece of paper
2. a stinging insect *and also* is a well-known acronym, an abbreviation whose letters stand for the name of a group
3. a condition caused by overeating *and* comes from a Latin word meaning "to eat away"
4. can be used *but* figuratively can mean able to be clearly seen or noticed
5. a person who defaces or damages public property *and is* based on the name of a German tribe that destroyed Rome in A.D. 455

6. gradually decrease to a vanishing point *and* rhymes with *swindle*
7. move like a dazed boxer *and also* may refer to the trembling or shaking of one's voice
8. saturate or wet through and through *and* is closely related to the word *drink*
9. a story handed down from early times *as well as* a key or explanation on a map, or picture
10. restore a person to usefulness and normalcy *as well as* restore a building or a neighborhood that has fallen upon bad times

Answer key, p. 199

E. **Writing a Feature Article.** The following article uses 10 words that appeared in Lessons 37–42. Fill in the blanks with those words, selected from the group below:

abide	deprived	heed	obstacle	transparent
amend	drastic	heir	potential	tumult
customary	drenched	indifference	rehabilitate	tyrant
deliberate	dwindling	legend	surplus	wrath

The 20th century is ___1___ to the most memorable events in world history—skyrocketing population, fantastic advances in medicine, science, and technology, two world wars and, shamefully, the greatest stain on the record of mankind, the Holocaust. This incredible calamity that took the lives of six million innocent people, almost one-third of them children, was the brainchild of Adolf Hitler, the head of the Nazi Party in Germany from 1933 to 1945.

With thoroughness and efficiency, this ___2___ and his willing henchmen organized and carried out a ___3___ program of annihilation against the Jewish people in Germany and the countries he conquered during World War II. The Holocaust ___4___ the soil of Europe with Jewish blood, as the Nazis, often with the cooperation of the local population, built concentration camps where the killing took place.

At first, the Nazis ___5___ the Jews of their civil rights. Then they adopted more ___6___ measures, ending with the notorious concentration camps. Then came the roundups. Jewish families were brutally dragged from their homes in the dead of night, packed into cattle cars, and sent to distant concentration camps throughout Europe, primarily in Poland.

Many thousands died from starvation, disease, and torture even before they reached their destination. The survivors were divided into two groups. Those capable of working were assigned to Nazi factories, where they were literally worked to death, and the others were immediately sent to the gas chambers. The mass killings, at first carried out by death squads in front of open graves, were speeded up with more sophisticated killing devices. Desperate efforts made by Jewish groups in the United States and elsewhere to stop the senseless slaughter of their kinsmen were met with ___7___ by the Allies.

This tragic event is no myth or ___8___, though some skeptics pay no ___9___ to the mountains of evidence—the ___10___ number of survivors who still have their concentration camp number tattooed on their arms, the pictures from the daily papers of that time, the mounds of shoes, hair, gold teeth discovered by the Allied soldiers who liberated the concentration camp inmates, and, most convincing of all, the disappearance of six million Jews who once lived in hundreds of cities and towns throughout Europe.

Answer key, p. 199

F. **Words That Do Double Duty.** The following words in Lessons 37–42 are capable of serving as more than one part of speech.

surplus (n., adj.)	negative (n., adj.)
deliberate (adj., v.)	pension (n., v.)
summit (n., adj.)	parole (n., v.)
swarm (n., v.)	snub (n., v.)
wobble (n., v.)	ballot (n., v.)

Make up two sentences for each of the above words, showing how it could be used as two different parts of speech.

Examples: My little brother seems to have a *surplus* (adj.) of energy that he must exhaust before he goes to sleep.

Our recent walkathon left us with a handy *surplus* (n.) that we will donate to a charitable cause.

100 Frequently Misspelled Words

A good technique for mastering these spelling words is to write each one five times and then to have a friend ask you to spell them aloud. Note the clues to correct spelling.

1. access (cc, ss)	**51. laudable** (aud)
2. acme (no k)	**52. lax** (ax)
3. acquainted (cq)	**53. license** (c, s)
4. adroit (oi)	**54. lieutenant** (ieu)
5. alleged (lleg)	**55. lightning** (bolt, no e)
6. ascend (sc)	**56. legion** (gi)
7. asset (ss)	**57. lethal** (al)
8. barrel (rr, l)	**58. liable** (able)
9. benefited (one t)	**59. medieval** (eval)
10. bias (ia)	**60. mortgage** (t)
11. bigot (got)	**61. naive** (ai)
12. cache (ch)	**62. noise** (oi)
13. cemetery (three e's)	**63. occasionally** (cc, ll)
14. changeable (ea)	**64. oust** (ou)
15. circuit (ui)	**65. pamphlet** (ph)
16. coerce (oe)	**66. parallel** (ll, l)
17. colossal (l, ss, l)	**67. perceive** (ei)
18. concur (cur)	**68. personnel** (nn, l)
19. cope (no k)	**69. phlegm** (ph, gm)
20. coup (ou)	**70. picnicking** (ck)
21. dearth (ear)	**71. plague** (gue)
22. debris (ris)	**72. possession** (ss, ss)
23. defendant (ant)	**73. procedure** (ced)
24. devout (ou)	**74. puny** (un)
25. diptheria (pth)	**75. questionnaire** (nn)
26. discern (sc)	**76. quell** (qu)
27. dismissal (miss)	**77. racist** (ci)
28. dissent (ss)	**78. raze** (z)
29. dupe (up)	**79. realm** (ea)
30. elapse (pse)	**80. remembrance** (ran)
31. embarrass (rr, ss)	**81. rue** (ue)
32. existence (en)	**82. scissors** (ciss)
33. exult (ul)	**83. seize** (ei)
34. fatal (tal)	**84. senile** (ile)
35. forfeit (ei)	**85. senior** (io)
36. frail (ai)	**86. sergeant** (ser)
37. frugal (al)	**87. siege** (ie)
38. fulfill (l, ll)	**88. sophomore** (pho)
39. grammar (mma)	**89. source** (our)
40. guarantee (ua, tee)	**90. sulphur** (phur)
41. harass (r, ss)	**91. superintendent** (ent)
42. hoard (oa)	**92. surge** (ur)
43. hoax (oa)	**93. surpass** (pass)
44. hosiery (ie)	**94. usurp** (sur)
45. inane (ane)	**95. vacuum** (uu)
46. indispensable (able)	**96. venom** (om)
47. irate (ate)	**97. vigil** (il)
48. jewelry (lr)	**98. waitress** (ess)
49. junior (io)	**99. yield** (ie)
50. labeled (l)	**100. yolk** (lk)

BONUS LESSON

125 More Difficult (But Essential) Words
Move up on the vocabulary ladder. Try adding these specially selected words to your collection.

1. abate (ə bāt') to decrease in force or intensity; to decrease in value or amount
- a. When the wind changed direction, the air grew quiet and the storm **abated**.
- b. The salesman could not **abate** the price of the automobile, without conferring with the manager.
- c. Although the doctors hoped the epidemic would **abate**, the number of hospital admissions did not decrease.

2. abhor (ab hôr') to regard with extreme distaste
- a. Many people **abhor** handling snakes, but most snakes are quite harmless.
- b. The interior decorator **abhorred** the thought of painting the kitchen walls purple.
- c. After dining at the Japanese restaurant, the tourist exclaimed, "I love most Japanese food, but I **abhor** eating uncooked fish."

3. acclimate (ak' lim āt) to adapt, to adjust
- a. It is difficult for the human body to **acclimate** to abrupt changes in temperature.
- b. Dogs and cats usually **acclimate** easily to living in a home with small children.
- c. Most zookeepers think animals **acclimate** successfully to a simulated natural environment.

4. adage (ad' aj) a proverb
- a. We often find out that the **adage** "haste makes waste" is true.
- b. Parents often teach their children by reciting **adages**, such as, "a stitch in time saves nine."
- c. If you want to get rich, remember the **adage**, "a penny saved is a penny earned."

5. aegis (ē' jis) defense; sponsorship, a shield
- a. In Greek mythology Apollo, the god of the sun, carried an **aegis** that provoked fear in his opponents.
- b. Freedom of speech is sheltered by the **aegis** of the Constitution's first amendment.
- c. Under the **aegis** of the fire department, the Fourth of July committee arranged a magnificent fireworks display.

6. affluent (af' flu ənt) rich; having material wealth
- a. Some parents think that children are living in an **affluent** society with too many games and toys.
- b. The number of **affluent** people with assets of more than one billion dollars has increased every year.
- c. The recent growth of the computer industry created a large number of **affluent** company presidents.

7. alleviate (ə lēv' ē āt) relieve; lessen; make more bearable
- a. Pharmaceutical manufacturers are always seeking new drugs to **alleviate** pain.
- b. After a death in a family, counselors may be able to **alleviate** the sorrow of the deceased's relatives.
- c. The government tried to **alleviate** the problems faced by the people who lost their homes during the mountain wildfire.

8. altercation (äl ter kā' shən) a noisy angry argument
- a. The judge cited the two lawyers with contempt after their lengthy **altercation** in the courtroom.
- b. A policeman had to intervene when two motorists became involved in an **altercation** after a traffic accident.
- c. During a major league baseball playoff game, a pitch that struck the batter started an **altercation** that involved players from both teams.

9. antithesis (ãn' ti thə səs) opposite; contrast
   a.   Some religions teach that free will, that is, our ability to determine our actions, is the **antithesis** of fatalism.
   b.   Hitting below the belt in a boxing match is the **antithesis** of fair play.
   c.   The **antithesis** of live Broadway dramatic theater is a television sitcom.

10. atheist (ā' thē ist) a person who denies the existence of God
   a.   The **atheist** is quite different from the agnostic, who is not sure whether there is a God.
   b.   During World War II, soldiers in life-threatening combat often proclaimed: "There are no **atheists** in foxholes."
   c.   When the judge asked the witness to swear that she would tell the truth, the witness replied that she could not, since she was an **atheist**.

11. avid (a' vid) extremely eager, enthusiastic
   a.   The candidate was accused of having an **avid** desire for personal power.
   b.   High school English teachers encourage their students to be **avid** readers.
   c.   The football team's **avid** approach to training resulted in a winning season.

12. belligerent (bə lij' ə rənt) a fighting attitude; warlike
   a.   The boxing coach urged his fighter to be more **belligerent** at the beginning of the match.
   b.   The most **belligerent** television talk show guests were in favor of the war.
   c.   A truce was arranged between the two **belligerent** nations.

13. benevolent (bə ne' vō lənt) disposed to doing good; generous; charitable
   a.   The **benevolent** heat of the sun is used to supply large parts of the worldwide solar power.
   b.   Mother Theresa's **benevolent** work in Third World nations made her famous.
   c.   **Benevolent** philanthropies have contributed millions of dollars toward cancer research.

14. benign (bə nīn') favorable; good-hearted; kind
   a.   Although there can be fierce rainstorms and windstorms and droughts in California, the weather there is usually **benign**.
   b.   Some tumors are virulent and therefore must be treated at once, but many tumors are of a **benign** nature.
   c.   The **benign** personality of the professor made him a favorite on campus.

15. bizarre (bə zär') fantastically out of the ordinary; odd
   a.   The church entrance was decorated with **bizarre** figures of outlandish gargoyles.
   b.   Many people believe in **bizarre** superstitions, such as, don't walk under ladders.
   c.   Writers for television dramas hope to attract viewers by offering **bizarre** stories.

16. cajole (kə jōl') to persuade with flattery; to coax
   a.   In order to convince his girlfriend to marry him, the man **cajoled** her by using sweet words and soft tones.
   b.   The candidate for mayor, a skillful speaker, **cajoled** the voters to vote for him.
   c.   When the small child ran into the busy street, the mother sometimes **cajoled** and sometimes threatened the child to be careful.

17. candor (kãn dər') honest, or sincere expression
   a.   An open mind and **candor** are qualities that we look for in a candidate for president.
   b.   It was the professor's placid temper and **candor** that made him the most popular teacher on campus.
   c.   A film critic must exhibit exceptional **candor** when writing a review of a motion picture.

18. caustic (käs tik') extremely sarcastic; corrosive
   a.   In the debate one speaker attacked his opponent with sharp, **caustic** remarks.
   b.   Automobiles wear out quickly from the **caustic** effect of salt spread on icy roads.
   c.   By avoiding **caustic**, stingingly mean humor, the television talk host was able to conduct a successful interview.

19. chronological (krän ə lä' ji kl) arranged in the order of time
   a. The writer of the famous novelist's biography needed to determine the **chronological** order of the subject's novel.
   b. Scholars have differed about the **chronological** order of Shakespeare's plays.
   c. In tracing the effectiveness of the knee operation he recently completed, the physician kept a **chronological** record of the patient's rehabilitation therapy.

20. clandestine (klan des' tən) secret; undercover
   a. Romeo and Juliet had a **clandestine** meeting under her balcony because their parents did not approve of their romance.
   b. James Bond has a series of **clandestine** affairs with beautiful women in most of the James Bond films.
   c. The police sometimes use **clandestine** sting operations in order to reduce criminal activity.

21. cliché (klē shā') an expression that has become overly familiar or commonplace
   a. Most television programs have become **clichéd**, following worn-out formulas.
   b. The writer's stories were rejected by the magazine editor because they contained plots that were filled with **clichés**.
   c. The new wave of architects have been trying to vary the same, lookalike, old-fashioned **clichéd** house plans.

22. coerce (kō ės') to restrain or dominate by force
   a. Policemen were stationed along the parade route to **coerce** the crowd and keep order.
   b. When the prisoners would not obey the guards, they were **coerced** into their cells.
   c. Since the candidate for office could not **coerce** the voters to vote for her, she used persuasion.

23. coherent (kō hir' ənt) logical; consistent; understandable
   a. The president wanted to write a **coherent** speech about the economy that would be easy to understand.
   b. The creative writing instructor explained that a good story should be **coherent**; it should be focused on one theme, and not divert from that theme.
   c. The motion picture director told the writer that the screenplay was not **coherent** because there were too many scenes that were not related to the plot.

24. condone (kən dōn') to excuse; pardon; overlook
   a. Public school authorities do not **condone** the use of force by the teacher.
   b. Because the basketball star led the team to a championship, many of his social shortcomings were **condoned**.
   c. Most dog trainers do not **condone** the use of spiked choke collars to control dogs.

25. connive (kə nīv') to conspire; to cooperate secretly to perform a wrong act
   a. It was revealed that foreign spies **connived** with criminals to gather information about atomic weapons.
   b. Even though the legislators opposed the bill to use government money to fund an obsolete military weapon, they **connived** with other members of congress to pass the bill.
   c. In planning the bank robbery, the thieves **connived** with the drivers of the armored truck to drive away after they made their delivery.

26. corpulent (kôr' pū lənt) having a large bulky body; obese; fat
   a. A recent survey revealed that many Americans are **corpulent** because they eat large portions at meals.
   b. Nutritionists disagree about which foods have made young children so **corpulent**.
   c. Fast-food restaurants have denied that their food has made Americans **corpulent**.

27. covert (kō vėrt') not openly shown; secret; clandestine
   a. The lioness placed her kittens in a **covert** cave to keep them safe.
   b. Before introducing herself to the charming-looking man at the party, the young woman glanced at him **covertly**.
   c. To maintain the security of the nation, **covert** investigations by the CIA are sometimes necessary.

28. **criterion** (krī tə' rē ən) a standard on which a judgment may be based; a measure
    a. Tasty food is the **criterion** for a popular fast-food restaurant
    b. Professional organizations usually determine the major **criterion** for membership.
    c. Motion picture reviewers have always maintained that fast action is the **criterion** for an Academy Award nomination.

29. **culpable** (kəl' pə bəl) guilty; able to be blamed
    a. A trial will take place to determine whether the Olympic committee member who was accused of bribery is actually **culpable**.
    b. Since the company treasurer was out of the country at the time the money was stolen, he was not **culpable**.
    c. The hunter thought the field he hunted on was not private; therefore he was not **culpable** of trespassing.

30. **cursory** (kûr' sə rē) rapidly and superficially performed; hasty
    a. During the **cursory** inspection of the restaurant kitchen, the inspector did not find any violations of the rules for cleanliness.
    b. Because the students had given the textbook only a **cursory** reading, they were unable to pass the examination.
    c. Since the train passed so quickly through the magnificent gorge, the tourist could get only a **cursory** glimpse of its beauty.

31. **decadent** (dek' ə dənt) marked by decay or decline
    a. A large amount of money was donated by the philanthropist, who hoped to have the **decadent** opera house restored.
    b. The rooms in the house we rented were old, worn out, dark, and dusty; there was a **decadent** air about them.
    c. Some art critics pointed out that modern paintings lacked vitality and freshness, and that a **decadent** artistic age had begun.

32. **devious** (dē' vē əs) cunning; deceptive; roundabout
    a. Since reindeer cannot be steered when pulling a sled, they will always take a **devious** route to the driver's destination.
    b. It was difficult to determine the truth of the witness' contradictory statements because of his **devious** manner.
    c. When the professor's **devious** lecture constantly strayed from the main topic, no one in the classroom understood what he was saying.

33. **digress** (d ī gres') to turn aside from the main subject; stray
    a. The members of the debating team were warned that they would lose the debate if they continued to **digress** from the proposed subject.
    b. After the minister had spoken for ten minutes about the pleasures of playing basketball, he said he had **digressed** too long and should return to his sermon.
    c. The small creek in front of our house **digressed** from the main river that had been formed by the melting snow on the mountains.

34. **dormant** (dôr' mənt) inactive; temporarily suspended
    a. The **dormant** buds of certain types of plants may remain buried during the winter and still be able to grow in the spring.
    b. The middle-aged musician who had just become famous said that talent may lie **dormant** during one's youth.
    c. The injured worker's lawyer asked the judge why his client's claim had lain **dormant** for so many months.

35. **duress** (də ress') forcible restraint: coercion
    a. During World War II, American prisoners of war in Bataan were marched 55 miles under **duress**.
    b. After arguing violently with the referee, the basketball coach was escorted out of the area under **duress**.
    c. It is illegal for a person to sign a contract while under a form of **duress**, such as loss of life, imprisonment, or fine.

36. egotist (ē' gō tist) a person who talks too much about himself; a conceited person
   a. Because **egotists** are always talking about their own lives, their friends become bored in their company.
   b. **Egoists** rarely listen to advice from friends or family because they feel certain that they know everything.
   c. The **egoist's** e-mail address was "thegreatest.com."

37. elusive (ēlo͞o' səv) tending to evade; hard to understand or define
   a. Despite years of research by famous specialists, the cure for cancer has proved to be **elusive**.
   b. When questioned by the police, the suspect, who had actually committed the crime, gave his questioners **elusive**, insubstantial answers.
   c. None of the football players on the all-star team could tackle the famous quarterback, one of the most **elusive** ball carriers in professional football.

38. emulate (em' ū lāt) to copy or imitate
   a. The Microsoft Windows system is regarded as the most efficient program for personal computers; therefore, all software companies want to **emulate** it.
   b. The basketball player admired his coach so much that he **emulated** his manner of speaking, walking, and dressing
   c. Eager for success, the newly hired newspaper reported tried to **emulate** the managing editor's writing style.

39. eulogy (ū' lə jē) a speech or writing of high praise
   a. The **eulogy** the student delivered at his teacher's funeral brought tears to the eyes of the mourners.
   b. At her inauguration the newly elected governor's **eulogy** listed the accomplishments of the previous governor.
   c. When the famous author Ernest Hemingway was thought to have died in an airplane accident, he was amused to read many **eulogies** in the newspapers.

40. exacerbate (eks as' ə bāt) to make more violent, bitter, or severe
   a. The pain in the pitcher's sore elbow was **exacerbated** when he pitched a full game after only one day's rest.
   b. In an argument with the basketball referee, the loud voice of the player **exacerbated** the intensity of the disagreement.
   c. The mood of the protesters was **exacerbated** when the police would not allow them to march down the main street of the town.

41. exhort (eks ôrt') to incite by argument or advice, urge strongly
   a. The candidate **exhorted** members of his party to be certain to vote for him on election day.
   b. In his speech, the president **exhorted** citizens to ask what they could do for their country.
   c. When the actors on the stage could not be heard by the director, who was sitting in the balcony of the theater, they were **exhorted** to speak louder.

42. expedite (eks' pə dīt) to execute promptly; speed up
   a. The company's large number of orders were **expedited** when the shipping clerk decided to use an airborne delivery company.
   b. By passing the initiative to raise ten million dollars for a new library, the voters **expedited** the building schedule.
   c. The new dam on Provo River will **expedite** the flow of water to the fields where sugar beets are grown.

43. fallacious (fə lā' shəs) deceiving or misleading
   a. Evidence that rests solely upon isolated facts is usually **fallacious**.
   b. The medical study was carelessly prepared, full of inaccurate data, and was, therefore, **fallacious**.
   c. In a desperate effort to gather votes, the candidate employed **fallacious**, invalid, unreasonable arguments.

44. fracas (frā' kəs) a noisy quarrel; brawl
   a. When we see more than two professional wrestlers in the ring at one time, we might think we are watching a **fracas** more than a wrestling match.
   b. A **fracas** took place between the two students after they bumped against each other on the stairs.
   c. Because there is so much pushing and shoving in professional ice hockey games, they rarely end without a **fracas**.

45. furtive (fėr' təv) underhanded; secret; stealthy
   a. Although photographing paintings was prohibited in the museum, the tourist **furtively** snapped a picture.
   b. Having been taught by her mother not to stare at anyone, she allowed herself only a **furtive** glance at the motion picture star.
   c. Spy stories always seem to feature a **furtive** and sinister enemy agent.

46. garrulous (ga' rū ləs) talkative; wordy
   a. The talk show host could not seem to stop the **garrulous** guest from telling one uninteresting story after another.
   b. The invited speaker's lengthy, **garrulous** speech at the graduation exercises put some members of the audience to sleep.
   c. If you need to take a nap, hope that you are not sitting next to a **garrulous** neighbor on a long airplane flight.

47. gesticulate (jes tik' ū lāt) to make gestures especially when speaking
   a. Englishmen think that French people speak louder and **gesticulate** more than English people.
   b. The candidate for the United States Senate **gesticulated** violently with his hands and arms in order to add passion to his remarks.
   c. When U.S. President Harry Truman wanted to stress an opinion, he **gesticulated** by making a chopping movement with his open hands.

48. heterogeneous (het ə ro jē' nəs) consisting of dissimilar ingredients; mixed
   a. Teaching a **heterogeneous** group of skiers, beginners, and intermediates in one class, for example, is extremely difficult.
   b. The entomologist's **heterogeneous** collection of insects, featuring both flying and crawling insects, was on display at the museum.
   c. The **heterogeneous** religious population of postwar Iraq is made up of Shiite Muslims, Sunni Muslims, and Christians.

49. imbibe (im bī b') to receive into the mind and retain; drink
   a. The more cigarettes the inmates smoked, the more they wanted to **imbibe** brandy and soda.
   b. The roots of plants are able to **imbibe** fluids from the soil, although we cannot see it happening.
   c. The heat of the sun's rays was **imbibed** by the sunbathers.

50. impasse (im' pas) no obvious escape; deadlock
   a. The two negotiators in the newspaper strike reached an **impasse** when they could not agree on a salary package for the delivery personnel.
   b. At the edge of the river, the general realized that his army was at an **impasse** because the bridge had been destroyed.
   c. As soon as the bank robber found himself in a dead end alley without a way out, he realized that he was at an **impasse**.

51. impeccable (im pek' əbl) free from fault or blame; flawless
   a. Although we had studied French for only one year, our pronunciation was **impeccable**.
   b. After driving a bus for 40 years without an accident, the driver received an award for **impeccable** service.
   c. When you engage an interior decorator, you should be able to be sure of **impeccable** taste in furniture and window treatment.

52. incarcerate (in kä' sə rāt) to put in prison
   a. After the jury pronounced the defendant guilty, the judge determined that the defendant should be **incarcerated** for ten years.
   b. The bank robbers **incarcerated** the bank manager and the hostages in the large vault while they made their escape.
   c. Many lawyers believe that children under the age of 16 should not be **incarcerated** in the same prisons as adults.

53. incriminate (in krim' ə nāt) to show evidence of involvement in a crime
   a. When faced with the fear of being sent to jail, criminals will sometimes offer evidence that will **incriminate** their associates.
   b. Because the detectives believed a murder had been committed, they searched the house for **incriminating** information.
   c. The investigators found an **incriminating** e-mail message on the suspect's computer, offering to plan a bank robbery.

54. incumbent (in kumb' ənt) the holder of an office; occupant
   a. The City Council voted to provide an adequate salary for the mayor, so that the **incumbent** could live comfortably.
   b. It is generally believed that in a congressional election **incumbents** have a significant advantage over their opponent.
   c. The minister of the church was eager to take over the duties of the present **incumbent**.

55. indigent (in' di jint) poor; impoverished
   a. The **indigent** population in the United States has benefited from the liberal welfare laws.
   b. During the nineteenth century each town or parish was responsible for its own disabled and **indigent** citizens.
   c. The wealthy Alaskan businessman set up a philanthropic organization designed to help the **indigent** in Alaska find jobs.

56. indolent (in' də lənt) disliking activity; habitually lazy
   a. The fact is, said the character in the novel, I don't like to exert myself; I have a naturally **indolent** disposition.
   b. The **indolent** boy scout would not take part in the difficult, hard task of gathering wood for the campfire.
   c. It was his **indolent** nature that allowed him to lie in the sun all day and avoid any kind of sport or game.

57. inept (in ept') lacking in fitness or aptitude; incompetent
   a. The **inept** lawyer was fired when his client found out he had not graduated from law school.
   b. When it was revealed that the truck driver was not wearing his eyeglasses, the police investigating the accident reported that he was **inept**.
   c. It was obvious that the battleship captain's **inept** maneuvers to avoid ramming the pier were going to cause an accident.

58. innocuous (in nək' ū əs) harmless
   a. You can add a cool green color to foods safely by using the **innocuous** coloring in spinach.
   b. People who keep snakes as pets wonder why so many of their friends tend to fear one of the most **innocuous** animals.
   c. Most bungee jumpers think it is an exciting experience, and a relatively safe, **innocuous** sport.

59. insolent (in' sō lənt) exhibiting boldness; impudent; arrogant
   a. **Insolent** behavior toward an officer in the armed forces will result in a court martial.
   b. When the taxi driver received a small tip from his customer, she gave him an **insolent**, haughty stare.
   c. The personnel manager of the company decided to fire the **insolent**, disrespectful sales manager for arguing with a customer.

60. intrepid (in tre' pəd) fearless; brave; bold
   a. During the forest fire in the San Bernardino Mountains, the firefighters displayed **intrepid** courage when they saved the children trapped in a burning house.
   b. In the Special Olympics the handicapped skiers showed **intrepid** determination when racing on the steep slopes.
   c. Trapeze artists in the circus perform **intrepid** maneuvers high above the circus floor.

61. inundate (in' ən dāt) to cover with a flood; overflow; overwhelm
   a. Some educators believe that it is never too early to **inundate** young children with a love of music.
   b. The gardener was chagrined to find that the owner of the house had **inundated** the cactus plant with too much water.
   c. If you watch television, be prepared to be **inundated** by a myriad of advertisements.

62. irrelevant (i rel' ə vant) not relating to the subject at hand
   a. Earl's **irrelevant** remarks embarrassed his wife at the party.
   b. The lawyer objected to the testimony, claiming it was **irrelevant**.
   c. Since we were discussing recipes, Chloe's cosmetics comment was **irrelevant**.

63. itinerary (ī tin' ə rer ē) a travel plan; proposed route of a journey
   a. The **itinerary** for the class trip would start in Buffalo.
   b. No matter what our **itinerary** says, Dad has the last word about our destination.
   c. Our **itinerary** indicates that if it's Tuesday, it must be Paris.

64. judicious (jōō dish' əs) showing good judgment
   a. A **judicious** investment brought Carlos considerable profit.
   b. King Solomon is said to have made a **judicious** decision.
   c. Dropping physics turned out to be a **judicious** move on my part.

65. lament (lə ment') to mourn; express grief
   a. The national **lament** for the dead leader was genuine.
   b. A loud **lament** was heard when the grades were posted.
   c. Do something in haste and **lament** in leisure.

66. lethargy (leth' ər jē) forgetfulness; drowsy indifference
   a. We could not arouse Irwin from his state of **lethargy**.
   b. After a big meal, I sometimes give in to **lethargy**.
   c. Shaking off his usual **lethargy**, Spencer got right to work.

67. lucid (lōō' sid) easily understood; clear; mentally sound
   a. Professor White's explanations are always commendably **lucid**.
   b. I have never heard a **lucid** explanation of Einstein's theory.
   c. The detective's **lucid** analysis led him to the murderer.

68. lucrative (lōō' kra tiv) profitable
   a. The business that had been so **lucrative** was now bankrupt.
   b. Edna's investment in real estate was happily **lucrative**.
   c. When his invention proved to be **lucrative**, Ralph retired.

69. ludicrous (lōō' di kras) silly; absurd
   a. Teachers hear many flimsy excuses but Andre's was truly **ludicrous**.
   b. "I find your proposal to be **ludicrous**," Rosita's boss declared.
   c. It's simply **ludicrous** to think that a copper bracelet could cure arthritis.

70. magnanimous (mag nan' ə məs) unselfish; generous
   a. Bertha's **magnanimous** act won praise from the community.
   b. In a **magnanimous** ruling, Judge Dicker released the sick convict.
   c. It's **magnanimous** of my cousin to support an orphan in Kenya.

71. malevolent (mə lev′ ə lənt) evil
   a.   Warren's **malevolent** behavior was attributed to his illness.
   b.   Dickens' portrayal of the **malevolent** Uriah Heep is a masterpiece.
   c.   None of us were aware of Murdoch's **malevolent** intentions.

72. mediate (mē′ dē āt) to bring about a settlement; resolve differences
   a.   Lawyer Harper was asked by both sides to **mediate**.
   b.   When my sister and I quarrel, Mom steps in to **mediate**.
   c.   The **mediator's** ruling was seen as favorable to management.

73. metaphor (met′ ə fôr) figure of speech in which different things are compared without using the words <u>as</u> or <u>like</u>
   a.   Her "battleship husband" sailed into the room is a **metaphor**.
   b.   Good authors often use **metaphors** in their prose.
   c.   In a beautiful **metaphor**, the child was likened to a butterfly.

74. meticulous (mə tik′ yə ləs) very careful about details
   a.   The **meticulous** housewife was hard to please.
   b.   Professor Harbage gave **meticulous** attention to our portfolios.
   c.   When packing parachutes, one must be **meticulous**.

75. militant (mil′ ə tənt) ready to fight; warlike
   a.   We are **militant** in defense of our freedom.
   b.   Phil's **militant** posture in the schoolyard kept the bullies away.
   c.   **Militant** parents picketed in front of the district office.

76. morbid (môr′ bid) unhealthy; pertaining to disease; gruesome
   a.   Doctor Grill spared us the **morbid** details.
   b.   I was in the mood for a comedy, but the **morbid** tone of the movie did not help me.
   c.   Poe's poem, "The Raven," strikes me as totally **morbid**.

77. mundane (mun dān′) concerned with the ordinary
   a.   The president has little time for **mundane** matters.
   b.   **Mundane** details bore me.
   c.   I hate biographies when they focus on **mundane** events.

78. nefarious (nə far′ ē əs) wicked; sinful; evil
   a.   The **nefarious** deeds of the serial killer shocked the nation.
   b.   Mr. Hyde committed a string of **nefarious** murders.
   c.   District Attorney Trop labeled the Hogans as **nefarious** criminals.

79. nemesis (nem′ ə səs) an unbeatable rival; person or thing that punishes
   a.   Roger can't beat me in chess because I'm his **nemesis**.
   b.   Acting as Jean Valjean's **nemesis**, Javert pursued him relentlessly.
   c.   Little Bellmore High, our **nemesis**, whipped us again.

80. nomad (nō′ mad) wanderer
   a.   Having lived in six different states, you might call us **nomads**.
   b.   The **nomadic** tribe constantly searched for fresh water.
   c.   Since buying the mobile home, we live the lives of **nomads**.

81. nonchalant (non′ shə lənt) cool; indifferent; calmly unconcerned
   a.   Surprisingly, Lorenzo took the news in a **nonchalant** manner.
   b.   We were all excited about the game but Eileen remained **nonchalant**.
   c.   The actress puffed on her cigarette in a **nonchalant** fashion.

82. nostalgia (no stal′ jə) yearning for the past
   a.   A wave of **nostalgia** swept over us at Thanksgiving time.
   b.   Giving in to **nostalgia**, Susan wept for the days of her youth.
   c.   In the poem, Miniver Cheevy had **nostalgic** yearnings for the Middle Ages.

83. oblivion (ə bliv' ē ən) a state of being forgotten; unaware of what is going on
   a.   His once-famous novel has now sunk into **oblivion**.
   b.   Ella rescued that song from **oblivion**.
   c.   The candidate arose from **oblivion** to become the leading contender.

84. obsolete (ob sə lēt') no longer in use; worn out
   a.   The government is auctioning **obsolete** computers.
   b.   It seems that typewriters are now considered **obsolete**.
   c.   New medicines have rendered some of the standard pills **obsolete**.

85. odious (ō' dē əs) hateful; disgusting
   a.   Violet was upset by Joe's **odious** remarks.
   b.   The zookeeper's **odious** treatment of the animals got him fired.
   c.   Shelley's **odious** table manners caused the breakup of our friendship.

86. omnipotent (om nip' ə tənt) all-powerful
   a.   In his tiny country, the king was **omnipotent**.
   b.   The successful police chief was **omnipotent** in our town.
   c.   **Omnipotent** is the word of the comic book dictator.

87. onus (ō' nəs) burden; obligation
   a.   The hospital bore the **onus** for the patient's death.
   b.   My partner reluctantly agreed to share the **onus** for our bankruptcy.
   c.   Judge Meyers ruled that the **onus** for the fire was correctly placed on the security guard.

88. ostensible (ə sten' sə bəl) apparent; on the surface; professed
   a.   The **ostensible** reason for the investment was to help the airline.
   b.   **Ostensibly**, Alec took the job to gain experience.
   c.   I refused to believe Maria's **ostensible** innocence.

89. panacea (pan' ə sē ə) cure-all; remedy for everything
   a.   Researchers are close to finding a **panacea** for asthma.
   b.   We cannot give up the search for a **panacea** for Middle East peace.
   c.   The drug was useful, but it was no **panacea** for the troublesome disease.

90. paradox (par' ə doks) statement that seems to contradict itself
   a.   Calling the coward the bravest man in the room is a **paradox**.
   b.   It was **paradoxical** for the weakest team to be leading the league.
   c.   In the state with the lowest yearly rainfall, the downpour was a **paradox**.

91. pariah (pə' rī ə) outcast; person who is shunned by others
   a.   Labeled a **pariah** by his colleagues, Davis resigned from the company.
   b.   Formerly respected as a businessman, today Arnold is regarded as a **pariah**.
   c.   For falsifying his stories, the reporter became a **pariah**.

92. parsimonious (pär sə mō' nē əs) stingy, cheap
   a.   The millionaire resented being called **parsimonious**.
   b.   **Parsimonious** all his life, Miller left all his wealth to the Red Cross.
   c.   "I prefer 'thrifty' to '**parsimonious**,'" my uncle said.

93. paucity (pô' sə tē) shortage; scarceness
   a.   Because of the **paucity** of migrant workers, the fruit remained unpicked.
   b.   The critics referred to the **paucity** of dancing talent in the show.
   c.   There was no **paucity** of courage in the Marine group.

94. penitent (pen' ə tənt) sorry for wrongdoing and willing to make amends
   a.   In the principal's office, the **penitent** sophomore confessed.
   b.   The parole board sensed that Evans was **penitent** and gave him a break.
   c.   When his sloppy play led to our loss, the quarterback was **penitent**.

95. pensive (pen' siv) thoughtful; thinking seriously
   a. In a **pensive** mood, Picasso started to paint his masterpiece.
   b. Dean Wermuth became **pensive** as she listened to the faculty complaints.
   c. "A penny for your thoughts," Clara said to her **pensive** husband.

96. perjury (pûr' jə rē) lying under oath
   a. Carole's attorney cautioned her about committing **perjury**.
   b. Facing **perjury** charges, Monte confessed tearfully.
   c. If there was one crime that the judge detested, it was **perjury**.

97. peruse (pə rōōz') to read carefully
   a. "I'd like you to **peruse** these documents tonight," my boss said.
   b. After I **peruse** the chapter, I'll deal with the questions.
   c. Eloise never signed anything that she hadn't **perused** at least twice.

98. phlegmatic (fleg mat' ik) slow to respond; not easily excited
   a. Ben's **phlegmatic** behavior irritated his wife no end.
   b. Because Darryl was generally **phlegmatic**, we were surprised by his lively response.
   c. Someone so **phlegmatic** could never succeed in our high-pressure business.

99. plagiarize (plā' je rīz) using another's words as your own
   a. The author was embarrassed when he was found to have **plagiarized** widely.
   b. If you **plagiarize**, you are committing a theft.
   c. Van Dyck took out a newspaper ad to apologize for his **plagiarism**.

100. plausible (plo' zə bəl) seemingly true; apparently believable
   a. I'll admit that Cabot's alibi was **plausible**.
   b. The scientist's **plausible** theory collapsed under serious scrutiny.
   c. There was only one thing wrong with Ron's **plausible** explanation—it was a lie.

101. posthumous (pos' cho məs) arising or occurring after one's death
   a. The **posthumous** award was presented to Hartley's widow.
   b. Melville's last novel was published **posthumously**.
   c. Van Gogh's fame grew **posthumously**.

102. precocious (pri kō' shəs) showing advanced development at an early age
   a. The literal meaning of **precocious** is half-baked.
   b. Since Lulu was so **precocious**, she was skipped twice at school.
   c. Only 14, the **precocious** violinist stopped the show.

103. potpourri (pō poo rē') mixture; medley
   a. The composer performed a **potpourri** of his hits.
   b. A **potpourri** of Faulkner's stories was a welcome gift.
   c. Reading a **potpourri** of Llncoln's speeches heightened my appreciation of Honest Abe.

104. procrastinate (prə kras' tə nāt) delay
   a. We were warned not to **procrastinate** about doing the term paper.
   b. Jerry is quite forceful but his kid brother loves to **procrastinate**.
   c. One cannot **procrastinate** when paying income taxes.

105. prognosticate (prog' nos tə kāt) predict
   a. The thunder and lightning **prognosticated** a huge storm.
   b. Judging from his stock market losses, my uncle can't **prognosticate** too well.
   c. **Prognosticating** the Academy Award winners is Marge's favorite pastime.

106. prolific (prə lif' ik) producing much; fertile
   a. The **prolific** author produced three best-sellers last year.
   b. We adopted the **prolific** cat's entire litter.
   c. Renoir was one of the world's most **prolific** painters.

107. quandary (kwon' də rē) dilemma; condition of doubt
   a. When he had to choose a new car, my father was in a **quandary**.
   b. Eloise admitted to being in a **quandary** over a new hairstyle.
   c. Vince was in a **quandary** when his neighbor asked to borrow his guitar.

108. rabid (rab' id) fanatical; furious; infected with rabies
   a. The **rabid** fans caused a riot when their soccer team lost.
   b. Clyde and Cleo are **rabid** antique enthusiasts.
   c. Having been bitten by a possibly **rabid** dog, Jeff needed immediate treatment.

109. rendezvous (rän' dā vōō) meeting place; meeting by arrangement
   a. We will **rendezvous** with the 82nd Airborne at dawn.
   b. Our secret **rendezvous** turned out to be not so secret.
   c. Let's **rendezvous** at the hotel's swimming pool.

110. rescind (ri sind') to cancel; to repeal
   a. General Moore tried to **rescind** his order but it was too late.
   b. Congress plans to **rescind** the unworkable new tax code.
   c. Before his appointment could be **rescinded**, Li Chen withdrew.

111. sanguine (sang' gwən) confident; hopeful; optimistic
   a. I'm not **sanguine** about our team's chances this year.
   b. **Sanguine** about Wall Street, Alfredo invested heavily.
   c. Paulette wasn't **sanguine** about her SAT score.

112. simile (sim' ə lē) figure of speech using *as* or *like* in which two different things are compared
   a. The poet's strength was in his creation of memorable **similes**.
   b. To say that a joke is as old as the hills is to use a tired **simile**.
   c. Mrs. Ford cautioned our English class about an overreliance on **similes**.

113. skeptic (skep' tik) one who doubts consistently; one who is hard to convince
   a. I couldn't convince Uncle Henry, a born **skeptic**.
   b. Ruth is **skeptical** about Sid's promise.
   c. Everyone is convinced except Bradley the **skeptic**.

114. slander (slan' dər) false oral statement designed to damage a person's reputation
   a. Those who have tried to **slander** the actor have paid for it in court.
   b. Calling Jackson a communist was a cruel **slander**.
   c. Frederick denied that he had committed **slander** but there were witnesses.

115. sporadic (spə rad' ik) occurring at irregular times
   a. **Sporadic** gunfire kept the troops awake all night.
   b. At the end of his speech there was **sporadic** applause.
   c. Dr. Kolitz noted the **sporadic** outbreak of measles in our community.

116. superficial (sōō pər fish' əl) not deep; on the surface only
   a. The play was filled with **superficial** characters.
   b. Since the bullet merely grazed his arm, it was a **superficial** wound.
   c. Despite her **superficial** knowledge of accounting, Eliza got the job.

117. taciturn (tas' ə tûrn) silent; reserved; uncommunicative
   a. **Taciturn** President Coolidge was a man of few words.
   b. Cindy is a great talker, the least **taciturn** person I know.
   c. In court, the **taciturn** witness didn't help the prosecution.

118. terse (tûrs) brief; to the point
   a. Al's **terse** report endeared him to the company president.
   b. The **terse** statement by the bridegroom was "I do."
   c. Normally talkative, Will startled us with his **terse** replies.

119. thwart (thwort) to hinder; block
   a. If you **thwart** Andre, you do it at your risk.
   b. The inmates' attempt to escape was **thwarted** by an alert guard.
   c. It took a Republican filibuster to **thwart** the Democrats' proposal.

120. trite (trīt) overused; commonplace
   a. The compositions' **trite** expressions disappointed the teacher.
   b. "He works like a dog" is a **trite** remark.
   c. It's impossible to find a **trite** description in Sylvia Plath's poetry.

121. utopia (yōō tō' pē ə) paradise; a place where everything is perfect
   a. The reformers hoped to set up a **utopia** in Arizona.
   b. The Garden of Eden's **utopia** was upset by a serpent.
   c. While we were freezing in Maine, our parents were in a warm **utopia** in Florida.

122. vacillate (vas' ə lāt) to waver back and forth
   a. If you **vacillate**, the broker said, the opportunity will disappear.
   b. He who **vacillates** is lost, the proverb says.
   c. Once Anthony's mind is made up, he never **vacillates**.

123. verbose (vər bōs') wordy; using more words than is necessary
   a. The judge cautioned the witness about giving **verbose** replies.
   b. By being **verbose**, Jon had huge phone bills.
   c. I wouldn't mind his being **verbose** if he had something worthwhile to say.

124. vindicate (vin' di kāt) clear; acquit; exonerate
   a. The lawyer asked the jury to **vindicate** his client.
   b. Javier presented his case so skillfully that his actions were **vindicated**.
   c. "Now I feel **vindicated**," the freed man declared.

125. volatile (vol' ə təl) explosive; changeable
   a. The stock market has been quite **volatile** this year.
   b. Bert's family was fearful of his **volatile** moods.
   c. In a **volatile** speech, the dictator incited his people to violence.

Panorama of Words

In this new section, you will find the 504 Words in a variety of sources—newspapers, magazines, TV, speeches, and books. It shows that our select group of vocabulary words has been widely used by all manner of writers.

Most issues of your local newspaper, for example, will contain a number of the words you have met in these pages. Wherever else you come in contact with useful vocabulary words, you are likely to find many of the words that appear in *504 Absolutely Essential Words*.

Now, for a useful summary of what you have learned in these forty-two lessons, read through the Panorama of Words, taking note of the different ways these familiar words are used. Be aware that some of these entries have been adapted or edited.

LESSON 1

1. **abandon** They followed him, racing through the trees for a long distance, but finally, one by one, they had to **abandon** the chase."
   Tarzan of the Apes, Edgar Rice Burroughs.

2. **keen** "When he looked into her eyes, he felt a **keen** sense of enjoyment."
   The Explorer, W. Somerset Maugham.

3. **jealous** "She felt extremely **jealous** of her brother and his friend because they laughed together happily."
   The Girl Who Kicked the Hornest's Nest, Stieg Larsson.

4. **tact** "A number of commenters suggest that Summers' resignation was due to his lack of **tact** in dealing with the faculty."
   BeckerPosner Blog, January 28, 2011.

5. **oath** "She has stated under **oath** that she was pressured to lie about Mooney's job performance in an attempt to get him fired."
   City Weekly, March 1, 2001.

6. **vacant** "They sat down at a **vacant** table and waited for the omelet to be served."
   The Explorer, W. Somerset Maugham.

7. **hardship** "At a time of war and economic **hardship**, the last thing we need is a tax cut for Americans who don't need them."
   Barack Obama's Address, January 25, 2011.

8. **gallant** "The General spoke of the **gallant** work of the people who tried to save the horses from the fire."
   Life on the Mississippi, Mark Twain.

9. **data** "It is just not scientific to take **data** after an explosion and expect it to be meaningful in any way."
   Los Angeles Times, January 28, 2011.

10. **unaccustomed** "The National Hockey League players are **unaccustomed** to different colored uniforms when they play in foreign cities."
    The Daily News, February 24, 2010.

11. **bachelor** "Quiet to the point of shyness and a lifelong **bachelor**, the lawyer needed an outgoing partner to handle the difficult cases."
    Scorpions, Noah Feldman.

12. **quality** "In most countries, where people worry about air **quality** and discuss ways of reducing carbon emissions, coal is not fashionable."
    The Economist, January 27, 2011.

LESSON 2

1. **corpse** "Her husband was sentenced last June to life in prison after being convicted of second-degree murder and abandonment of a **corpse**."
   Los Angeles Times, January 29, 2011.

2. **concealed** "A majority of states require a permit to carry a **concealed** weapon. Only two other states allow concealed weapons."
   New York Times, January 10, 2011.

3. **dismal** "The quarterback wasn't worried when his University of Connecticut Huskies football team suffered through a **dismal** offensive first half."
   mercurynews.com, January 26, 2011.

4. **frigid** "The weather was **frigid** this week, especially in Florida. Air temperatures ranged from the upper 20s to low 50s, and surfers all wore wet suits."
   Times Union, January 29, 2011.

5. **inhabited** "In a certain part of the country there were villages **inhabited** by numerous and angry settlers."
   Life on the Mississippi, Mark Twain.

6. **numb** "At one freezing tailgate party at a Bears playoff game, Jeff Meyer, 32, of Lake in the Hills, said his fingers were 'a little **numb**.'"
   The Hartford Courant, January 16, 2011.

7. **peril** "The **peril** was different, of course, perhaps more clear than ever. We were in the nuclear arms race of the Cold War."
   The Stamford Advocate, January 2, 2011.

8. **recline** "In Toyota's new Crossover, all you had to do is pull the lever on the seat bases and the seatbacks **recline** up to 14 degrees."
   Houston Chronicle, December 3, 2010.

9. **shriek** "They're going to have to find a way to measure decibels to calculate the **shrieks** that greeted the performers at the concert."
   New York Daily News, September 1, 2008.

10. **sinister** "The darkest of Shakespeare's comedies, *Measure for Measure*, combines slapstick comedy with **sinister** dealings."
    Dallas-Fort Worth Register, January 2, 2011.

11. **tempt** "It's a sure thing that fall is in full swing when retailers **tempt** shoppers with special retail bargains."
    Post Kansas, October 26, 2010.

12. **wager** "There will be no-limit poker games at the new casino in Atlantic City, and players will probably **wager** large amounts of money."
    Time magazine, May 8, 2009.

LESSON 3

1. **typical** "The appearance of our visitor was a surprise to me, since I had expected a **typical** country doctor."
   The Hound of the Baskervilles, Sir Arthur Conan Doyle.

2. **minimum** "I am perfectly willing to act as business manager at a **minimum** salary of $500."
   Memoirs of Sherlock Holmes, Sir Arthur Conan Doyle.

3. **scarce** "The homeless population is rising in Jacksonville as affordable housing becomes **scarcer** and assistance options decrease."
   jacksonvilleherald.com, August 31, 2010.

4. **annual** "The two daring explorers then embarked for England, and the Geographical Society of Paris awarded them the society's **annual** medal."
   Five Weeks in a Balloon, Jules Verne.

5. **persuade** "She is perfectly well-bred, indeed, and has the air of a woman of fashion, but no one can **persuade** me to fall in love with her."

   Lady Susan, Jane Austen.

6. **essential** "After the blizzard the mayor came out first with warnings to the public to stay home, except for **essential** trips."

   New York Times, January 20, 2011.

7. **blend** "Having collected an army and concentrated his forces, the general must **blend** the different elements before pitching his camp."

   Art of War, Sun Tzu.

8. **visible** "Everyone got up and began watching the movements of our troops below, as plainly **visible** as if but a stone's throw away."

   War and Peace, Leo Tolstoy.

9. **expensive** "Zeena always came back laden with **expensive** remedies, paying twenty dollars for an electric battery."

   Ethan Frome, Edith Wharton.

10. **talent** "No, I do not have the **talent** for managing people, but I see what ought to be done."   *An Old-Fashioned Girl*, Louisa May Alcott.

11. **devise** "The mice summoned a council to decide how they might best **devise** means of warning themselves of the approach of their great enemy the Cat."   *Fables*, Aesop.

12. **wholesale** "**Wholesale** sales offered fresh evidence that demand strengthened as the holiday shopping season began."

    Reuters, January 12, 2011.

LESSON 4

1. **vapor** "Houseplants give off water **vapor** like a living humidifier, helping the indoor air feel more comfortable."

   latimes.com, January 31, 2011.

2. **eliminate** "Without additional revenue, vital public services may be severely diminished or **eliminated**."   *nydailynews.com*, January 30, 2011.

3. **villain** "He was always a **villain**, smooth-spoken and clever, but a dangerous villain all the same."   *Beyond the City*, Arthur Conan Doyle.

4. **dense** "You can expect the fog to be quite **dense** tonight."

   NBC-TV, Al Roker.

5. **utilize** "He had never before seen such a tool, but he was quick to see its virtues and to **utilize** it."   *Burning Daylight*, Jack London.

6. **humid** "It was now fully night-fall, and a thick **humid** fog hung over the city, soon ending in a settled and heavy rain."

   The Man of the Crowd, Edgar Allan Poe.

7. **theory** "I have a **theory** that it is always the women who propose to us, and not we who propose to the women."

   The Picture of Dorian Gray, Oscar Wilde.

8. **descend** "In the next two winters, an Arctic chill may **descend** on Europe, burying that continent in snow and ice."

   mercurynews.com, January 27, 2011.

9. **circulate** "With LeBron James playing poorly at the beginning of each basketball game, rumors began to **circulate** about the job security of the coach."   *nypost.com*, November 30, 2010.

10. **enormous** "The surface of the valley was dotted with **enormous** trees, a strange sight so far from a Martian waterway."

    Thuvia, Maid of Mars, Edgar Rice Burroughs.

11. **predict** "He didn't **predict** the future, he knew the past—often a more dangerous thing."   *Twenty Years After*, Alexandre Dumas.

12. **vanish** "She felt as if all her morning's gloom would **vanish** if she could see her husband smile when she helped him with his work."

    Middlemarch, George Eliot.

LESSON 5

1. **tradition** "President Obama made an appearance on YouTube as part of the State of the Union **tradition**."

    New York Times, January 27, 2011.

2. **rural** "The average Chinese income is pennies on the dollar because more than 3/4 of their billion people population still live in **rural** areas."

    New York Times, January 31, 2011.

3. **burden** "It was with the greatest difficulty that prevented the men from throwing away their **burdens** and fleeing."

    The Return of Tarzan, Edgar Rice Burroughs.

4. **campus** "A sixth location of the Manhattan-based cafe opened today on the university **campus**, with a barista whose sole job is to brew coffee to order."   *New York Times*, January 24, 2011.

5. **majority** "By 7 o'clock in the evening, dinner was about over; a promenade; then a large **majority** of the party retired to their cabin."

    The Innocents Abroad, Mark Twain.

6. **assemble** "Congress shall make no law to deny the right of the people peaceably to **assemble**."   *The Bill Of Rights, United States Constitution*.

7. **explore** "Mets owners acknowledged Friday they will **explore** selling a minority stake in the team."   *New York Daily News*, January 31, 2011.

8. **topic** "It has always been a common **topic** of popular discussion whether animals think."   *The Analysis of Mind*, Bertrand Russell.

9. **debate** "After a long **debate**, it was agreed that they should be disarmed and not permitted to have either gun, sword or any weapon."

    Adventures of Robinson Crusoe, Daniel Defoe.

10. **evade** "A driver who was trying to **evade** bullets fired from a pursuing sport-utility vehicle Wednesday noon smashed into a car."

    jacksonville.com, July 15, 2009.

11. **probe** "The Georgia Bureau of Investigation is conducting a **probe** that began in late January when the company's audit was completed."

    jacksonville.com, December 11, 2001.

12. **reform** "You want to cure men of their old habits and **reform** their will in accordance with science and good sense."

    Notes from the Underground, Fyodor Dostoyevsky.

LESSON 6

1. **approach** "My **approach** is simply this: You've got to slow the growth of spending by all the taxing authorities and make them live within a budget."   *Time magazine*, December 2010.

2. **detect** "And often, from the side of my eye, I could **detect** her raising a hand, and brushing something off her cheek."
   Wuthering Heights, Emily Bronte.

3. **defect** "There was a radical **defect** somewhere, and I must search it out and cure it."   *Pudd'nhead Wilson*, Mark Twain.

4. **employee** "I think Juan is the best **employee** that I have ever hired, said his boss."   *New York Post*, December 27, 2010.

5. **neglect** "The doctor told him that he should not **neglect** taking his medications regularly."   *Salt Lake Tribune*, October 30, 2009.

6. **deceive** "Some Senators may **deceive** the public by not expressing their true position on a subject."   *New York Times*, February 2, 2011.

7. **undoubtedly** "While the menu guidelines are for consumers and federal programs, they will **undoubtedly** put pressure on the food industry."
   New York Times, February 2, 2011.

8. **popular** "The owners of the **popular** Inwood Road Restaurant have prepared a list of their recipes for their customers."
   dallasnews.com, February 1, 2011.

9. **thorough** "In a **thorough** and decisive win over Utah University's basketball team, Brittney had fifteen rebounds."
   dallasnews.com, January 2, 2011.

10. **client** "As a stockbroker, I want to know where each **client** has invested his money in the past."   *New York Times*, February 1, 2011.

11. **comprehensive** "Hubbard Hospital is a certified, **comprehensive** center providing programs and services to more than 6,000 families annually."   *jacksonville.com*, December 1, 2009.

12. **defraud** "An eminent Justice of the Supreme Court of Patagascar was accused after an investigation of having obtained his appointment by **defrauding** the committee."   *Patagascar News*, January 12, 2011.

LESSON 7

1. **postpone** "Rock band Kings of Leon has been forced to **postpone** several international tour dates because their drummer was injured in a car accident."   *Washington Post*, February 1, 2011.

2. **consent** "The mayor said she couldn't release information on an individual's nationality without their **consent**."
   Washington Post, October 21, 2010.

3. **massive** "The dwellings of the islanders were almost always built upon **massive** stone foundations."   *Typee*, Herman Melville.

4. **capsule** "E-Ink uses black and white particles with opposite electrical charges, floating in tiny **capsules** of liquid."
   latimes.com, January 31, 2001.

5. **preserve** "The Pentagon would undoubtedly like to **preserve** its working relationship with the Egyptian military."   *latimes.com*, February 1, 2011.

6. **denounce** "I confess that I expected to see my unhappy sister **denounce** him, and that I was disappointed by her praise."
Great Expectations, Charles Dickens.

7. **unique** "The shooting of a member of Congress cast a harsh spotlight on Arizona's **unique** politics." *nytimes.com*, January 23, 2011.

8. **torrent** "One night there was a dreadful storm; it thundered and lightened and the rain streamed down in a dreadful **torrent**."
The Yellow Fairy Book, Andrew Lang.

9. **resent** "Charles never complained, he asked for nothing, he was perfectly silent; but he seemed to **resent** the care that was taken of him."
Moon and Sixpence, W. Somerset Maugham.

10. **molest** "It has been difficult to understand why people do certain things like murder other people, **molest** children, commit suicide, or commit robberies." *jacksonville.com*, May 7, 2001.

11. **gloomy** "There is the **gloomy**, dreary prospect of going out to buy gifts and finding your bank account empty."
Florida Times-Herald, June 7, 2009.

12. **unforeseen** "The project will take approximately three months to complete, barring any **unforeseen** conditions such as rainy weather."
jacksonville.com, November 1, 2006.

LESSON 8

1. **exaggerate** "It was silliness on your part to **exaggerate** this little trifle of love-making into something serious." *Adventure*, Jack London.

2. **amateur** "The twins had accepted several invitations, and had also volunteered to play some duets at an **amateur** entertainment for the benefit of a local charity." *Pudd'nhead Wilson*, Mark Twain.

3. **mediocre** "Although she had always praised her friend's performances, she said that in this film her friend was merely a commonplace **mediocre** actress." *The Picture of Dorian Gray*, Oscar Wilde.

4. **variety** "You can now download and print a **variety** of puzzles from the Sunday magazine free online." *New York Times*, February 5, 2011.

5. **valid** "There may only be about four **valid** title contenders in any given N.B.A. season, but those four contenders change every few years."
New York Times, February 5, 2011.

6. **survive** "The owners of failed businesses have a million stories about why they failed, why they did not **survive**."
New York Times, February 5, 2011.

7. **weird** "Florida officially has a **weird** deer season, one of the longest, in the nation. With careful planning, one could hunt deer in Florida from July to February." *Florida Times Union*, February 5, 2011.

8. **prominent** "Cuba freed a **prominent** political prisoner Friday and the Roman Catholic Church said another would be released."
Washington Post, February 5, 2011.

9. **security** "But domestic production alone cannot end the threat to national **security** because of the high price of oil."
Washington Post, February 5, 2011.

10. bulky "Although battery technology has improved in recent years, both nickel-metal hydride and the more powerful lithium ion batteries are still too **bulky**." *Business Day*, January 7, 2011.

11. reluctant "Photographers who were traveling around the city of Cairo on their own a few days ago are now **reluctant** to take their cameras into the crowded center of the city." *New York Times*, February 4, 2011.

12. obvious "To keep her from marrying, he took the **obvious** course of keeping her at home and forbidding her to seek the company of people of her own age."

The Adventures of Sherlock Holmes, Sir Arthur Conan Doyle.

LESSON 9

1. vicinity "Representative Peter King of New York introduced a bill to ban anyone from carrying a gun in the **vicinity** of a federal official."
New York Times, February 1, 2011.

2. century "Though Debussy was born in 1862 and died in 1918, this leading composer has to be considered a giant of the present **century**."
New York Times, January 12, 2011.

3. rage "Road **rage** is a common conflict on Florida Roads. It takes two drivers to be drawn into a conflict."
Florida Times Union, December 30, 2010.

4. document "I have brought copies of the **documents** with me. He opened a small valise and took out several bundles tied with pink tape."
Tom Swift in the Land of Wonders, Victor Appleton.

5. conclude "Although I attach no sort of credit to the fantastic Indian legend, I must **conclude** that I am influenced by a certain superstition of my own in this matter." *The Moonstone*, Wilkie Collins.

6. undeniable "Miranda has quickly become one of a handful of go-to musicians for chamber groups that need a violinist who can play thorny works with **undeniable** musicality. *New York Times*, January 20, 2011.

7. resist "How much longer can the European Central Bank **resist** the pressure to raise interest rates?" *New York Times*, February 7, 2011.

8. lack "The **lack** of electric lines has been the reason for reduced wind-power construction in Texas." *New York Times*, January 21, 2011.

9. ignore "The use of cell phones and laptops may cause people to **ignore** real life as it unfolds in front of them."
New York Times, February 6, 2011.

10. challenge "The New York Knicks' only **challenge** will be from the Boston Celtics, who have won 20 of their last home games."
New York Daily News, February 7, 2011.

11. miniature "A rare **miniature** cow with markings similar to a panda bear was born on a farm in northern Colorado."
New York Daily News, February 7, 2011.

12. source "The main question for the online encyclopedia, Wikipedia, is this: How can a **source** be reliable when anyone can edit it?"
New York Times, January 20, 2011.

LESSON 10

1. **excel** "What the ancients called a clever fighter is one who not only wins, but **excels** in winning with ease."   *The Art of War*, Sun Tzu.

2. **feminine** "Those were the days when a stylish woman would not wear slacks, and would wear only the most **feminine** styled dresses or skirts."
The Golden Road, L.M. Montgomery.

3. **mount** "A kind of steward appeared just as D'Artagnan and his companions were prepared to **mount** their horses."
Twenty Years After, Alexandre Dumas.

4. **compete** "You can't try to ski in your middle forties and expect to **compete** with those who have been at it from childhood."
Uneasy Money, Pelham Grenville Wodehouse.

5. **dread** "He felt too restless to sleep, and he had a horrible **dread** of being arrested by the police."
Of Human Bondage, W. Somerset Maugham.

6. **masculine** "Women were always absent from noisy town meetings and the purely **masculine** gatherings at the store or tavern."
Rebecca of Sunnybrook Farm, Kate Douglas Wiggin.

7. **menace** "He was an animal, lacking in intelligence and spirit, a **menace** and a thing of fear, as the tiger and the snake are menaces and things of fear."   *The Game*, Jack London.

8. **tendency** "People who have worked very hard for their money have a **tendency** to invest in conservative savings accounts rather than the stock market."   *New York Post*, January 25, 2000.

9. **underestimate** "Do not **underestimate** the importance of cultivating friendly relations with your next-door neighbor."
Snow Country, April 2000.

10. **victorious** "They therefore entrenched themselves on a hill over against the enemy's camp, and though **victorious**, were under greatly disadvantaged."
A Voyage to Abyssinia, Father Lobo.

11. **numerous** "We visited **numerous** overseas communities."
Language Arts & Discipline, Marlis Hellinger.

12. **flexible** "One trick for getting the best airline flight deals online is to have **flexibility** when and where you travel."
New York Daily News, April 15, 2004.

LESSON 11

1. **evidence** "The **evidence** which I have collected from various sources leads me to believe that the person who committed this murder was an American."   *The Illustrious Prince*, E. Phillips Oppenheim.

2. **solitary** "The neighborhood was a dreary one at that time; as sad and **solitary** by night, as any about London."
David Copperfield, Charles Dickens.

3. **vision** "In one serious eye disease, **vision** may become blurred, or a completely dark area may appear in the center of the vision."
Newsweek, May 3, 1999.

4. **frequent** "But besides his **frequent** absences, there was another barrier to friendship with him: he seemed to have a brooding nature."
Jane Eyre, Charlotte Bronte.

5. **glimpse** "The first **glimpse** of her new home was a delight to eye and spirit—it looked so like a big, creamy seashell stranded on the harbor shore.   *Anne's House of Dreams*, Lucy Maud Montgomery.

6. **recent** "Although there have been many voters for **recent** presidential elections, voting has been on a steady decline since Kennedy vs. Nixon in 1960."   *Jacksonville Herald*, May 8, 2010.

7. **decade** "While she slept, six **decades** or more had rolled back, and she was again in her girlhood."   *Margaret Ogilvy*, James Barrie.

8. **hesitate** "It has been so nice to have you here, but if you only knew how difficult it was to arrange, you'd understand why I **hesitate** to ask you to come again."   *The Kingdom of the Blind*, E. Phillips Oppenheim.

9. **absurd** "His father thought that it would be **absurd** for him to marry a woman who he did not love."   *The Picture of Dorian Gray*, Oscar Wilde.

10. **conflict** "During the uprising in Algeria's main square, a smaller **conflict** took place down a side street."   *Salt Lake City Tribune*, February 2, 2001.

11. **minority** "Ruby Gillis was voted the handsomest girl of the year, but a small **minority** voted in favor of Anne Shirley."
Anne's House of Dreams, Lucy Maud Montgomery.

12. **fiction** "The newspaper columnist suspected that the report that the man was injured was **fiction** because no one had seen the accident."
City Weekly, January 4, 2011.

LESSON 12

1. **ignite** "The speaker during the popular peaceful protest was reluctant to **ignite** popular fury by discussing the failures of the government."
Newsweek magazine, February 12, 2011.

2. **abolish** "The world is very different now, for man holds in his hands the power to **abolish** all forms of human poverty and all forms of human life."   *John F. Kennedy's Inaugural Address*.

3. **urban** "The mono-rail cable car became a new and unusual method of transportation in the future **urban** sections of the country."
The War in the Air, H.G. Wells.

4. **population** "How comes it, sir, that the **population** of the valley has been trebled in ten years?"   *The Country Doctor*, Honoré de Balzac.

5. **frank** "Fred insisted that he was a victim of fraud, and that his **frank** opinion of the team's owner's behavior was that they had handled the situation incorrectly."   *New York Daily News*, February 18, 2011.

6. **pollute** "We have overpopulated the earth, and we **pollute** the waterways, cut down the forests and fill the atmosphere with CO_2."
Mercury Press, February 3, 2011.

7. **reveal** "Some day it may seem worthwhile to take up the story of the younger ones again; therefore, it will be wisest not to **reveal** any of that part of their lives at present."   *Tom Sawyer*, Mark Twain.

8. prohibit "There is an act to **prohibit** the killing of deer in the mating season."   *The Pioneers*, James Fenimore Cooper.

9. urgent "Profound and powerful forces are shaking and remaking our world, and the **urgent** question of our time is whether we can make change our friend and not our enemy."   *Bill Clinton's Inaugural Address.*

10. adequate "Without an **adequate** income, half the possibilities of life are shut off."   *Of Human Bondage*, W. Somerset Maugham.

11. decrease "Proceeding northward, the quantity of rain does not appear to **decrease** in strict proportion to the distance toward the Arctic Circle."   *The Voyage of the Beagle*, Charles Darwin.

12. audible "At long intervals, as he turned the corner of a distant canal, the warning cry of a gondolier was just **audible**."

The Haunted Hotel, Wilkie Collins.

LESSON 13

1. journalist "'But I do enjoy finding an interesting story to write about,' said a **journalist** of considerable local fame."

Can Such Things Be?, Ambrose Bierce.

2. famine "Just after the great war, during which no man could sow or reap, a **famine** came upon the land, and the people complained because of lack of food, and looked round like a starved lion."

King Solomon's Mines, Rider Haggard.

3. revive "She fainted one evening in her husband's arms, and he carried her to the open window to **revive** her with the fresh air."

The Posthumous Papers of the Pickwick Club, Charles Dickens.

4. commence "His strokes were long and easy—it would be many hours before those giant muscles would **commence** to feel fatigue."

The Return of Tarzan, Edgar Rice Burroughs.

5. observant "For a week Tarzan and his ape friends remained there near the camp, and the ape-man, keenly **observant**, learned much of the ways of men."   *Tarzan*, Edgar Rice Burroughs.

6. identify "He would be able to disguise himself so effectually that ninety-nine people out of a hundred would fail to **identify** him, either by his voice or his manner."   *I Say No*, Wilkie Collins.

7. migrate "I think he had a dim idea that if he could **migrate** to a distant parish, he might find neighbors worthy of him."

Adam Bede, George Eliot.

8. vessel "When the maneuver had been completed, the **vessel** which bore the admiral saluted France by twelve discharges of cannon, which were returned, discharge for discharge, from Fort Francis I."

Ten Years Later, Alexandre Dumas.

9. persist "He has been punished, not because he said he saw a ghost last night, but because he **persists** in saying he saw the ghost after I have told him that no such thing can possibly be."

The Woman in White, Wilkie Collins.

10. hazy "It happened, to my further misfortune, that the weather proved **hazy** for three or four days while I was in the valley, and not being able to see the sun, I wandered about very uncomfortably, and at last was obliged to find the seaside."   *Robinson Crusoe*, Daniel Defoe.

11. **gleam** "Detecting the **gleam** of Governor Bellingham's lamp, the old lady quickly extinguished her own, and vanished."
The Scarlet Letter, Nathaniel Hawthorne.

12. **editor** "'It seems a pity to let the dinner spoil,' said the **editor** of a well-known daily paper; and thereupon the doctor rang the bell."
The Time Machine, H.G. Wells.

LESSON 14

1. **unruly** "Jo Frost, star of *Supernanny*, tames **unruly** kids and administers discipline advice to parents." *Parents magazine*, 2011.

2. **rival** "You can dive your kite around a **rival's** string, cutting the string and setting the kite flying free." *The Kite Runner*, Khaled Hosseini.

3. **violent** "Thousands of Yemeni pro- and anti-government protestors threw stones at each other in **violent** clashes in the city of Sanaa."
news.yahoo.com, February 19, 2011.

4. **brutal** "With the **brutal** murder of Simon, the last vestige of civilized order on the island is stripped away." *Lord of the Flies*, William Golding.

5. **opponent** "An Iowa wrestler became the first girl to win a state tournament match when her **opponent** refused to face her."
ABC News/ESPN Sports, February 18, 2011.

6. **brawl** "The NHL suspended 3 New York Islanders and issued a $100,000 fine for their actions in a **brawl** with the Pittsburgh Penguins."
The Associated Press, February 12, 2011.

7. **duplicate** "Making **duplicate** copies and printouts of things no one wants is giving America a new sense of purpose."
Andy Rooney, *www.brainyquote.com*.

8. **vicious** "When I get really angry and I feel like my back is up against the wall, I will say **vicious** things." Howard Stern, *www.brainyquote.com*.

9. **whirling** "**Whirling** winds piling up drifts of snow near the highway couldn't keep the young at heart from braving the cold."
www.katu.com, December 21, 2008.

10. **underdog** "Everyone expects the favorite to win; therefore, when an **underdog** wins, it comes as a surprise."
American Sports Analysts, www.asawins.com.

11. **thrust** "He seemed to be crouched down, hands splayed on the floor, his head **thrust** out, nose to the stone." *The Hobbit*, J.R.R. Tolkien.

12. **bewildered** "If a father feels **bewildered** and even defeated, let him take comfort from the fact that whatever he does has a fifty percent chance of being right." Bill Cosby, *www.thinkexist.com*.

LESSON 15

1. **expand** "The Japanese brewer plans to spend $1.5 billion dollars as he seeks to **expand** his business in North America."
Bloomberg News, February 20, 2011.

2. **alter** "When friends asked me, 'Can we help?' I say not unless you can **alter** time or teleport me off this rock."
Charlie Sheen, *www.brainyquote.com*.

3. **mature** "A well-cared for property with **mature**, healthy trees gives the best kind of first impression as a car pulls up to the house."
The Tree Book, Jeff Meyer.

4. **sacred** "I pledge myself to the **sacred** cause, hoping this little book may hasten the day of deliverance to my brethren in bonds."
Narrative of the Life of Frederick Douglass, An American Slave,
Frederick Douglass, 1845.

5. **revise** "The College Board said it intended to **revise** all of its Advanced Placement science, history and language courses to emphasize how students can use the knowledge."   *New York Times*, January 29, 2011.

6. **pledge** "The world's leading nations **pledge** to support the new governments arising in revolution-torn Egypt and Tunisia."
CNN, February 19, 2011.

7. **casual** "Shelving allows for the display of books, collections and decorative objects, which enhances the **casual**, homey feel of this alcove."   *www.silive.com*, Sepetmber 10, 2009.

8. **pursue** "I hope he can help us **pursue** our future education."
The Freedom Writers Diary, 1999.

9. **unanimous** "The National Academy of Sciences is unable to give a **unanimous** decision if asked whether the sun would rise tomorrow."
Paul Ehrlich, *www.brainyquote.com*.

10. **fortunate** "To the Beaudelaire orphans, having each other in the midst of their unfortunate lives felt very **fortunate** indeed."
The Wide Window: A Series of Unfortunate Events, Lemony Snicket.

11. **pioneer** "Molly faces the greatest challenge of her life as she prepares for the **pioneer** journey to Arizona Territory."
Fried-Egg Quilt, Laura Ostrom.

12. **innovative** "The Boeing company, a global aviation leader, has grown through decades of **innovative** aircraft designs and the acquisition of McDonnell Douglas and Rockwell International."
New York Times, July 29, 2010.

LESSON 16

1. **slender** "I counted the miles until I'd see her...silver bracelets jingling around her **slender** wrists."   Soraya in *The Kite Runner*, Khaled Hosseini.

2. **surpass** "Few if any of our duties **surpass** our obligation to provide for the common defense of our nation."
Joe Lieberman, *www.brainyquote.com*.

3. **vast** "Simon found he was looking into a **vast** mouth. There was blackness within, a blackness that spread."   *Lord of the Flies*, William Golding.

4. **doubt** "Recently I began to have odd, flitting **doubts**. Did I still believe him?"   *Sarah's Key*, Tatiana de Rosnay.

5. **capacity** "American Airlines announced it would strip 7,200 coach-class seats to cut **capacity** and make its resulting coach class roomier."
NY Reuters, February 3, 2010.

6. **penetrate** "The detector would have to be in space, because gamma rays cannot **penetrate** the atmosphere."
A Brief History of Time, Stephen Hawking.

7. **pierce** "I am armoured above and below with iron scales and hard gems. No blade can **pierce** me."   Dragon in *The Hobbit*, J.R.R. Tolkien.

8. **accurate** "As years passed, he grew interested in preserving an **accurate** record of the region's rich heritage."
   Pioneer Days in the Black Hills, John McClintock.

9. **microscope** "Under the **microscope**, I found that snowflakes were miracles of beauty."   *www.silive.com*, January 21, 2010.

10. **grateful** "I have benefited greatly from the freedom that exists in my country and for this I am eternally **grateful**."
    Johnny Depp, *www.thinkexist.com*.

11. **cautious** "**Cautious** my precious! More haste less speed. We mustn't risk our necks!"   *The Two Towers*, J.R.R. Tolkien.

12. **confident** "Remember how **confident** and cared about you feel when someone smiles at you."
    Be True to Yourself: A Daily Guide for Teenage Girls, Amanda Ford.

LESSON 17

1. **appeal** "For a unique experience, vacation cruises with a theme are growing in **appeal** to travelers interested in art, photography, and science."   *New York Times*, February 11, 2011.

2. **addict** "I'll admit it...I'm a college **addict**, addicted to the freedom, the social aspect, the entertainment, and yes, even the classes! I loved it from the very first day."
   Bing News, www.associatedcontent.com, February 17, 2011.

3. **weary** "When at last they halted and dismounted, even Aragorn was stiff and **weary**."   *The Two Towers*, J.R.R. Tolkien.

4. **aware** "I am well **aware** that the superheated station wagon is not an automotive staple in the United States."
   Automobile Magazine, April 2009.

5. **misfortune** "Acceptance of what has happened is the first step to over-coming the consequences of any **misfortune**."
   William James, *www.quotationsbook.com*.

6. **avoid** "Rudy, who was farthest away, caught up quickly, but not quickly enough to **avoid** being last."   *The Book Thief*, Markus Zusak.

7. **wretched** "So poor Harry spent a **wretched** Veterans' Day weekend after that. But Dwayne spent a worse one."
   Breakfast of Champions, Kurt Vonnegut.

8. **keg** "Vintage wine by the **keg** is now available to New York City eateries."
   www.silive.com, October 28, 2010.

9. **nourish** "Once you see how easy it is to **nourish** your heart, you'll be inspired to indulge in these delicious power meals regularly."
   Prevention magazine, November, 2010.

10. **harsh** "Her voice was softer now, less **harsh**."
    Sarah's Key, Tatiana de Rosnay.

11. **quantity** "There was Mrs. Weasley's usual package, including a new sweater and a large **quantity** of homemade mince pies."
Harry Potter and the Goblet of Fire, J.K. Rowling.

12. **opt** "The accused stalker will **opt** to stay in jail and go to trial rather than see a shrink."   *New York Daily News*, February 14, 2011.

LESSON 18

1. **tragedy** "Particularly in light of the recent **tragedy**—the death of that poor little girl—you will be safer by far at your orphanage."
Harry Potter and the Chamber of Secrets, J.K. Rowling.

2. **pedestrian** "They walked back into the thick of the **pedestrian** traffic, making their way to the soiled old Cafe du Monde."
The Witching Hour, Anne Rice.

3. **glance** "He fell silent for a moment, and his little eyes darted suspicious **glances** from side to side before he proceeded."
Animal Farm, George Orwell.

4. **budget** "The governor unveiled a **budget** that shows $33.9 billion in revenue and $35.3 billion in expenses."
The Daily Journal, February 17, 2011.

5. **nimble** "The doctor, by comparison, was like a balding rodent; small and **nimble**, pacing the school office."   *The Book Thief*, Markus Zusak.

6. **manipulate** "Voldemort attempted to force his way into your mind, to **manipulate** and misdirect your thoughts."
Harry Potter and the Order of the Phoenix, J.K. Rowling.

7. **reckless** "After striking and killing a man with his car in November 2001, Mr. Long testified that he was a **reckless** driver of automobiles."
New York Times, April 20, 2010.

8. **horrid** "Last night I had a dream, a **horrid** dream, fighting with things."
Phil, a "littlun" in *Lord of the Flies*, William Golding.

9. **rave** "The shows were not as bad as movies, but nothing to **rave** about."
Catcher in the Rye, J.D. Salinger.

10. **economical** "Here are recipes for quick, easy, **economical** meals without using complicated procedures or fancy equipment."
Slapdash Cooking, Carol Barkin and Elizabeth James.

11. **lubricate** "**Lubricate** car doors every time you get an oil change to avoid squeaky car doors."   *Happy Living magazine*, 2009.

12. **ingenious** "You seem to have given this a great deal of thought, Moody, and a very **ingenious** theory it is."
Karkaroff in *Harry Potter and the Goblet of Fire*, J.K. Rowling.

LESSON 19

1. **harvest** "Everywhere there was so much corn that at **harvest** time every barn was stuffed."   *The Return of the King*, J.R.R. Tolkien.

2. **abundant** "The guests had a very pleasant feast: rich, **abundant**, varied; and prolonged."   *The Fellowship of the Ring*, J.R.R. Tolkien.

3. **uneasy** "Wahid finally broke the **uneasy** silence that followed and began to speak."   *The Kite Runner*, Khaled Hosseini.

4. **calculate** "Rowan started to **calculate** how old the baby would be at Christmas."   *The Witching Hour*, Anne Rice.

5. **absorb** "The two cart-horses could **absorb** everything that they were told and passed it on to the other animals."   *Animal Farm*, George Orwell.

6. **estimate** "Aristotle even quoted an **estimate** that the distance around the earth was 400,000 stadia."   *A Brief History of Time*, Stephen Hawking.

7. **morsel** "Gollum watched every **morsel** from hand to mouth, like an expectant dog by a diner's chair."   *The Two Towers*, J.R.R. Tolkien.

8. **quota** "NYPD cops have a **quota** of summonses which they are expected to issue every month."   *Staten Island Advance*, September 13, 2010.

9. **threat** "The children were startled. They expected **threats**, blows, anything but kindness."   *Sarah's Key*, Tatiana de Rosnay.

10. **ban** "Mayor Bloomberg made a meddling move on nutrition by issuing a **ban** on trans fats."   *New York Daily News*, February 22, 2011.

11. **panic** "The double attack turned what had hitherto been nervousness into real **panic**."   *Harry Potter and the Chamber of Secrets*, J.K. Rowling.

12. **appropriate** "Mrs. Weasley threw him a look, upon which he became immediately silent and assumed an expression **appropriate** to the sickbed of a close friend."   *Harry Potter and the Deathly Hallows*, J.K. Rowling.

LESSON 20

1. **emerge** "As soon as they were well inside the yard, the animals who had been lying in ambush in the cowshed suddenly **emerged** in their rear, cutting them off."   *Animal Farm*, George Orwell.

2. **jagged** "The machines evinced the only vitality with their tiny monotonous beeps and **jagged** neon lines."   *The Witching Hour*, Anne Rice.

3. **linger** "His glance **lingered** admiringly on my leather coat and my jeans."   *The Kite Runner*, Khaled Hosseini.

4. **ambush** "There seemed no chance of reaching the Ford before he was cut off by the others that had lain in **ambush**."   *The Fellowship of the Ring*, J.R.R. Tolkien.

5. **crafty** "He is a wizard both cunning and **crafty**, having many guises."   *The Two Towers*, J.R.R. Tolkien.

6. **defiant** "Some children may be more **defiant**, stubborn, and negative than others."   *www.scholastic.com*, 2011.

7. **vigor** "The Prefect got up and shook his hand with **vigor**."   *Harry Potter and the Sorcerer's Stone*, J.K. Rowling.

8. **perish** "The day will come when they will **perish** and I shall go back!"   *The Hobbit*, J.R.R. Tolkien.

9. **fragile** "It was the trade name for wood shavings used to protect **fragile** objects inside packages."   *Breakfast of Champions*, Kurt Vonnegut.

10. **captive** "They comforted the **captive** that was aboard, and bade him put aside fear."   *The Return of the King*, J.R.R. Tolkien.

11. **prosper** "No race can **prosper** till it learns that there is as much dignity in tilling a field as in writing a poem."
Booker T. Washington, *www.brainyquote.com*.

12. **devour** "He set two carrots aside and **devoured** the third, making an astounding noise as he crushed it in his mouth."
The Book Thief, Markus Zusak.

LESSON 21

1. **plea** "His lawyer planned to enter a **plea** of temporary insanity."
Breakfast of Champions, Kurt Vonnegut.

2. **weary** "The dwarves were sick and **weary**, and they could not go much better than a hobble and a wobble."   *The Hobbit*, J.R.R. Tolkien.

3. **collide** "The taxi which took me to my hotel nearly **collided** with another car as we pulled up to the curb."   *The Witching Hour*, Anne Rice.

4. **confirm** "He looked over his shoulder to **confirm** that he was utterly alone."   Simon in *Lord of the Flies*, William Golding.

5. **verify** "Applications may be reviewed to **verify** qualifications and eligibility."   *www.silive.com*, February 14, 2011.

6. **anticipate** "Do not **anticipate** trouble, or worry about what may never happen. Keep in the sunlight."
Benjamin Franklin, *www.brainyquote.com*.

7. **dilemma** "That's the **dilemma**—we can eat anything but how do we know what to eat?"
The Omnivore's Dilemma for Kids: The Secrets Behind What You Eat, Michael Pollan.

8. **detour** "Harry made his usual **detour** along the seventh-floor corridor."
Harry Potter and the Half-Blood Prince, J.K. Rowling.

9. **merit** "He served as a salaried clerk of the parish and enjoyed status enough to **merit** his name on a pew."
Charity and Merit: Trinity School at 300, Timothy Jacobson.

10. **transmit** "You love your pet, but you won't love an illness your dog or cat might **transmit** to you."   *Prevention magazine*, October 2009.

11. **relieve** She dragged him to the steps at the side of the church where they rested, both **relieved**."   *The Book Thief*, Markus Zusak.

12. **baffle** "Doctors were at first **baffled** by the disease, which they report is extremely rare."   *The Joy Luck Club*, Amy Tan.

LESSON 22

1. **warden** "There's really only one rule at Camp Green Lake: Don't upset the **warden**—he's the boss."   *Holes*, Louis Sachar.

2. **acknowledge** "Then the old warrior would walk to the young one, embrace him, **acknowledge** his worthiness."
The Kite Runner, Khaled Hosseini.

3. **justice** "Beregond, perceiving the mercy and **justice** of the King, was glad...and departed in joy and content."
The Return of the King, J.R.R. Tolkien.

4. **delinquent** "I wrote down mostly typical **delinquent**-girl stuff—fighting, lying, stealing." *Something Like Hope*, Shawn Goodman.

5. **reject** "A young boy must decide whether to go along with his father, who is a thief, or **reject** his father's way of life and risk losing him." *It Ain't All for Nothin'*, Walter Dean Myers.

6. **deprive** "They are waiting to celebrate with you, and it would be a shame to **deprive** them of this excellent excuse to make a great deal of mess and noise." *Harry Potter and the Goblet of Fire*, J.K. Rowling.

7. **spouse** "A house is not a home when a **spouse** is not home." *The Joy Luck Club*, Amy Tan.

8. **vocation** "An inheritance and a fancy house in New Orleans had lured her away from her true **vocation**." *The Witching Hour*, Anne Rice.

9. **unstable** "The woman who pushed Pope Benedict XVI appeared to be mentally **unstable** and was arrested by Vatican police." *www.silive.com*, December 24, 2009.

10. **homicide** "The Los Angeles County coroner said Friday in a statement that Michael Jackson's death was a **homicide** primarily caused by two drugs." *New York Times*, August 28, 2009.

11. **penalize** "The referee may **penalize** the other team for misuse of the paint check rule." *Ultimate Paintball Field Guide*, John R. Little and Curtis Wong.

12. **beneficiary** "Little Stone is the sole **beneficiary** to all his insurance and property." *Wolf Hunter*, Tracie Nix.

LESSON 23

1. **reptile** "The snakes, and everything in the **Reptile** Room, were the last reminders the Baudelaires had of the few happy days they'd spent at the house." *The Reptile Room*, Lemony Snicket.

2. **rarely** "The rangers had strange powers of sight and hearing, and roamed at will; but they were now few and **rarely** ever seen." *The Fellowship of the Ring*, J.R.R. Tolkien.

3. **forbid** "Nina Khan faces the pain of having a crush when her parents **forbid** her to date." *Skunk Girl*, Sheba Karim.

4. **logical** "If Mr. Pendanski only thought about it, he'd realize it was very **logical**." *Holes*, Louis Sachar.

5. **exhibit** "He wanted the **exhibit** to show how machines evolved just as animals did, but with much greater speed." *Breakfast of Champions*, Kurt Vonnegut.

6. **proceed** "He would **proceed** to say what he really wanted, which was more despicable than all the terrible things I had imagined." *The Joy Luck Club*, Amy Tan.

7. **precaution** "Not a punishment, Hagrid, more a **precaution**, said Fudge." *Harry Potter and the Chamber of Secrets*, J.K. Rowling.

8. **extract** "Ron struggled for a moment before managing to **extract** his wand from his pocket." *Harry Potter and the Deathly Hallows*, J.K. Rowling.

9. **prior** "**Prior** studies of weight loss surgeries suggested that gastric banding was safer than gastric bypass surgery."
    New York Daily News, February 21, 2011.

10. **embrace** "Her arms halfway stretched out as though she would have liked to **embrace** me but dared not."
    Jacob Have I Loved, Katherine Paterson.

11. **violent** "A great rumbling noise rolled in the ground and echoed in the mountains;...it seemed unbearably **violent** and fierce."
    The Two Towers, J.R.R. Tolkien.

12. **partial** "They decided against it, since there was at least a **partial** threat that their presence would be felt."   *The Book Thief*, Markus Zusak.

LESSON 24

1. **fierce** "He rolled over and peered into Jack's **fierce**, dirty face."
    Simon in *Lord of the Flies*, William Golding.

2. **detest** "Much as he **detested** Filch, Harry couldn't help feeling a bit sorry for him."   *Harry Potter and the Chamber of Secrets*, J.K. Rowling.

3. **sneer** "Strider had heavy black brows and dark scornful eyes; his large mouth curled in a **sneer**."   *The Fellowship of the Ring*, J.R.R. Tolkien.

4. **scowl** "She smiled, looking pleased for a moment before the **scowl** came back."   *The Joy Luck Club*, Amy Tan.

5. **encourage** "The Hawaiian Festival was Harry's golden opportunity to loosen up, to have some fun, to **encourage** other people to have some fun, too."   *Breakfast of Champions*, Kurt Vonnegut.

6. **consider** "Though the goblins of Gringotts will **consider** it base treachery, I have decided to help you."
    Harry Potter and the Deathly Hallows, J.K. Rowling.

7. **vermin** "Foxes, rats, stoats, weasels and all manner of **vermin** could be seen fleeing from the armoured mouse."   *Triss*, Brian Jacques.

8. **wail** "Before the old lady could answer, there was a long **wail** from upstairs."   *Sarah's Key*, Tatiana de Rosnay.

9. **symbol** "It was this **symbol** of married love that started everyone talking about the desirability of marriage."
    Across the Nightingale Floor, Lian Hearn.

10. **authority** "I'll be on my third honeymoon, so I'm more of an **authority** than I care to be."   Alan Thicke, *www.brainyquote.com*.

11. **neutral** "The College of Staten Island has new gender-**neutral** bathrooms to accommodate different students, including those with small children."
    Staten Island Advance, September 7, 2010.

12. **trifle** "Out came a long file of pigs, all walking on their hind legs; one or two were even a **trifle** unsteady and looked as though they would have liked the support of a stick."   *Animal Farm*, George Orwell.

LESSON 25

1. **architect** "Chris Hoy worked with designers and **architects** in preparing the 6,000-seat, $152 million Velodrome in London as the main venue for the upcoming Olympic Games."
Washington Post, February 22, 2011.

2. **matrimony** "Without thinking highly either of men or **matrimony**, marriage had always been her object; it was the only honourable provision for well-educated young women of small fortune."
Pride and Prejudice, Jane Austen.

3. **baggage** "Check with your airline regarding checked and carry-on **baggage** allowances and restrictions."
www.tripadvisor.com, February 2011.

4. **squander** "Michael's mother's paternal grandmother **squandered** the entire fortune, leaving behind one carved chair and three heavily framed landscape paintings."
The Witching Hour, Anne Rice.

5. **abroad** "Parents had the right to teach witches and wizards at home or send them **abroad** if they preferred."
Harry Potter and the Deathly Hallows, J.K. Rowling.

6. **fugitive** "Illinois law considered a person of color without freedom papers to be a **fugitive** and thus subject to arrest."
Adventures of Huckleberry Finn, Mark Twain.

7. **calamity** "The **calamity** that comes is never the one we had prepared ourselves for."
Mark Twain, *www.thinkexist.com*.

8. **pauper** "The clothes of all the **paupers**, which fluttered on their shrunken forms after a week or two's gruel, was rather expensive."
Oliver Twist, Charles Dickens.

9. **envy** "The brand new Schwinn Stingray was sure to make me the **envy** of every kid in the neighborhood."
The Kite Runner, Khaled Hosseini.

10. **collapse** "Emboldened by the **collapse** of the windmill, the human beings were inventing fresh lies about Animal Farm."
Animal Farm, George Orwell.

11. **prosecute** "Merchants are encouraged to **prosecute** shoplifters and not consider loss from theft a cost of doing business."
www.silive.com, January 10, 2010.

12. **bigamy** "A reality TV show *Sister Wives* featuring a 41-year-old salesman and his 4 wives, 13 children and 3 stepchildren led to a **bigamy** investigation."
New York Times, September 28, 2010.

LESSON 26

1. **possible** "There was more silence than she ever thought **possible**."
The Book Thief, Markus Zusak.

2. **compel** "Her laments always **compel** Harold to explain things to my mother in simple terms."
The Joy Luck Club, Amy Tan.

3. **awkward** "There was a long and **awkward** silence, which was broken at last by Mrs. Weasley."
Harry Potter and the Deathly Hallows, J.K. Rowling.

4. **venture** "You need rest before your **venture** Frodo; if go you must."
Boromir in *The Two Towers*, J.R.R. Tolkien.

5. **awesome** "The Discovery Channel show *Out of the Wild* took city dwellers out of their element, into the jungle, for an **awesome** wasp-eating experience."   *www.nydailynews.com*, February 15, 2011.

6. **guide** "Here you are...*Unfogging the Future*—a very good **guide** to all your basic fortune-telling methods."
Harry Potter and the Prisoner of Azkaban, J.K. Rowling.

7. **quench** "Club soda contains sodium and might not **quench** your thirst."
Self magazine, January 7, 2009.

8. **betray** "E-cards cover up your lateness, since they take no time to send and don't **betray** that you've forgotten a thing."
Washington Post, February 14, 2011.

9. **utter** "And by the time the sheep had quieted down, the chance to **utter** any protest had passed."   *Animal Farm*, George Orwell.

10. **pacify** "They kept the students and doctors in jail for their own safe-keeping, and to **pacify** the crowd."   *It Happened in New York*, Fran Capo.

11. **respond** "Nailer was almost too tired to **respond**, but he mustered a grin for the occasion."   *Ship Breaker*, Paolo Bacigalupi.

12. **beckon** "Professor McGonagall lowered the megaphone and **beckoned** Harry over to her."   *Harry Potter and the Chamber of Secrets*, J.K. Rowling.

LESSON 27

1. **despite** "These great green sea eagles eventually became extinct, **despite** anything anyone could do."   *Breakfast of Champions*, Kurt Vonnegut.

2. **disrupt** "The house is sleek, spare and 'fluid,' nothing to **disrupt** the line, meaning none of my clutter."   *The Joy Luck Club*, Amy Tan.

3. **rash** "By the time Halloween arrived, Harry was regretting his **rash** promise to go to the deathday party."
Harry Potter and the Chamber of Secrets, J.K. Rowling.

4. **rapid** "It only took me about two minutes since I'm a very **rapid** packer."
Catcher in the Rye, J.D. Salinger.

5. **exhaust** "No need to **exhaust** yourself! MODERATE exercise is best."
Healing Daily, 2002.

6. **severity** "Evidence has been accumulating that zinc could reduce the **severity** and duration of the common cold."
Washington Post, February 15, 2011.

7. **feeble** "The **feeble** attempt at magic was too much for Harry's wand, which split into two again."
Harry Potter and the Deathly Hallows, J.K. Rowling.

8. **unite** "Let both sides explore what problems **unite** us instead of belaboring those problems which divide us."
John F. Kennedy's Inaugural Address, January 20, 1961.

9. **cease** "This doom shall stand for a year and a day, and then **cease**."
The Two Towers, J.R.R. Tolkien.

10. **thrifty** "It is **thrifty** to prepare today for the wants of tomorrow."
Aesop, *www.brainyquote.com*.

11. **miserly** "A **miserly** fellow named Joe was obsessed with his weekly cash flow. The guy was so petty, he ordered wife Betty to flush once a day. She said, 'No!'" Madeleine Begun Kane, *www.madkane.com*.

12. **monarch** "As expected, Colin Firth won best actor for his portrayal of the reluctant **monarch** in *The King's Speech* at Britain's top film awards."
www.nydailynews.com, February 14, 2011.

LESSON 28

1. **outlaw** "No member of our family was ever an **outlaw**."
The Summer of the Beautiful White Horse, William Saroyan.

2. **promote** "Mr. Fotheringay tried to **promote** himself as a miracle man."
The Man Who Could Work Miracles, H.G. Wells.

3. **undernourished** "When Donovan was released, he was badly **undernourished**."
Guns, Germs, and Steel, Jared Diamond.

4. **illustrate** "I can **illustrate** my method of establishing law in science very easily."
We Are All Scientists, T.H. Huxley.

5. **disclose** "Meshenka **disclosed** that the brooch was worth a thousand kopecks."
An Upheaval, Anton Chekov.

6. **excessive** "My Irish teacher showed **excessive** irritability about my questions on religion."
The Saint, V.S. Pritchett.

7. **disaster** "Unable to breathe properly from nervousness, I was facing **disaster**."
Breaking With Music, Boris Pasternak.

8. **censor** "Chinese Journalist Defies the **Censor**."
New York Times, January 27, 2011.

9. **culprit** "When my roommates were the **culprits**, I was not backward with my revenge."
A Room of My Own, Mary Ellen Chase.

10. **juvenile** "As a **juvenile**, I learned to write to help me to survive."
Why I Write, William Saroyan.

11. **bait** "I wouldn't take the **bait** from Sylvester, and I turned away."
The Jockey, Carson McCullers.

12. **insist** "For those Americans like myself who **insist** on improving the quality of education, there is good news."
Reds Have the Edge in Science, Inez Robb.

LESSON 29

1. **toil** "He undertook all manner of **toil** because he dreamed of wealth."
Dreams, Walt Whitman.

2. **blunder** "Esmond didn't correct the old man's **blunder**."
The History of Henry Esmond, William Thackeray.

3. **daze** "I awoke in a **daze** to see several natives bending over me."
Typee, Herman Melville.

4. **mourn** "Hundreds came to **mourn** for the 9-year-old who was killed in Tucson, Arizona."
Newsday, January 21, 2011.

5. **subside** "After the second whiskey, the pain **subsided**."
The Man of the House, Frank O'Connor.

6. **maim** "The bullet **maimed** Morris terribly, and he bled to death."
Can We See the Future?, Alison Smith.

7. **comprehend** "He knows as much of what he talks about, as a blind man **comprehends** colors."
On the Ignorance of the Learned, William Hazlitt.

8. **command** "The major gave the **command** to dig in for the night."
The Courting of Dinah Shadd, Rudyard Kipling.

9. **final** "Regis Philbin said that his decision to retire is **final**."
CBS Nightly News, January 18, 2011.

10. **exempt** "No Longer **Exempt** From Taxes."
Newsday, February 16, 2011.

11. **vain** "Oliver had every reason to be **vain** but he wasn't."
A Friend from Ireland, Ben Lucien Burman.

12. **repetition** "In tense silence, they listened to a **repetition** of the sound."
The Outlaw of Tom, Edgar Rice Burroughs.

LESSON 30

1. **depict** "Officially produced ads that **depict** Israel as Palestine and vice versa must be ended."   *New York Times*, January 26, 2011.

2. **mortal** "The jaguar mother lashed out and delivered a **mortal** wound."
Jungle War, Tom Gill.

3. **novel** "My father had a **novel** way of running his buisness."
My First Boss, Ralph McGill.

4. **occupant** "You can't decline an invitation from the **occupant** of the White House."   *The Magnificent Yankee*, Emmet Lavery.

5. **appoint** "Becky teased her mother to **appoint** the next day for the long-delayed picnic."   *The Adventures of Tom Sawyer*, Mark Twain.

6. **quarter** "Joel opened his deli in the Jewish **quarter**."
Save the Deli, David Sax.

7. **site** "The Under Secretary chose a convenient **site** for the meeting."
Graven Image, John O'Hara.

8. **quote** "May I **quote** you on that?"   *Public Lives*, Joyce Wadler.

9. **verse** "Tear him for his bad **verses**."
Julius Caesar, Act III, William Shakespeare.

10. **mortality** "I could not accept the **mortality** of treating the untouchables as inferior."   *The Untouchables*, Mohandas Gandhi.

11. **roam** "Mr. Offord allowed his eyes to **roam** over the quests."
Brooksmith, Henry James.

12. **attract** "The screaming is sure to **attract** the police."
The Good Bad Movie, Norman Holland.

LESSON 31

1. **commuter** "Today's snowstorm left thousands of **commuters** stranded."
   Weather Channel, January 27, 2011.

2. **confine** "Little Penelope was **confined** to her room after the surgery."
   Merry Christmas, Jimmy Cannon.

3. **idle** "The hours from seven to midnight are an **idle** time for the toll takers."
   The Law, Robert Coates.

4. **idol** "It is only in the past century that art historians have been able to discard the fake **idols**."   *Cleopatra: Last Queen of Egypt*, Joyce Tyldesley.

5. **jest** "Bounderby's **jest** failed to entertain us."
   Hard Times, Charles Dickens.

6. **patriotic** "The President saluted the **patriotic** men and women of our armed forces."   *Barack Obama's State of the Union Address*.

7. **dispute** "They agreed to settle their **dispute** in my office."
   Living in the Law, Jeremy Weinstein.

8. **valor** "He is as full of **valor** as of kindness."
   Henry V, Act IV, William Shakespeare.

9. **lunatic** "The **lunatic** brought her a watermelon with his initials carved on it."   *A Good Man Is Hard to Find*, Flannery O'Connor.

10. **vein** "He held forth in a **vein** that recalled the pulpit."
    The Man Who Shot Snapping Turtles, Edmund Wilson.

11. **uneventful** "Although Cap't. Wentworth was there, breakfast was **uneventful**."   *Persuasion*, Jane Austen.

12. **fertile** "The land along the Nile River was made **fertile** because of the annual flooding."   *Cleopatra: Last Queen of Egypt*, Joyce Tyldesley.

LESSON 32

1. **refer** "For that, I will **refer** you to the Old Testament."
   Deuces Are Wild, Archer Lamont.

2. **distress** "I was greatly **distressed** to learn that my mail was opened in Nairobi."   *Out of Africa*, Isak Dinesen.

3. **diminish** "Interest in Lord Strawberry's **diminished** quickly."
   The Phoenix, Sylvia T. Warner.

4. **maximum** "The minister's black veil had a **maximum** effect upon the congregation."   *The Minister's Black Veil*, Nathaniel Hawthorne.

5. **flee** "Wilder decided to **flee** before the helicopter landed."
   White Noise, Don DeLillo.

6. **vulnerable** "We were **vulnerable** to a highly organized war machine."
   Their Finest Hour, Winston Churchill.

7. **signify** "Slips of paper **signified** a change from the chips of wood."
   The Lottery, Shirley Jackson.

8. **mythology** "Hemingway's simplicity was part of his **mythology**."
   Ernest Was Very Simple, Robert Ruark.

9. **provide** "When it comes to food, you will have to **provide** for yourself."
Army Now, Col. Maxwell Forbes.

10. **colleague** "His new **colleague** chased the butterfly culture wih a net."
A Visit to America, Dylan Thomas.

11. **torment** "Mr. Martin decided to rub out Mrs. Barrows and end the **torment** she had caused." *The Catbird Seat*, James Thurber.

12. **loyalty** "The state commands the complete **loyalty** of the prosecutor."
Should a Lawyer Defend a Guilty Man?, Joseph Welch.

LESSON 33

1. **volunteer** "Nick **volunteered** to bring the logs in"
The Three-Day Blow, Ernest Hemingway.

2. **prejudice** "Red didn't inherit the **prejudice** of his parents."
Friday with Red, Bob Edwards.

3. **shrill** "He heard the **shrill** voice of the governess calling him a liar."
Main Currents of American Thought, Irwin Shaw.

4. **jolly** "Roger and June had a **jolly** time, driving across the country."
The Call of the Open Road, John Keats.

5. **witty** "Mercutio's speech is full of **witty** puns."
The Development of Shakespeare's Imagery, Wolfgang Clemen.

6. **hinder** "'I won't **hinder** you from making a living,' said Bossett."
The Man Higher Up, O'Henry.

7. **lecture** "After the **lecture**, we left Genacht alone while we went to lunch."
Dark, Josephine Johnson.

8. **abuse** "The Dodger knew the meaning of child **abuse**."
Oliver Twist, Charles Dickens.

9. **mumble** "'Hello, Mom?...Oh, I'm sorry,' Jerry **mumbled**."
Snake Dance, Corey Ford.

10. **mute** "He was born quietly, he remained **mute** throughout and died quietly." *Buntcheh the Silent*, I.L. Peretz.

11. **wad** "Mr. Herder took the **wad** of tobacco out of his mouth."
How Beautiful with Shoes, Wilbur D. Steele.

12. **retain** "Although fired, Maxwell was allowed to **retain** certain privileges."
Wall Street Folly, Timothy Foster.

LESSON 34

1. **candidate** "I could not support him as a **candidate**."
The Growth of the Law, Benjamin Cardozo.

2. **precede** "I saw that is was my brother who had **preceded** me through the hedge." *The Other Side of the Hedge*, E.M. Forster.

3. **adolescent** "Because I was an **adolescent**, I suffered more than the others."
Looking Back, Guy DeMaupassant.

4. **coeducational** "He was in the first class when Skidmore went **coeducational**."   *The College for You*, Martin G. Blatt.

5. **radical** "He's no **radical**, but he'll represent the working class."
   Ivy Day in the Committee Room, James Joyce.

6. **spontaneous** "On July 10, a **spontaneous** strike of conductors and trainmen closed the railroad down."   *The Press*, A.J. Liebling.

7. **skim** "An attempt to **skim** the editorial proved unsatisfactory."
   Hot Words for the S.A.T., Murray Bromberg.

8. **vaccinate** "Their religious beliefs kept them from getting their children **vaccinated**."   *Time magazine*, August 17, 2010.

9. **untidy** "He didn't think the guy on the **untidy** porch would pay any attention to him."   *Out of Sight*, Elmore Leonard.

10. **utensil** "He had a brown pot, which he held as his most precious **utensil**."   *Silas Marner*, George Eliot.

11. **sensitive** "Because I was so **sensitive**, I felt the terror of being different."
    The Neglected Art of Being Different, Arthur Gordon.

12. **temperate** "He found himself in the **temperate** zone."
    The Other Two, Edith Wharton.

LESSON 35

1. **vague** "**Vague** thoughts of strange hypnotic things ran through my head."
   The Ghosts, Lord Dunsany.

2. **elevate** "Woods to **Elevate** His Game."   *Golf Digest*, February 10, 2011.

3. **lottery** "Carlos invested five dollars on **lottery** tickets—but lost it all."
   Real Stories, Milton Katz.

4. **finance** "Laura, who prided herself on a knowledge of **finance**, did not believe the pearls to be worth forty thousand pounds."
   A String of Beads, Somerset Maugham.

5. **obtain** "I had to **obtain** a number of specimens before we could start the project."   *Eleven Blue Men*, Berton Roueché.

6. **cinema** "We used to go to the movies but now we attend the **cinema**."
   The Truth of the Matter, Evelyn L. Dannen.

7. **event** "Hillary baked cookies for the pre-convention **event**."
   The Inside Story, Judith Warner.

8. **discard** "Laura felt she should have **discarded** the big hat with the velvet streamer."   *The Garden Party*, Katherine Mansfield.

9. **soar** "**Soar** above the split-level house and the two-car garage."
   To a Young Doctor, Dr. Thomas Dooley.

10. **subsequent** "A **subsequent** story sees Cleopatra poisoning the flowers in her crown."   *Cleopatra: Last Queen of Egypt*, Joyce Tyldesley.

11. **relate** "Tremaine's words **related** to the simple truth."
Simple Truth, David Baldacci.

12. **stationary** "Hightower remained **stationary** while Byron moved to the door." *Light in August*, William Faulkner.

LESSON 36

1. **prompt** "The teacher should receive a **prompt** report after your classroom visit." *Supervising Instruction*, Robert L. Schain.

2. **hasty** "During his sister's **hasty** maneuvers, he was dragged by the arm." *The Red Badge of Courage*, Stephen Crane.

3. **scorch** "Anyone who got near the burning pit could have been **scorched**." *Fire Walking in Ceylon*, Leonard Feinberg.

4. **tempest** "The **tempest** in the soul of Augusto ended in a terrible calm." *Mist*, Miguel de Unamuno.

5. **soothe** "We had to **soothe** her or tell her the truth." *Primary Colors*, Joe Klein.

6. **sympathetic** "I was **sympathetic** to P. who has lived in Hollywood with humor and dignity for thirty years." *Hollywood*, Truman Capote.

7. **redeem** "He could fix up Lizzie, **redeem** all of his promises, and still have enough left to build his grass-walled castle." *Martin Eden*, Jack London.

8. **resume** "**Resume** your seat; keep yourself fresh for the gentlemen callers." *The Glass Menagerie, Act I*, Tennessee Williams.

9. **harmony** "Such **harmony** is in immortal souls." *The Merchant of Venice, Act V*, William Shakespeare.

10. **refrain** "After six years in the navy, I learned how to **refrain** from volunteering." *Our Seven-Mile Drive*, Lt. Don Walsh.

11. **illegal** "Mr. Bloomberg formed a special group called Mayors Against **Illegal** Guns." *New York Times*, January 25, 2011.

12. **narcotic** "I was pleased to be transferred to the **Narcotic** Squad." *Drugs in the City*, A.J. Drexler.

LESSON 37

1. **heir** "We dare not forget today that we are the **heirs** of that first revolution." *John F. Kennedy's Inaugural Address*.

2. **majestic** "The parade in Alexandria was a **majestic** spectacle." *Antony and Cleopatra*, Adrian Goldsworthy.

3. **dwindle** "The days **dwindle** down to a precious few." "September Song" in *Knickerbocker Holiday*, Kurt Weill.

4. **surplus** "The United States corn **surplus** before the next harvest will be 5.6 percent larger than estimated a month ago." *businessweek.com*, April 11, 2010.

5. **traitor** "Every **traitor** must be hanged." *Macbeth, Act IV*, William Shakespeare.

6. **deliberate** "A great deal of **deliberate** cheating goes on in schools."
What About Cheating?, Thaddeus B. Clark.

7. **vandal** "**Vandals** Damage Church Relics."
New York Daily News, December 1, 2010.

8. **drought** "Father always broke the **drought** with a glass of cold ice water."
Father Wakes Up the Village, Clarence Day.

9. **abide** "I couldn't **abide** the nonsense of the fraternity's pledges."
My Crusade Against Fraternities, Wade Thompson.

10. **unity** "Make me happy in your **unity**."
Richard III, Act II, William Shakespeare.

11. **summit** "From the beginning, we expected Streisand to reach the **summit** of stardom."   *Song and Dance: the Musicals of Broadway*, Ted Sennett.

12. **heed** "Stan paid no **heed** to the nurse."
He Gave Him a Stone, Charles Ferguson.

LESSON 38

1. **biography** "Each **biography** gives a detailed account of the scientist's life."   *100 Great Scientists*, Jay Greene.

2. **drench** "When Paganini finished, his face was **drenched** with sweat."
A Portrait of Paganini, Heinrich Heine.

3. **swarm** "If you read a **swarm** of criticism, you encounter many different opinions."   *A Critique of Criticism*, Francois Mauriac.

4. **wobble** "He began to trot, then **wobbled** to a walk."
The Giaconda Smile, Aldous Huxley.

5. **tumult** "What had been lost in the **tumult** is the meaning of obligation."
Freedom of Speech, Walter Lippmann.

6. **kneel** "The trees would stoop and **kneel** in the wind."
A Haunted House, Virginia Woolf.

7. **dejected** "Our women become **dejected** because they don't have enough dresses."   *The Terrors of T.V.*, William Taylor.

8. **obedient** "Bashan is most **obedient**, responding to my whistle."
A Man and His Dog, Thomas Mann.

9. **recede** "Dixon was depressed when he saw his hairline **receding**."
Nature, March 2009.

10. **tyrant** "'Tis time to fear when **tyrants** seem to kiss."
Pericles, Act I, William Shakespeare.

11. **charity** "The doctor was told it would be an act of **charity** to visit the poor man."   *The Death of a Bachelor*, Arthur Schnitzler.

12. **verdict** "Of course the judge handed down a **verdict** of guilty."
The Evening Sun, William Faulkner.

LESSON 39

1. **unearth** "We attempted to **unearth** the source of the hate material."
Deflating the Professional Bigot, S. Andhil Fineberg.

2. **depart** "At the stroke of midnight, the guests began to **depart**."
The Masque of the Red Death, Edgar Allan Poe.

3. **coincide** "Annabel and Midge's tastes **coincided**."
The Start of Living, Dorothy Parker.

4. **cancel** "Unless we receive your check by August 30, we will have to **cancel** your policy."   *Letter from Geico Insurance Company*, no date.

5. **debtor** "Hubert refused to be a **debtor** where Rotary was concerned."
The Apostate, George Milburn.

6. **legible** "The way young people hold their pens certainly does nothing to promote any kind of **legible** writing."
standard.net, December 27, 2011.

7. **placard** "Hundreds waving **placards** filled the streets of Lebanon."
New York Post, January 28, 2011.

8. **contagious** "I must spend a few more weeks here until I am no more **contagious**."   *The Curfew Tolls*, Stephen Vincent Benét.

9. **clergy** "He was one member of the **clergy** who struck terror in the hearts of his followers."   *Thrawn Janet*, Robert Louis Stevenson.

10. **customary** "The rats knew where it was **customary** to find the food."
The Door, E.B. White.

11. **transparent** "We promise a more **transparent** government."
Eric Cantor, *Meet the Press*, January 21, 2010.

12. **scald** "Rachel Ray **scalded** her hand during the food show."
The New Julia Childs, Sally Benson.

LESSON 40

1. **epidemic** "I returned after the influenza **epidemic**."
A.V. Laider, Max Beerbohm.

2. **obesity** "Schools Serious About Childhood **Obesity**."
C.S.A. News, January 6, 2011.

3. **magnify** "That's an actor's technique—to be able to recall and **magnify** pain."   *quotesandpoems.com*, Erika Sleezak.

4. **chiropractor** "I'm a licensed **chiropractor** and can relieve your pain."
Two and a Half Men, T.V. broadcast, August 7, 2009.

5. **obstacle** "No **obstacle** can come between me and the full prospect of my hopes."   *Twelfth Night, Act III*, William Shakespeare.

6. **ventilate** "She tried to **ventilate** the room but it was impossible."
The Bucket Rider, Franz Kafka.

7. **jeopardize** "Our men and women in uniform put their lives on the line for our nation; they should not have to **jeopardize** their financial well-being as well."   *cleverquotes.com*, Mark Pryor.

8. **negative** "She had **negative** feelings about the janitress."
Theft, Katherine Anne Porter.

9. **pension** "He believed he had his **pension** money in five different banks."
A Girl from Red Lion P.A., H.L. Mencken.

10. **vital** "West African leaders moved to cut off **vital** sources of cash."
New York Times, January 25, 2010.

11. **municipal** "There's a U.S. state that has so reformed the way its **municipal** employees purchase health insurance that cities will now save taxpayers a whopping $100 million for years."
nydailynews.com, January 1, 2012.

12. **oral** "**Oral** swab testing tells life insurance companies how healthy you are."
nasdaq.com, January 4, 2012.

LESSON 41

1. **complacent** "You can't be **complacent** when you get a telegram like that."
The Late Christopher Bean, Sidney Howard.

2. **wasp** "When you have the honey, let not the **wasp** outlive us."
Titus Andronicus, Act II, William Shakespeare.

3. **rehabilitate** "In an attempt to **rehabilitate** his campaign, Gingrich spent two million in TV ads."
CNN, Anderson Cooper.

4. **parole** "One of those thieves was out on **parole**."
Reckless Abandon, Stuart Woods.

5. **vertical** "Above the terrace was a **vertical** stone parapet."
The Bridge on the Drina, Ivo Andric.

6. **multitude** "Among the **multitude** of biographies, this is the only one whose validity is confirmed."
Saint Joan of Arc, Mark Twain.

7. **nominate** "It will be my pleasure to **nominate** you for the state's governorship."
Albany Minutes, Terry O'Reilly.

8. **potential** "Miss Hope's arrival caused a **potential** embarrassment."
The Schartz-Metterklume Method, H.H. Munro.

9. **morgue** "When Buntcheh was carried to the **morgue**, his corner of the cellar was rented quickly."
Buntcheh the Silent, I.L. Peretz.

10. **preoccupied** "Miss Abbey was too **preoccupied** to pay attention to Bob Gliddery."
Our Mutual Friend, Charles Dickens.

11. **upholstery** "The first thing we gotta do is change this rotten **upholstery**."
Mincing Words, Edward Osborne.

12. **indifference** "Our country's **indifference** toward the growing Nazi strength can no longer be tolerated."
1938 speech to Parliament, Winston Churchill.

LESSON 42

1. **maintain** "Harrison found it hard to **maintain** his calm."
Not Him, Robert Wallace.

2. **snub** "I deeply resented the royal family's **snub** of Wallis."
The Duke's Last Secrets, Clive Fletcher.

3. **endure** "Benny's warm coat helped him **endure** the cold."
The Boy in the Dark, MacKinlay Kantor.

4. **wrath** "When we write about an error the player made, we are likely to incur his **wrath**." *Intellectuals and Ballplayers*, Roger Kahn.

5. **expose** "Those who were **exposed** to the heat of the explosion suffered greatly." *The Bombing of St. Louis*, Florence Moog.

6. **legend** "Elisa's chrysanthemums were a **legend** in our town." *The Chrysanthemums*, John Steinbeck.

7. **ponder** "I **pondered** my father's advice: the taller the bamboo grows, the lower it bends." *Best Advice*, Carlos Romulo.

8. **resign** "No one knew the cause that had led him to **resign** from the service." *The Shot*, Alexander Pushkin.

9. **drastic** "The parish council had to face **drastic** budget cuts." *In the Parish House*, Selma Lagerlöf.

10. **wharf** "It was the seediest dive on the **wharf**." *Macho Bygrande*, Ted Striker.

11. **amend** "We will **amend** the law." *Speech in Congress*, John Boehner, February 6, 2011.

12. **ballot** "The proud Yemenite said it was his first **ballot** ever." *New Jersey Star Ledger*, May 12, 2010.

Bonus Review

After learning the 504 Absolutely Essential Words contained in the 42 lessons and having challenged yourself with the exercises and extra Word Review exercises throughout this book, here is an extra challenge to see how you have mastered these words. Place one vocabulary word that makes the most sense in all three samples on the answer line.

1. I'm thinking of a word (awesome, commence, mature, temperate, vocation)
   a. Gentlemen, start your engines.
   b. Let the games begin.
   c. At the opening there was a prayer.

   Answer _____

2. I'm thinking of a word (abandon, appeal, burden, chiropractor, vain)
   a. That's a load off my back.
   b. Six infants to care for.
   c. I was happy to put that package down.

   Answer _____

3. I'm thinking of a word (frigid, legend, logical, massive, unique)
   a. "Baby, it's cold outside."
   b. The polar bears love this climate.
   c. Our warm friendship took a 360 degree turn.

   Answer _____

4. I'm thinking of a word (beneficiary, endure, obstacle, radical, subside)
   a. When it comes to politics, he's far out.
   b. His brain surgery had never been tried before.
   c. She's always carrying the banner for lost causes.

   Answer _____

5. I'm thinking of a word (ban, bigamy, brawl, conflict, sacred)
   a. "Do you take this woman and that woman?"
   c. A tale of two households.
   c. Double your pleasure.

   Answer _____

6. I'm thinking of a word (audible, appoint, complacent, disrupt, heed)
   a. "Did I hear you correctly?"
   b. The librarian said, "No talking."
   c. Speak up, young man.

   Answer _____

7. I'm thinking of a word (molest, peril, rehabilitate, vain, valiant)
   a. Railroad crossing
   b. TNT—handle with care!
   c. Walking on thin ice

   Answer _____

8. I'm thinking of a word (charity, drench, expose, ingenious, toil)
   a. "I've been working on a railroad.
   b. "Tote that barge, lift that bale."
   c. Up in the morning, out on the job

   Answer _____

9. I'm thinking of a word (obesity, pension, refrain, subside, vital)
   a. Living off the fat of the land
   b. New Year's resolution to lose weight
   c. I'll skip the whipped cream.

   Answer _____

10. I'm thinking of a word (legible, monarch, urban, vulnerable, witty)
   a.   Home of the skyscrapers
   b.   So long to the farm.
   c.   That's where the capitol is.

   Answer _____

11. I'm thinking of a word (absurd, mute, nimble, snub, partial)
   a.   I never heard something so foolish.
   b.   You can't be serious.
   c.   Harold's plan was laughable.

   Answer _____

12. I'm thinking of a word (alter, sacred, source, vital, wrath)
   a.   The dress needed to be shortened.
   b.   Don hid behind a mustache and a hairpiece.
   c.   My original design for the kitchen had to changed.

   Answer _____

13. I'm thinking of a word (annual, baffle, contagious, crafty, jealous)
   a.   We get together every Christmas.
   b.   The years are flying by so quickly.
   c.   A lot of money is raised by the Labor Day telethon.

   Answer _____

14. I'm thinking of a word (awesome, brutal, delinquent, venture, wasp)
   a.   The Grand Canyon
   b.   A great fireworks display
   c.   Niagara Falls was fantastic.

   Answer _____

15. I'm thinking of a word (ban, dread, extract, keen, scorch)
   a.   You can't do that!
   b.   No smoking!
   c.   There ought to be a law!

   Answer _____

16. I'm thinking of a word (cautious, lecture, morsel, prohibit, prosper)
   a.   Wearing a belt and suspenders
   b.   Entering on tiptoes
   c.   Afraid to take a chance

   Answer _____

17. I'm thinking of a word (minority, potential, untidy, venture, verify)
   a.   Fewer than half of our members were present.
   b.   Jason got 49 percent of the vote but Jane got 51 percent.
   c.   A few people from El Salvador moved into our neighborhood.

   Answer _____

18. I'm thinking of a word (observant, ponder, surpass, tradition, tumult)
   a.   Police had to be called.
   b.   So noisy we couldn't sleep
   c.   Loud celebration at the winner's hotel

   Answer _____

19. I'm thinking of a word (abroad, century, dispute, endure, evade)
   a.   My parents left for London.
   b.   The news from overseas was bad.
   c.   I showed them my passport.

   Answer _____

20. I'm thinking of a word (harsh, jagged, patriotic, vital, weird)
    a.   It's a grand old flag.
    b.   Stand for the Pledge of Allegiance.
    c.   We're proud of our country.

Answer _____

21. I'm thinking of a word (abolish, casual, culprit, dilemma, decade)
    a.   President Lincoln put an end to slavery.
    b.   No more death penalty.
    c.   The law against Sunday shopping was done away with.

Answer _____

22. I'm thinking of a word (menace, soar, survive, vague, vertical)
    a.   Did he say what I thought he said?
    b.   Without my glasses I couldn't see who was in the picture.
    c.   Please make yourself clear.

Answer _____

23. I'm thinking of a word (budget, debtor, nimble, opponent, placard)
    a.   The Orioles beat the Braves.
    b.   I was up against a 6'5" player.
    c.   It looks like a two-man race.

Answer _____

24. I'm thinking of a word (multitude, quantity, surplus, tragedy, vandal)
    a.   9/11
    b.   Serious business on the stage
    c.   The three-year-old was badly hurt.

Answer _____

25. I'm thinking of a word (linger, miserly, prohibit, quench, symbol)
    a.   The drinks are on the house.
    b.   Water boy, where are you hiding?
    c.   Yes, I'll have a Dr. Pepper.

Answer _____

26. I'm thinking of a word (data, defect, penalize, rave, reckless)
    a.   There was just one slight thing wrong with the diamond.
    b.   The radio had to be repaired.
    c.   Harry's heart problem kept him out of the army.

Answer _____

27. I'm thinking of a word (abide, dwindle, famine, jest, oath)
    a.   Raise your right hand.
    b.   When Dad is angry, he will swear.
    c.   I do, I do.

Answer _____

28. I'm thinking of a word (alter, capacity, debtor, keg, lubricate)
    a.   I owe everything to my parents.
    b.   Buy now, pay later.
    c.   Lend me your ears.

Answer _____

29. I'm thinking of a word (parole, ponder, squander, thrifty, vermin)
    a.   Watch your pennies; your dollars will take care of themselves.
    b.   My mom has a Christmas Club at the bank.
    c.   Those supermarket coupons come in handy.

Answer _____

30. I'm thinking of a word (appoint, coincide, expand, heed, matrimony)
   a.   Do you take this woman?
   b.   "Love and Marriage"
   c.   My parents celebrated their 20th anniversary.

   Answer _____

31. I'm thinking of a word (calamity, coeducational, economical, finance, obvious)
   a.   The earthquake took many lives.
   b.   Our dog ate my homework.
   c.   Uncle Morty closed the car door with the keys inside.

   Answer _____

32. I'm thinking of a word (penetrate, accurate, microscope, essential, device)
   a.   It looks cloudy in there.
   b.   The mirror part needs cleaning.
   c.   I had one, but I couldn't see anything.

   Answer _____

33. I'm thinking of a word (expensive, amateur, guide, pleasure, profession)
   a.   Won't make the major leagues
   b.   Better than a beginner
   c.   Singing is just a pastime.

   Answer _____

34. I'm thinking of a word (conclusion, scarce, document, computer, beau)
   a.   The Constitution of the United States
   b.   Does anyone here have a printing press?
   c.   I'm glad I have my driver's license.

   Answer _____

35. I'm thinking of a word (glimpse, hesitate, recent, frequent, numerous)
   a.   If I turn on the light for a second
   b.   It's all you get with a fastball pitch.
   c.   That bird flew by so fast.

   Answer _____

36. I'm thinking of a word (mount, tendency, miniature, wholesale, addict)
   a.   Let's buy a toy car.
   b.   The locket has a picture.
   c.   Put the furniture in the dollhouse.

   Answer _____

37. I'm thinking of a word (action, conflict, success, evidence, opinion)
   a.   Essential in a good movie
   b.   Let's not have a big argument.
   c.   My friend never agrees with me.

   Answer _____

38. I'm thinking of a word (fiction, predict, information, candid, clarity)
   a.   That story can't be true.
   b.   I don't believe a word you wrote.
   c.   A novel reply

   Answer _____

39. I'm thinking of a word (decreased, urban, locomotive, defect, polluted)
   a.   Let's go downtown.
   b.   There's not one farm nearby.
   c.   Too crowded for an automobile

   Answer _____

40. I'm thinking of a word (vapor, circulate, ignite, prohibit, urgent)
   a. Time for the fire department.
   b. Where are the matches I bought?
   c. Boy scouts rub two sticks together.

Answer _____

41. I'm thinking of a word (decrease, sufficient, audible, theory, utilize)
   a. Do you need a hearing aid?
   b. We sat too far from the stage.
   c. Where is the volume control on this radio?

Answer _____

42. I'm thinking of a word (persist, migrate, identify, revive, prohibit)
   a. Are those birds up there?
   b. No one seems to stay where he is born.
   c. When it's cold go to Florida.

Answer _____

43. I'm thinking of a word (underdog, jealous, idol, thorough, opponent)
   a. I'm usually not a winner.
   b. Some people are sorry for me.
   c. Sportswriters never root for me.

Answer _____

44. I'm thinking of a word (nimble, vermin, utter, maim, wasp)
   a. Watch out, it can sting.
   b. That's not a bird nest up there.
   c. I guess it's too small for a bird.

Answer _____

45. I'm thinking of a word (alter, upholstery, wretched, morsel, wad)
   a. I love to wrap around something.
   b. SIlk is best, of course.
   c. You need a special sewing machine.

Answer _____

46. I'm thinking of a word (vertical, visible, obstacle, vital, negative)
   a. It's got its ups and downs.
   b. My favorite venetian blinds.
   c. You didn't say horizontal.

Answer _____

47. I'm thinking of a word (debtor, transparent, depart, customary, placard)
   a. The invisible man
   b. People in glass houses . . .
   c. It's really easy to know me.

Answer _____

48. I'm thinking of a word (comprehend, discard, cancel, wobble, legible)
   a. Now, that's beautiful handwriting.
   b. I can tell the difference in the letters.
   c. As clear as any word processor

Answer _____

49. I'm thinking of a word (obedient, dejected, tyrant, neutral, compete)
   a. It's best to listen to your parents.
   b. The dog everyone loves.
   c. Your classmates will appreciate you.

Answer _____

50. I'm thinking of a word (vandal, bachelor, radical, lunatic, oath)
   a.   He knows how to avoid a wedding.
   b.   Female version: spinster
   c.   Very eligible

   Answer _____

51. I'm thinking of a word (tempest, narcotic, subside, illegal, extract)
   a.   Dangerous without a prescription
   b.   Gangs are involved
   c.   You might fall asleep easily.

   Answer _____

52. I'm thinking of a word (bigamy, employee, conflict, ballot, hazy)
   a.   We used to drop them in a box.
   b.   Everyone in the office decided to vote.
   c.   Let's use machines, no more chads.

   Answer _____

53. I'm thinking of a word (scowl, plea, witty, mute, sensitive)
   a.   Do you want to hear a joke?
   b.   It helps to be clever.
   c.   They laughed until their sides ached.

   Answer _____

54. I'm thinking of a word (warden, monarch, wad, lunatic, site)
   a.   King or queen
   b.   I am also a butterfly.
   c.   My plan is to refurnish the palace.

   Answer _____

55. I'm thinking of a word (postpone, volunteer, plea, utter, soar)
   a.   Never do today what you can do tomorrow.
   b.   I'll do my homework tomorrow.
   c.   It's raining too hard for the baseball game to continue.

   Answer _____

56. I'm thinking of a word (slender, prior, nimble, mortal, merit)
   a.   No one here needs to go on a diet.
   b.   You don't need to make that doorway wider.
   c.   If you want to look your best in the new styles

   Answer _____

57. I'm thinking of a word (circulate, fertile, devour, drastic, daze)
   a.   The desert after a rainfall
   b.   Rabbits produce many bunnies
   c.   Can you imagine a tree with 500 apples?

   Answer _____

58. I'm thinking of a word (campus, event, innovative, keen, maim)
   a.   The engineer was badly hurt in the train wreck.
   b.   Permanent damage
   c.   He was rushed to the hospital after being rescued from the fire.

   Answer _____

59. I'm thinking of a word (abundant, betray, descend, reform, venture)
   a.   Take the elevator to the ground floor.
   b.   Seeing the balloon land was exciting.
   c.   Come on down!

   Answer _____

60. I'm thinking of a word (biography, candidate, fierce, variety, wail)
   a.   Running for office?
   b.   Election night was wild.
   c.   I'm asking for your vote.

   Answer _____

61. I'm thinking of a word (pioneer, relate, retain, undeniable, valiant)
   a.   She made a fantastic effort.
   b.   The medal winners were truly brave.
   c.   That took courage.

   Answer _____

62. I'm thinking of a word (capsule, client, defraud, epidemic, idle)
   a.   The counterfeiter was caught.
   b.   People lost millions to the swindlers.
   c.   You have to read the small print to avoid being cheated.

   Answer _____

63. I'm thinking of a word (disrupt, dread, expose, mature, molest)
   a.   Really grown up
   b.   I thought he was much older.
   c.   Time to put aside childish games.

   Answer _____

64. I'm thinking of a word (loyalty, scorch, subside, vanish, vocation)
   a.   Out in the blazing sun
   b.   Take that pot off the stove!
   c.   115° in Phoenix

   Answer _____

65. I'm thinking of a word (pension, pollute, prejudice, surpass, talent)
   a.   Our big car is a gas guzzler.
   b.   Too many chemicals in the river
   c.   Secondhand smoke

   Answer _____

66. I'm thinking of a word (beckon, clergy, confirm, vigor, wary)
   a.   Father Duffy performed the ceremony.
   b.   Our priest has a free parking spot.
   c.   He came back from confession.

   Answer _____

67. I'm thinking of a word (frank, ignore, indifference, persuade, torrent)
   a.   They talked me into it.
   b.   I'll listen to your argument.
   c.   She tried to get me to change my mind.

   Answer _____

68. I'm thinking of a word (pauper, reform, theory, vigor, vital)
   a.   I promised never to do it again.
   b.   Our committee will change things.
   c.   My New Year's resolution

   Answer _____

69. I'm thinking of a word (authority, confident, discard, rural, vanish)
   a.   I'm sure we'll win.
   b.   I know it will work out.
   c.   Have no doubts

   Answer _____

70. I'm thinking of a word (dejected, exaggerate, ignore, jagged, jeopardize)
   a.   Alfie must have won a million dollars on the slot machine.
   b.   The fish I caught was eight feet long.
   c.   My grandfather probably owned 60 motorcycles.

   Answer _____

71. I'm thinking of a word (consent, hinder, menace, multitude, promote)
   a.   Parents had to approve of the school trip.
   b.   If you agree to the operation, sign here.
   c.   My mom allowed me to try out for the cheerleaders.

   Answer _____

72. I'm thinking of a word (morality, mythology, reveal, severity, untidy)
   a.   Vinny is a sloppy dresser.
   b.   The butcher's apron was a mess.
   c.   I got a stain on my tie.

   Answer _____

73. I'm thinking of a word (cancel, emerge, grateful, justice, vulnerable)
   a.   No show—the star is sick.
   b.   Without more students, we'll have to call off the trip.
   c.   My brother doesn't want *Sports Illustrated* anymore.

   Answer _____

74. I'm thinking of a word (misfortune, pacify, reluctant, verdict, vicious)
   a.   Guilty!
   b.   We decided that the movie was rotten.
   c.   After tasting the soup, what do you think?

   Answer _____

75. I'm thinking of a word (abandon, distress, fragile, linger, precaution)
   a.   The infant was left at the church door.
   b.   Home alone
   c.   The lookouts ran away.

   Answer _____

76. I'm thinking of a word (merit, mourn, pauper, resent, vandal)
   a.   Can you spare a quarter?
   b.   She lost a fortune in the stock market.
   c.   The homeless man was given a hot meal.

   Answer _____

77. I'm thinking of a word (duplicate, obvious, security, variety, weird)
   a.   It was as plain as the nose on your face.
   b.   We didn't have to guess about who stole the money.
   c.   The test questions were just what we expected.

   Answer _____

78. I'm thinking of a word (blunder, illustrate, legible, respond, wad)
   a.   One picture was worth a thousand words.
   b.   Let me show you what I mean.
   c.   The teacher went to the board with chalk.

   Answer _____

79. I'm thinking of a word (neutral, perish, refrain, sacred, valid)
   a.   The cow has a special place in India.
   b.   We saw a huge statue of the Buddha.
   c.   Let us pray.

   Answer _____

80. I'm thinking of a word (appoint, circulate, estimate, finance, insist)
    a.   The TV repairman gave us a price.
    b.   How long do you think it will take you to finish the job?
    c.   The charge will probably be between $75 and $100.

Answer _____

81. I'm thinking of a word (defiant, hardship, insist, legend, scarce)
    a.   It was painful to be without food for 48 hours.
    b.   The early settlers faced a cruel winter.
    c.   We were the poorest family on the block.

Answer _____

82. I'm thinking of a word (confident, manipulate, opt, vain, victorious)
    a.   Our team won the final game.
    b.   The young boxer was declared the winner.
    c.   The chess expert beat the computer.

Answer _____

83. I'm thinking of a word (coincide, depart, hasty, neutral, verify)
    a.   The ship sails at midnight.
    b.   After the wedding, the couple left for Hawaii.
    c.   Good-bye.

Answer _____

84. I'm thinking of a word (abide, adequate, negative, venture, wrath)
    a.   Minus one
    b.   She was against the plan.
    c.   Count me out!

Answer _____

85. I'm thinking of a word (devour, duress, shrill, signify, vulnerable)
    a.   His chin was his weak spot.
    b.   Eleanor was open to infection.
    c.   The city could be attacked easily.

Answer _____

86. I'm thinking of a word (magnify, oral, reluctant, unanimous, valid)
    a.   The vote was 56 to zero.
    b.   Everyone, but everyone, agreed.
    c.   All hands went up when they called for volunteers.

Answer _____

87. I'm thinking of a word (pledge, redeem, reluctant, utter, visible)
    a.   Anita was unwilling to invest.
    b.   We couldn't convince them to join us.
    c.   The 45-year-old hesitated about getting married.

Answer _____

88. I'm thinking of a word (dismal, neglect, prohibit, summit, wary)
    a.   I forgot to pay the electric bill.
    b.   Was the homework due today?
    c.   There wasn't enough in my account to cover the check.

Answer _____

89. I'm thinking of a word (abundant, appropriate, fertile, redeem, soothe)
    a.   Gary had a plentiful supply of food.
    b.   The huge crop of wheat was shipped to Russia.
    c.   There were many chances to help the needy.

Answer _____

90. I'm thinking of a word (delinquent, illegal, partial, vicious, visible)
    a.   My neighbor's son is always in trouble.
    b.   We were warned about our late mortgage payment.
    c.   The teenagers were brought to Family Court.

    Answer _____

91. I'm thinking of a word (radical, rash, revive, unstable, vocation)
    a.   A wild personality
    b.   We had to put some paper under the table leg.
    c.   Ricky blew his top.

    Answer _____

92. I'm thinking of a word (authority, beneficiary, charity, famine, swarm)
    a.   Once poor, now he helps the poor.
    b.   Faith, hope, and _____
    c.   Our club's dinner raised $10,000 for the Red Cross.

    Answer _____

93. I'm thinking of a word (debate, expose, excessive, innovative, threat)
    a.   Sandy pays too much attention to TV.
    b.   Mrs. Tuttle gives two hours of homework each night.
    c.   I complained about the number of commercials.

    Answer _____

94. I'm thinking of a word (despite, dejected, deprive, embrace, variety)
    a.   The menu covered five pages.
    b.   Many different acts were on the telethon.
    c.   Sheila had all sorts of reasons to stay home.

    Answer _____

95. I'm thinking of a word (adolescent, narcotic, population, surplus, vandal)
    a.   They hang out in the mall.
    b.   They will be taking this year's SAT.
    c.   Big fans of hip-hop music

    Answer _____

96. I'm thinking of a word (detest, neutral, symbol, trifle, wail)
    a.   When my older brothers fight, I don't take sides.
    b.   I'm not sure how I feel about the death penalty.
    c.   "Don't get involved" turned out to be good advice.

    Answer _____

97. I'm thinking of a word (flexible, pacify, ponder, urgent, valor)
    a.   When Carmen was out of control, I calmed her down.
    b.   Sid settled the argument with flowers.
    c.   Collecting all the guns was a good idea.

    Answer _____

98. I'm thinking of a word (brutal, complacent, drastic, envy, frank)
    a.   Old-time detectives were shocked at the crime.
    b.   When drunk, he beat his wife.
    c.   The senator's attack on his opponent was unforgivable.

    Answer _____

99. I'm thinking of a word (accurate, disclose, dismal, endure, homicide)
    a.   Tell us what really happened.
    b.   Bernard's information helped solve the case.
    c.   She whispered the secret in his ear.

    Answer _____

100. I'm thinking of a word (beneficiary, morgue, penalize, pledge, snub)
   a.   The reading of the will
   b.   In case of accidental death
   c.   I hope you will profit from this advice.

Answer _____

Answers

Lesson 1: 1. data 2. tact 3. vacant 4. oath
5. jealous 6. gallant 7. hardship 8. abandon
9. qualify 10. keen 11. Unaccustomed
12. bachelor
1. oath 2. keen 3. abandon 4. hardship 5. qualify
6. jealous 7. gallant 8. bachelor 9. data 10. tact
11. vacant 12. unaccustomed
The illustration suggests the word **vacant.**

Lesson 2: 1. dismal 2. wager 3. peril 4. recline 5.
shriek 6. sinister 7. conceal 8. inhabit 9. frigid
10. numb 11. corpse 12. tempt
The illustration suggests the word **wager.**

Lesson 3: 1. annual 2. blend 3. minimum
4. talent 5. persuade 6. visible 7. typical 8. devise
9. essential 10. wholesale 11. scarce
12. expensive
The illustration suggests the word **expensive.**

Lesson 4: 1. humid 2. vanish 3. dense 4. predict
5. villain 6. Vapor 7. enormous 8. theory 9. utilize
10. descend 11. eliminate 12. circulate
1. b 2. b 3. d 4. b 5. c 6. a 7. b 8. c 9. c 10. c
11. c 12. b
The illustration suggests the word **predict.**

Lesson 5: 1. rural 2. campus 3. evade
4. majority 5. assemble 6. tradition 7. burden
8. explore 9. reform 10. topic 11. probe 12. debate
The illustration suggests the word **debate.**

Lesson 6: 1. thorough *or* comprehensive
2. undoubtedly 3. approach 4. popular 5. neglect
6. employee 7. defect 8. deceive *or* defraud
9. deceived 10. detect 11. client
12. comprehensive *or* thorough
1. popular 2. employees 3. detected
4. approached 5. comprehensive 6. defect
7. undoubtedly 8. thorough 9. neglect
10. defraud 11. deceive 12. clients
The illustration suggests the word **employee.**

Word Review #1: A. 1. typical 2. blend 3. peril
4. detected 5. neglect 6. sinister 7. qualify
8. unaccustomed 9. scarce 10. reform
B. 1. g 2. j 3. a 4. c 5. b 6. d 7. i 8. e 9. f 10. h
C. 1. abandon 2. minimum 3. dense 4. neglect
5. evade 6. campus 7. oath 8. descend 9. vacant
10. predict
D. 1. wholesale 2. villain 3. majority 4. probe
5. defraud 6. abandon 7. assemble 8. eliminate
9. comprehensive 10. tact
E. 1. annual 2. enormous 3. detected 4. defects
5. hardship 6. expensive 7. wholesale
8. employees 9. neglected 10. comprehensive

Lesson 7: 1. preserve 2. gloomy 3. consent
4. unique 5. resent 6. denounced 7. molested
8. unforeseen 9. torrent 10. postponed
11. capsule 12. massive
The illustration suggests the word **postponed.**

Lesson 8: 1. weird 2. valid 3. obvious 4. mediocre
5. reluctant 6. exaggerate 7. security 8. bulky
9. amateur 10. variety 11. prominent 12. survive
1. f 2. d 3. h 4. g 5. j 6. a 7. l 8. b 9. k 10. i 11. e
12. c
The illustration suggests the word **exaggerate.**

Lesson 9: 1. ignore 2. documents 3. century
4. challenge 5. source 6. conclude 7. undeniable
8. lack 9. vicinity 10. rage 11. miniature 12. resist
1. c 2. a 3. d 4. a 5. c 6. c 7. b 8. a 9. d 10. a
11. c 12. a
The illustration suggests the word **rage.**

Lesson 10: 1. menace 2. dread 3. tendency
4. underestimate 5. excel 6. flabby 7. numerous
8. feminine 9. compete 10. mount 11. victorious
12. masculine
The illustration suggests the word **victorious.**

Lesson 11. 1. decades 2. vision 3. minority
4. glimpse 5. absurd 6. frequent 7. hesitate
8. solitary 9. conflict 10. Recent 11. evidence
12. fiction
1. h 2. g 3. b 4. k 5. i 6. d 7. j 8. a 9. f 10. e 11. c
12. l
The illustration suggests the word **vision.**

Lesson 12: 1. frank 2. audible 3. urgent 4. urban
5. ignite 6. prohibited 7. pollute 8. decrease
9. abolish 10. population 11. reveals
12. adequate
1. urban 2. reveal 3. adequate 4. pollute
5. abolish 6. decrease 7. frank 8. urgent 9. ignite
10. population 11. audible 12. prohibit
The illustration suggests the word **pollute.**

Word Review #2: A. 1. postpone
2. underestimated 3. mediocre 4. menace
5. challenged 6. prominent 7. abolished
8. Unforeseen 9. adequate 10. ignores
B. 1. d 2. j 3. a 4. h 5. b 6. i 7. c 8. g 9. e 10. f
C. 1. absurd 2. prohibit 3. postpone 4. reveal
5. decade 6. prominent 7. menace 8. massive
9. urban 10. gloomy
D. 1. hesitate 2. fiction 3. massive 4. century
5. conclude 6. absurd 7. obvious 8. preserve
9. vision 10. unique
E. 1. frank 2. hesitate 3. dread 4. tendency
5. urban 6. security 7. glimpse 8. obvious
9. consent 10. conclude

Lesson 13: 1. commence 2. migrate 3. gleam 4. famine 5. vessel 6. identify 7. observant 8. editor 9. revive 10. persist 11. Hazy 12. journalist
The illustration suggests the word **journalist.**

Lesson 14: 1. unruly 2. brutal, violent, *or* vicious 3. brawl 4. thrust 5. duplicate 6. rival *or* opponent 7. rival *or* opponent 8. bewildered 9. underdog 10. brutal, violent, *or* vicious 11. whirling 12. brutal, violent, *or* vicious
1. T 2. F 3. T 4. T 5. T 6. F 7. F 8. T 9. F 10. F 11.T 12.T
The illustration suggests the word **bewildered.**

Lesson 15: 1. fortunate 2. sacred 3. revise *or* alter 4. innovative 5. pursue 6. mature 7. unanimous 8. pledge 9. revise *or* alter 10. pioneers 11. casual 12. expand
The illustration suggests the word **pledge.**

Lesson 16: 1. grateful 2. doubt 3. slender 4. cautious 5. accurate 6. penetrate *or* pierce 7. vast 8. surpass 9. capacity 10. confident 11. microscope 12. pierce
1. a 2. c 3. a 4. d 5. a 6. b 7. a 8. a 9. c 10. b 11. a 12. a
The illustration suggests the word **pierce** or **penetrate.**

Lesson 17: 1. avoid 2. aware 3. quantity 4. appeal 5. wretched 6. harsh 7. misfortune 8. opt 9. wary 10. keg 11. nourish 12. addict
1. j 2. i 3. k 4. l 5. a 6. h 7. c 8. e 9. b 10. f 11. g 12. d
The illustration suggests the word **wary.**

Lesson 18: 1. reckless 2. ingenious 3. economical 4. rave 5. glance 6. budget 7. manipulate 8. lubricate 9. tragedy 10. horrid 11. pedestrian 12. nimble
The illustration suggests the word **lubricate.**

Word Review #3: A. 1. famine 2. nimble 3. revive 4. mature 5. alter 6. reckless 7. pursue 8. economical 9. unanimously 10. capacity
B. 1. c 2. a 3. j 4. f 5. d 6. b 7. e 8. i 9. h 10. g
C. 1. famine 2. unanimous 3. pioneer 4. migrate 5. revive 6. wary 7. unruly 8. slender 9. reckless 10. vicious
D. 1. confidence 2. pioneer 3. rival 4. vessel 5. thrust 6. revise 7. capacity 8. nourish 9. tragedy 10. rave
E. 1. rave 2. innovative 3. confident 4. mature 5. pursue 6. journalist 7. aware 8. expand 9. identify 10. grateful

Lesson 19: 1. ban 2. quota 3. abundant 4. absorbed 5. appropriate 6. estimate 7. uneasy 8. panic 9. harvest 10. calculated 11. morsel 12. threat

1. abundant 2. threat 3. uneasy 4. panic 5. harvest 6. calculate 7. ban 8. morsel 9. absorb 10. quotas 11. estimate 12. appropriate
The illustration suggests the word **panic.**

Lesson 20: 1. perish 2. jagged 3. captive 4. crafty 5. linger 6. defiant 7. ambush 8. prosper 9. emerged 10. devour 11. vigor 12. fragile
1. a 2. b 3. a 4. b 5. d 6. b 7. b 8. d 9. a 10. a 11. a 12. b
The illustration suggests the word **captive.**

Lesson 21: 1. transmitted 2. confirm *or* verify 3. detour 4. weary 5. merit 6. plea 7. collide 8. relieved 9. dilemma 10. confirm *or* verify 11. baffled 12. anticipate
1. detour 2. plea 3. collide 4. transmit 5. baffle 6. merit 7. relieve 8. weary 9. confirm 10. dilemma 11. verify 12. anticipate
The illustration suggests the word **collide.**

Lesson 22: 1. delinquent 2. penalize 3. vocation 4. homicide 5. acknowledge 6. reject 7. warden 8. spouse 9. unstable 10. deprived 11. Justice 12. beneficiary
1. c 2. h 3. k 4. f 5. j 6. i 7. a 8. b 9. d 10. g 11. l 12. e
The illustration suggests the word **reject.**

Lesson 23: 1. embraced 2. forbid 3. proceed 4. reptile 5. partial 6. logical 7. rarely 8. exhibit 9. prior 10. precaution 11. valiant 12. extract
The illustration suggests the word **precaution.**

Lesson 24: 1. authority 2. encourage 3. symbol 4. vermin 5. neutral 6. consider 7. fierce 8. wail 9. trifle 10. detest 11. scowl 12. sneer
1. c 2. a 3. c 4. a 5. c 6. b 7. d 8. a 9. c 10. a 11. a 12. b
The illustration suggests the word **wail.**

Word Review #4: A. 1. quotas 2. reject 3. fragile 4. extract 5. dilemma 6. partial 7. linger 8. neutral 9. calculated 10. confirmed
B. 1. f 2. h 3. d 4. b 5. j 6. c 7. i 8. e 9. a 10. g
C. 1. exhibit 2. fragile 3. collide 4. dilemma 5. vermin 6. confirm 7. prosper 8. perish 9. quota 10. abundant
D. 1. ambush 2. beneficiary 3. symbol 4. harvest 5. panic 6. prosper 7. baffle 8. warden 9. precaution 10. trifle
E. 1. detour 2. appropriate 3. rarely 4. reptiles 5. precaution 6. emerge 7. abundant 8. anticipate 9. consider 10. confirm

Lesson 25: 1. baggage 2. calamity 3. paupers 4. collapse 5. architect 6. prosecuted 7. squander 8. fugitive 9. bigamy 10. abroad 11. envy 12. matrimony
The illustration suggests the word **baggage.**

Lesson 26: 1. quench 2. guide 3. respond
4. beckoned 5. venture 6. compelled 7. awesome
8. betrayed 9. possible 10. pacify 11. uttered
12. awkward
1. F 2. T 3. F 4. T 5. T 6. F 7. T 8. T 9. F 10. T
11. F 12. T
The illustration suggests the word **quench.**

Lesson 27: 1. feeble 2. ceased 3. rash
4. exhausted 5. monarch 6. disrupt 7. thrifty
8. rapidly 9. severity 10. unite 11. Despite
12. miserly
The illustration suggests the word **monarch.**

Lesson 28: 1. undernourished 2. disclose
3. disaster 4. outlaw 5. excessive 6. culprit
7. promote 8. illustrate 9. insist 10. censor
11. juvenile 12. bait
1. bait 2. promote 3. culprit 4. insist 5. outlaw
6. juvenile 7. censor 8. disclose 9. excessive
10. disaster 11. illustrate 12. undernourished
The illustration suggests the word **disaster.**

Lesson 29: 1. exempt 2. repetition 3. blundered
4. comprehend 5. toiled 6. maimed 7. commended
8. final 9. mourning 10. vain 11. subsided
12. daze
1. i 2. f 3. h 4. l 5.g 6. j 7. b 8. d 9. e 10. a 11. k
12. c
The illustration suggests the word **mourning.**

Lesson 30: 1. appointed 2. mortal 3. occupants
4. depict 5. site 6. verse 7. quartered 8. quoted
9. novel 10. attracted 11. morality 12. roam
The illustration suggests the word **novel.**

Word Review #5: A. 1. prosecuted 2. depict
3. blunder 4. mourn 5. squandered 6. utter
7. guide 8. matrimony 9. novel 10. unite
B. 1. f 2. a 3. i 4. j 5. h 6. d 7. b 8. c 9. e 10. g
C. 1. subside 2. juvenile 3. pacify 4. mourn
5. cease 6. monarch 7. unite 8. depict 9. thrifty
10. bigamy
D. 1. mortal 2. maim 3. calamity 4. thrifty
5. architect 6. bigamist 7. quench 8. monarch
9. censor 10. quarter
E. 1. attract 2. repetition 3. possible 4. promote
5. undernourished 6. thrifty 7. awkward
8. despite 9. architect 10. excessive

Lesson 31: 1. idle 2. dispute 3. commuter
4. valor 5. vein 6. uneventful 7. lunatic 8. jest
9. confine 10. patriotic 11. fertile 12. idol
The illustration suggests the word **commuter.**

Lesson 32: 1. distress 2. maximum 3. flee
4. tormenting 5. loyalty 6. apologize 7. colleagues
8. signified 9. refer 10. diminished 11. mythology
12. vulnerable
1. signify 2. flee 3. distress 4. maximum 5. refer

6. loyalty 7. colleague 8. mythology 9. vulnerable
10. torment 11. diminish 12. apologize
The illustration suggests the word **flee.**

Lesson 33: 1. mumbled 2. wad 3. retain
4. volunteers 5. jolly 6. prejudice 7. hindered
8. mute 9. abused 10. shrill 11. lecture 12. witty
The illustration suggests the word **lecture.**

Lesson 34: 1. adolescent 2. candidate
3. radical 4. spontaneous 5. vaccinated
6. utensil 7. sensitive 8. temperate 9. untidy
10. coeducational 11. precedes 12. skim
1. k 2. e 3. d 4. b 5. j 6. i 7. c 8. g 9. l 10. h
11. a 12. f
The illustration suggests the word **vaccinate.**

Lesson 35: 1. lottery 2. obtain 3. cinema
4. event 5. soaring 6. stationary 7. Subsequent 8.
discard 9. relate 10. vague 11. finance
12. elevate
1. elevate 2. subsequent 3. cinema 4. event
5. soar 6. vague 7. stationary 8. lottery 9. relate
10. obtain 11. finance 12. discard
The illustration suggests the word **lottery.**

Lesson 36: 1. prompt 2. soothed 3. redeemed
4. refrain 5. harmony 6. hasty 7. tempest
8. scorch 9. sympathetic 10. resumed 11. illegal
12. narcotics
The illustration suggests the word **scorch.**

Word Review #6: A. 1. relate 2. prompt 3. vague
4. obtain 5. resume 6. distressed 7. vulnerable
8. radical 9. uneventful 10. maximum
B. 1. g 2. j 3. a 4. i 5. e 6. b 7. h 8. c 9. f 10. d
C. 1. vaccinate 2. idle 3. diminished 4. resume
5. prejudice 6. radical 7. idol 8. vulnerable
9. uneventful 10. commuter
D. 1. lunatic 2. colleague 3. prejudice 4. vaccinate
5. cinema 6. mute 7. spontaneous 8. lottery
9. discard 10. redeem
E. 1. distress 2. relate 3. referred 4. sympathetic
5. dispute 6. fertile 7. signified 8. provide
9. radical 10. retain

Lesson 37: 1. dwindled 2. heir 3. deliberate
4. surplus 5. heeding 6. unified 7. vandals
8. abide 9. drought 10. summit 11. traitor
12. majestic
1. a 2. b 3. d 4. a 5. e 6. b 7. a 8. a 9. d 10. b
11. e 12. e
The illustration suggests the word **summit.**

Lesson 38: 1. tumult 2. swarm 3. verdict
4. biography 5. receded 6. charity 7. kneel
8. dejected 9. tyrant 10. drenched 11. wobbled
12. obedient
1. F 2. T 3. F 4. T 5. T 6. F 7. T 8. T 9. F 10. F
11. T 12. T
The illustration suggests the word **kneel.**

Lesson 39: 1. depart 2. cancelled 3. placard
4. contagious 5. unearthed 6. customary
7. scalded 8. transparent 9. legible 10. clergy
11. debtor 12. coincide
1. f 2. g 3. j 4. e 5. h 6. i 7. a 8. d 9. k 10. l 11. b
12. c
The illustration suggests the word **depart.**

Lesson 40: 1. obesity 2. epidemic 3. chiropractors
4. ventilated 5. oral 6. magnifying 7. obstacle
8. pension 9. jeopardize 10. negative
11. municipal 12. vital
The illustration suggests the word **obesity.**

Lesson 41: 1. wasp 2. parole 3. rehabilitate
4. multitude 5. potential 6. upholstery
7. indifference 8. preoccupied 9. vertical
10. nominated 11. morgue 12. complacent
1. e 2. a 3. c 4. a 5. d 6. d 7. a 8. a 9. c 10. a
11. a 12. b
The illustration suggests the word **parole.**

Lesson 42: 1. snubbed 2. wrath 3. pondered
4. maintained 5. endure 6. expose 7. legend
8. ballot 9. wharf 10. resigned 11. amend
12. drastic
The illustration suggests the word **ballot.**

Word Review #7: A. 1. customary 2. drastic
3. jeopardize 4. tumult 5. endure 6. drenched
7. receded 8. dwindled 9. summit 10. preoccupied
B. 1. a 2. d 3. b 4. j 5. e 6. c 7. f 8. g 9. h 10. i
C. 1. heir 2. expose 3. epidemic 4. deliberate
5. oral 6. tumult 7. abide 8. cancel 9. rehabilitate
10. biography

D. 1. ballot 2. wasp 3. obesity 4. legible 5. vandal
6. dwindle 7. wobble 8. drench 9. legend
10. rehabilitate
E. 1. heir 2. tyrant 3. deliberate 4. drenched
5. deprived 6. drastic 7. indifference 8. legend
9. heed 10. dwindling

Review of Reviews: 1. commence 2. burden
3. frigid 4. radical 5. bigamy 6. audible 7. peril
8. toil 9. obesity 10. urban 11. absurd 12. alter
13. annual 14. awesome 15. ban 16. cautious
17. minority 18. tumult 19. abroad 20. patriotic
21. abolish 22. vague 23. opponent 24. tragedy
25. quench 26. defect 27. oath 28. debtor
29. thrifty 30. matrimony 31. calamity
32. microscope 33. amateur 34. document
35. glimpse 36. miniature 37. conflict 38. fiction
39. urban 40. ignite 41. audible 42. migrate
43. underdog 44. wasp 45. upholstery 46. vertical
47. transparent 48. legible 49. obedient
50. bachelor 51. narcotic 52. ballot 53. witty
54. monarch 55. postpone 56. slender 57. fertile
58. maim 59. descend 60. candidate 61. valiant
62. defraud 63. mature 64. scorch 65. pollute
66. clergy 67. persuade 68. reform 69. confident
70. exaggerate 71. consent 72. untidy
73. cancel 74. verdict 75. abandon 76. pauper
77. obvious 78. illustrate 79. sacred 80. estimate
81. hardship 82. victorious 83. depart
84. negative 85. vulnerable 86. unanimous
87. reluctant 88. neglect 89. abundant
90. delinquent 91. unstable 92. charity
93. excessive 94. variety 95. adolescent
96. neutral 97. pacify 98. brutal 99. disclose
100. beneficiary

Index

The number indicates the lesson in which the word first appears. For the Bonus Lesson—125 More Difficult (But Essential) Words, see the index that follows on page 202.

Index of 125 More Difficult (But Essential) Words

The following index contains words found in the Bonus Lesson—125 More DIfficult (But Essential) Words beginning on page 142.